Walking from Inn to Inn

The San Francisco Bay Area

Jacqueline Kudler and Arlene Stark

The East Woods Press
Charlotte, North Carolina

Library of Congress Cataloging-in-Publication Data
Kudler, Jacqueline, 1935-
    Walking from inn to inn.

    Includes index.
    1. Walking — California — San Francisco Bay Area —Guide-
books. 2. San Francisco Bay Area — Description and travel —
Guide-books. I. Stark, Arlene, 1930-
II. Title.
GV199.42.C22S26945 1986   917.94'6   85-45697
ISBN 0-88742-068-0 (pbk.)

Cover design by Rick Petersen

Inside illustrations and maps by Rick Petersen
Typography by R. J. Publishing Co.
Printed in the United States of America

East Woods Press Books
Fast & McMillan Publishers, Inc.
429 East Boulevard
Charlotte, NC 28203

To Junie, who walked each mile with us.

Contents

Introduction

San Francisco

The North Bay

The South Bay

The Santa Cruz Mountains

The Wine Country

Walking from Inn to Inn

The San Francisco Bay Area

Introduction

Afoot and light-hearted, I take to
  the open road
Healthy, free, the world before me,
[The long brown path before me leading]
  wherever I choose.

                              Walt Whitman

Let's say the song of the open road has been calling to you as long as you can remember. On any especially golden kind of day, you're all for setting off. Or let's say it's not so much the wanderlust as the walking itself; you've given up trying to explain how so simple an activity can be so profoundly satisfying. Either way, if ever you've had an inclination to travel light, on foot, toward some particular unknown somewhere, consider the possibilities of weekend trekking.

With a light pack on your back, you embark on a small adventure — a journey on foot from your inn for the night before the trek to the inn that awaits you at trail's end. The distance between the two may be a 2-mile park stroll or a 15-mile mountain odyssey; a day's walk is defined only by which route you fancy and the pace you choose to set.

The weekend walking tours that we propose were not possible until quite recently on two counts. Although the trails themselves have been here as long as we can remember, they have been significantly expanded and interconnected during the past ten years, thanks to the visionary endeavors of such agencies as the East Bay Regional Parks District and the Golden Gate National Recreation Area. The current spate of comfortable country inns and "bed-and-breakfast" stops along the way provides the other important component. For centuries vacationing Europeans have rambled over moors and Alpine passes, stopping each night to enjoy the comforts of good company, a nourishing dinner and a soft bed. We welcome the opportunity to translate this delightful tradition into a Pacific idiom.

Weekend Trekking and Variations

Great weekend trekking involves two crucial elements: enjoyable hiking and good lodging. We have chosen routes that combine the best of each, but, because walking is such a universal activity, we have also tried to provide for a wide variety of tastes. We have included walks for novices or for those who wish to temper their physical activities with long afternoon picnics in cool meadows. There are also routes that will challenge the most experienced hiking enthusiast (see Appendix A). Lodgings vary, too, from simple cots in hostels to ornate, antique four-posters in elegant Victorian mansions (see Appendix B).

The excursion starts on Friday night at an inn near the beginning of the route. (Many of them can be reached by public transportation.) On Saturday morning you set out on the day hike that leads you to your new lodging, reaching it in plenty of time for a hot shower and cocktails before dinner. On Sunday you return to the original inn, either by public transportation or on foot, as the spirit moves you.

Of course, even this weekend prototype can be varied. For example, by arriving at the starting point on Saturday morning, you can eliminate the Friday night lodging entirely or you could begin with an inn stay but, by arranging a car shuttle, eliminate the stay at the other end. With opposite intentions, the ambitious hiker may combine contiguous weekend treks into a continuous walking tour, which can span three, four or more days (see Appendix C). Whatever your pleasure and pocketbook, you will certainly find here combinations of hiking and inns that will make your vacations memorable.

Getting Ready

When To Go

The most reliable period for one of these treks is between May and October, since this is the dry season. (During the other months take foul weather gear; the rains aren't always predictable, though they may insure your privacy on the trail.) As you choose your route, remember that the temperature range for these months varies from an average low of 50 degrees to an average high of 85 degrees, and that it is usually the presence of fog that determines the variation for the day. The foggy coastal areas, such as the western North Bay, the Santa Cruz Mountains and San Francisco, are therefore particularly good choices for the summer months. The East Bay, the South Bay and the Wine Country are at their best in spring and fall.

What To Take

We suggest taking the basic minimum, to keep your pack light. Dressing in layers is the strategy most compatible with the changing climate frequently found in the Bay Area. The items following should be sufficient:

- a light day pack
- a water canteen; this is crucial, because you cannot safely drink from the streams along the trails
- an appropriate clothing change, including clothes for the evening (outside San Francisco all of the inns are casual; jeans would be acceptable)
- comfortable lightweight hiking shoes
- a first aid kit (including treatment for snake bite and poison oak, optional but desirable)
- toilet articles

How to Start

It is absolutely necessary to make reservations well in advance at each inn. Guest houses, particularly, with their limited accommodations, require early planning, and some areas, such as San Francisco and the Wine Country, are notorious for this.

Since it will be necessary for you to leave your car overnight, you should inquire at your first night inn about parking facilities.

How to Use This Book

We have covered six sections of the Bay region, and each weekend trek is described in a separate chapter. Reservation information is included with each inn description at the beginning and end of the trek (see The Night Before and Jouney's End).

Unless the type of lodging offered is correctly reflected in the name of the establishment, its type is specified as one of these five:

Inn . . . . A small hotel
Guest house . . . A private residence that offers some rooms
Hotel-resort . . . A hotel that offers activities such as tennis, golf and swimming
Motel . . . . The basic overnight accommodation
Hostel . . . . A simple bunk-type lodging run by American Youth Hostels

For each, the room rate is described as follows (for a double room, per night):

Less than $41 . . .Inexpensive
$41 to $70 . . . . . .Moderately expensive
$71 to $100 . . . . .Expensive
More than $100 . .Very expensive

Public transportation information is also included; start with the information given in each chapter, then contact the transit companies for specific details.

Under each chapter's section, A Look at the Day's Walk, an overview of the day's route describes as well the flavor of the walk, to help you make choices among the 50 varied treks. Because of our own frustration with hiking books and trail maps that leave critical trails and junctions unmarked, we have provided route instructions in minute detail. Where useful, numbered instructions correspond with locations on the route maps, which are included for each walk. Despite our best intentions, we apologize for any changes in trail markings that may have occurred in the time elapsed between our writing and your reading of this book.

Each chapter ends with The Way Back, suggestions for returning to your inn of origin. In many cases public transportation is one alternative. For those preferring a second day's walk as the means of return, we have included, wherever possible, alternatives to merely retracing your steps. Because of space limitations, these routes are described briefly and without benefit of maps; they should be attempted only by the experienced hiker.

Our goal is to guide you from inn to inn with a minimum of confusion, even if we must neglect details of flora and fauna along the way. We hope this philosophy will give you the freedom to make discoveries for yourself, as you traverse these beautiful trails and back roads.

The Environment

One of the great pleasures of walking is the opportunity to experience nature at close range. In the Bay region, a day's hike can include the spectrum of local plant environments, which might be loosely categorized as shore, forest and open country. If you are not already familiar with the flora typical of these groupings, this brief overview will fill you in on some representative species.

Walking the shore where it is rocky, you will notice many varieties of surf grasses. And where the terrain becomes sandy beach and dune, you will find lupines, sand verbena, beach grass and sea rockets, as well as iceplant and beach morning glory. Near the beaches, in areas protected from wave action, salt marshes are formed; here glasswort, pickleweed, cord grass and sea blite flourish. Limantour Marsh at Point Reyes National Seashore is a prime example of such a marsh. Farther inland, near streams and ponds, such as freshwater marshes, Ledson Marsh in Annadel Park are home to cattails, bulrushes and tule.

Most any Bay area hike passes through one or another type of forestland; it's as characteristic of the Northern California coast as the shore itself. Bishop and Monterey pines cling to the ridges above the sea, and, just inland, the great coast redwood forests find an ideal environment in the coastal fog zone. Douglas fir forests occur less frequently, but the hikes on Inverness Ridge in Marin County route you through some of the finest stands in the area. The fir is most likely to appear in the company of compatible neighbors — oak, bay laurel and madrone — in the mixed evergreen forests that thrive alongside the redwood groves. Farther inland, on the drier and warmer slopes of the East Bay and the Wine Country, oak woodland predominates. Many of the trails in this book follow the sure course of a canyon stream, and here you can enjoy the shade of the sycamore, willow, maple and alder that flourish at the water's edge.

Soil and climate conditions that do not support the great forests are ideal for other common Bay area plant communities. Just above the sea, dry, rocky hillsides are covered in coastal scrub, with its pungent aromas of sage and coyote brush. Chaparral covers the high slopes and inland ridges with chamise, scrub oak, manzanita and wild lilac. And farther inland still, grassland prevails — mile after mile of bunch grass, sedge and wild oats, which, under the summer sun, color California's rolling hills golden.

San Francisco

Great cities reveal their innermost treasures to walkers, and San Francisco is no exception. The treks that follow allow you the pleasure of discovering some of these gems: a lane of midnineteenth-century sea cottages overlooking the San Francisco harbor, a procession of dim sum delicacies in a Chinatown tea room, a magnificent pair of Florentine-cast cathedral doors atop Nob Hill. But, apart from San Francisco's urban charms, what most distinguishes it as a walker's paradise is its superb natural setting. Many of the routes here clamber over the hills and around the open space preserves of the coastline. (Note also the route of chapter 15, in the following section on the North Bay, which also traces San Francisco's coastline but ends on the coastline of Marin County.) Because San Francisco is a tourist town, lodgings of all varieties are plentiful; the selections here are limited to those found most attractive and convenient to the routes.

Chapter 1
Union Square to North Beach

A 2¾-mile historic walk up and over
Telegraph Hill between city inns.

The Night Before

Getting There

By Public Transportation: Take Muni bus 2, 3, 4, 30, 38, 56 or 76.
The BART Powell Street Station is nearby. (Call (415) 673-6864 for
Muni or 788-BART for BART schedule.)

By Car: From Highway 101 along Van Ness Avenue, turn east on
Post Street and proceed to Union Square. Alternatively, follow
signs to downtown.

Union Square

When Elizabeth II of England graced San Francisco with a visit in
early 1983, she and Prince Philip stayed at the venerable Saint Francis Hotel on Union Square. No visitor, royal or otherwise, wishing
to be at the center of things in the city could have made a happier
choice of location. The square, a palm-fringed green crisscrossed by
walks and rimmed by the city's grandest department stores, both
pinpoints the downtown shopping district and defines the eastern
boundary of the theater district. Chinatown, Nob Hill and the
centers of high finance on Montgomery Street all lie within easy
walking distance. When done with exploring, the tourist may enjoy daytime viewing of the complete spectrum of San Franciscans
from the grandstand seat of a park bench in the square itself.

The Inns

The streets surrounding Union Square abound with hotels grand and small. The two following can best be described as inns.

The Adelaide Inn, 5 Adelaide Place, San Francisco 94102; (414) 442-2261. Continental breakfast included; inexpensive.

A European-style *pensione,* tucked away in a lane two blocks from Union Square. The 16 rooms are simply furnished; quiet and comfortable.

The Inn at Union Square, 440 Post Street, San Francisco 94102; (415) 397-3510. Continental breakfast included; expensive to very expensive.

This inn is the last word in charm, comfort and elegance and is a half block from Union Square. The 27 rooms are attractively decorated with Georgian antiques.

A Look at the Day's Walk

From Union Square, you stroll the length of elegant Maiden Lane and take a shortcut through the new Galleria shopping arcade at Crocker Center to arrive at the financial district. The route turns northward on Montgomery Street, where distinguished buildings vary in architectural style and period from the brick landmarks of the preearthquake era to today's towering prisms of glass and steel. From Levi Plaza, you ascend Telegraph Hill via a hidden pedestrian staircase, detouring to explore historic Napier Lane en route. Arriving at the Coit Tower summit, where once a telegraph advised the city of approaching ships, you take in a spectacular view of the city and Bay before descending Filbert Street to your North Beach inn.

The Route

Distance: 2¾ miles.
Walking Time: 1½ hours.
Grade: One steep uphill climb and descent.

From the Inn At Union Square, turn left and walk down Post. Cross Powell Street and walk through Union Square, an oasis of greenery amidst the hustle and bustle of the city's main shopping center. The monument in the center, dedicated to Theodore Roosevelt, commemorates Commodore Dewey's 1898 victory at Manila in the Spanish-American War.

Cross Stockton Street at either corner and find Maiden Lane, a narrow street between Post and Geary Street, walk the two-block span of this former red-light district that now attracts shoppers and tourists to its posh stores. The curvilinear design of number 140, an art gallery, is by Frank Lloyd Wright.

At Kearny Street, turn left and catch your first glimpse of the black-windowed, sleekly rectangular Bank of America building that dominates the landscape, about four blocks ahead on Kearny.

Turn right on Post; about halfway down the block, turn left into the Galleria, a new luxury shopping mall that provides a pleasant atrium walkway from Post to Sutter. When you have enjoyed window-shopping through the mall, turn right on Sutter Street and then left on Montgomery Street.

The route now traverses the length of the financial heart of the city — down Montgomery to the Transamerica Pyramid, which you can see straight ahead. Number 220, the Mills Building, on the right, dates from 1891 and was built by Darius Ogden Mills, whose wealth financed the Comstock silver lode and the Transcontinental Railroad. (Crossing Pine, look to the left to get a closer view of the Bank of America building.)

Turn right at California Street for a one-block detour to Sansome Street and back, worth taking because this area is the city's banking center. Number 465 California, on the right, is the Merchant's Exchange, dating from 1905 and serving as a gathering place for the business community of the city. Take a moment to go inside and examine the nautical paintings on the walls of the Grain Exchange Hall.

When you arrive at Sansome, stop to notice the red-brick Southern Pacific building ahead on Market Street, the headquarters for the first Transcontinental Railroad. Cross California and return to Montgomery, passing numbers 400 and 420, the headquarters of the Bank of California, dating from 1908. Within, you may visit the Museum of the Money of the American West, containing among other things a collection of precious metal from the Gold Rush days.

Before continuing north on Montgomery through the financial district, enjoy the choice view of the Mark Hopkins Hotel ahead on California at the top of Nob Hill.

The Wells Fargo Bank building, at 420 Montgomery, houses a fascinating History Room that is well worth a visit. Across the street, at number 505, a plaque commemorates the Hudson's Bay Company, which once occupied this site.

Proceed on Montgomery to the corner of Commercial Street. This was the center of the city in the midnineteenth century. You can see up ahead to the west the old brick pavement leading to Chinatown. To the east, you can pick out the Ferry Building on the Embarcadero.

Cross Commercial Street and continue to the corner of Clay, where the old Bank of America building still sits (number 552). At the corner of Montgomery and Merchant streets, notice the plaque where the first Pony Express rider arrived in the city in 1860.

Here you can see the unique Transamerica Pyramid up close before leaving the financial section and continuing on Montgomery past Clay Street. Cross Washington Street, being careful not to veer off on Columbus Avenue, and take note of the old Transamerica Building at number 701 and at 722, the Belli Building. The famous San Francisco attorney Melvin Belli has his offices in this charming vintage-1850 structure. In the midnineteenth-century, Bret Harte wrote *The Luck of Roaring Camp* in the Genella Building, number 728. The Knoll Building, number 732, dates from 1852. Across the street, next door to number 735, the first Jewish religious services in San Francisco were held on Yom Kippur in 1849.

At Jackson Street, turn right. You are in the heart of the Jackson Square Historical District, and the route takes you one block through this area of midnineteenth-century buildings that now house antique and other decorator showrooms. The Hotaling Buildings, numbers 445, 451 and 467-73 Jackson Street, were built in the 1860s by A. P. Hotaling, a wealthy liquor dealer. Unlike much of the town they survived the 1906 earthquate, much to the amusement of limerick writer Charles K. Field:

If, as they say, God spanked the town
For being over-frisky
Why did He burn the churches down
And save Hotaling's whiskey?

You may wish to detour into Hotaling Place, where the Villa Taverna, a private lunch club, attracts San Francisco society.

Continue to Sansome and turn left. Walk five blocks north and, just past Union Street, turn right into Levi Strauss Plaza for a rest or lunch stop before beginning the climb up Telegraph Hill. When you are ready for the only strenuous portion of this route, cross Sansome and find the Filbert Street steps directly across the street from the Plaza, just before number 1301 Sansome.

The steep ascent up to Telegraph Hill is accomplished pleasurably by taking frequent pauses along the lushly planted Filbert steps, enjoying the quaint old houses and lovingly planted gardens. Take Napier Lane to the right for a brief foray along the old wooden walkway lined with tiny nineteenth-century cottages.

Continue up the Filbert steps, crossing to the left at Darrell Place and then climbing the steps again at Montgomery Street, turn right to Greenwich Street, where the restaurant Julius' Castle sits on its fabulous peak overlooking the city and Bay. Turn left and follow the red-brick Greenwich steps up to the top of Telegraph Hill.

During the Gold Rush, a semaphore tower situated here was used to signal the arrival of ships through the Golden Gate. Thus Telegraph Hill got its name. Today, it is a tourist mecca famed for the 360-degree views from its summit and for Coit Tower, built in the 1930s with money donated by Lillie Hitchcock Coit.

You will certainly wish to make a slow circle of the parking area to enjoy bird's-eye views in all directions. For the tourist, this is a wonderful place to get a sense of the layout of the city as well as an appreciation of the beauty of the entire Bay Area.

Another, even more dramatic view is available from the top of the 210-foot tower, and, in addition, you should not miss the murals on the walls inside. They were done in 1934 by artists of the Works Progress Administration of the Roosevelt era and are a fascinating glimpse into the political and social life of those turbulent times.

To find the Filbert steps going down the west, take the pedestrain path alongside Telegraph Hill Boulevard past the small cottage marked number 115 and down the steps to Filbert Street. At the bottom, continue steeply down Filbert to Stockton. Turn left to the Washington Square Inn. For the Millefiore Inn, remain on Stockton to Columbus and turn left.

Journey's End

North Beach

No area in San Francisco has more sensual delights for the walker than North Beach. Restaurants redolent with tomato and garlic and espresso bars perfect for people-watching, plus the ethnic diversity of the population, provide an atmosphere reminiscent of Paris or New York. Like Greenwich Village, this center of the Italian community has long attracted artists and writers.

The Inns

Washington Square Inn, 1660 Stockton Street, San Francisco, 94133; (415) 981-4220. Continental breakfast included; expensive.

Fifteen large, comfortable guest rooms overlooking Washington Square — a smashing location right in the heart of North Beach.

Millefiore Inn, 444 Columbus Avenue, San Francisco, 94133; (415) 433-9111. Continental breakfast included; moderately expensive.

A genteel, European-style inn, one block from Washington Square. Sixteen rooms, distinctively furnished.

The Way Back

By Public Transportation: Take Muni bus number 30 down Columbus, then Stockton to Union Square. (Call (415) 673-6864 for schedule.)

By Foot: There are an infinite number of ways to wander back, depending on what you want to explore. One alternative is to walk down Columbus, then take Grand Avenue through Chinatown, turning right on Maiden Lane to return to Union Square. Another is to walk one block west of Washington Square to Mason, following Mason over Nob Hill and down to Union Square.

Chapter 2
North Beach to Pacific Heights

A 2¼-mile stroll including Chinatown
and Nob Hill between city inns.

The Night Before

Getting There

By Public Transportation: Take Muni buses 41 or 82. (Call (415) 673-6864 for schedules.)

By Car: From Highway 101 along Lombard Street take Union Street east to Stockton Street.

North Beach and the Inns

See the preceding chapter for description of the neighborhood and the Washington Square and Millefiore inns.

A Look at the Day's Walk

From North Beach to Pacific Heights is little more than one mile as the crow flies. You will take a more leisurely stroll, however, sampling the exotic flavors of Chinatown and the elegance of Nob Hill along the way.

The Route

Distance: 2¼ miles.
Time: 1½ hours.
Grade: Two short uphill climbs: mostly level terrain.

From the doorway of the Washington Square Inn you can enjoy the bustle of Washington Square, the hub of North Beach. The large Church of Saints Peter and Paul, the scene of many neighborhood weddings and baptisms, was built in 1924.

Turn left on Stockton and walk one block to the intersection with Columbus Avenue, the main street of North Beach. Turn left on Columbus and walk to Vallejo, where Saint Francis Church dominates the northeast corner. This Gothic Revival church was built in 1859 to serve the Italian immigrants who began arriving here during the Gold Rush. Here, Millefiore Inn patrons join the route which continues southeast.

Proceeding along Columbus past markets, coffeehouses and restaurants, arrive at Broadway and the center of North Beach nightlife. In the midnineteenth-century, before the Bay inlet was filled with land, new immigrants arrived at the Broadway Wharf a few blocks to the east. Now this area is crowded at night with people enjoying the topless clubs, as well as such famous night spots as the hungry i, where Mort Sahl began his career, the Purple Onion and Basin Street West. A half block to the left is Romolo Place, where a plaque locates the old Broadway jail.

Proceeding south on Columbus, you may wish to visit the City Lights Bookstore across the street. This literary and artistic landmark, owned by poet Lawrence Ferlinghetti, became the hub of the Beat Generation of the 1950s with the publication of such writers as Allen Ginsberg and Jack Kerouac.

At the next intersection, the meeting of Columbus, Pacific Avenue and Kearny Street, pause for a moment to recall the old Barbary Coast waterfront of which these blocks were a part. This notorious red-light district of the late nineteenth century was damaged by the 1906 fire and eventually finished off by Prohibition.

Straight ahead you can see the green flatiron building, Columbus Tower. Built after the big earthquake, it has witnessed a history of political corruption and reform. Beyond, the dramatic Transamerica Pyramid dominates the skyline. This marks the edge of the Jackson Square area, set aside by San Francisco as a historical district because it is the city's oldest intact commercial area.

Take Kearny to the right, heading south toward Chinatown. You will notice an immediate shift from the fettucine and prosciutto of North Beach storefronts to the long beans and Peking ducks displayed in Chinatown.

In the midnineteenth century the Chinese started arriving here, attracted in growing numbers by the Gold Rush and, later, imported by Charles Crocker to build the Central Pacific Railway. After the Exclusion Act was repealed, and following World War II, many more Chinese poured in, creating a Cantonese city within the city.

Turn right on Washington, noticing on the corner Buddha's Universal Church, which represents a modern approach to the religion of many Chinese-Americans. On the left, as you continue on Washington Street is Portsmouth Plaza, where elderly residents come to sit and children to play. Memorials in the park include a flagpole for Comdr. John Montgomery, who in 1846 landed his ship *Portsmouth* and raised the American flag here. At 743 Washington Street is the Kow Kong Benevolent Association building, built in 1909 in the style of an ancient Chinese temple.

At the intersection with Grant Avenue, turn left for a leisurely stroll through the heart of Chinatown. The novelty shops are fun to browse and, if you are ready for lunch, one of the wonderful restaurants and dim sum tearooms in this area would be an apt choice.

At 823 Grant, a bronze plaque marks the site of the first dwelling in Yerba Buena, built by Capt. William Richardson. Three blocks farther on Grant at the intersection with California Street is the Chinatown Wax Museum on the right, and, on the left, Old Saint Mary's Church, the first building erected as a cathedral in California.

At the corner of Grant and California, turn right and start your climb to old San Francisco's pinnacle of power — Nob Hill. Here, in the glittering twilight of the nineteenth century, the great railroad magnates and silver kings — Fair, Hopkins, Stanford, Flood, Crocker and Huntington — established their palatial residences. After the devastation of the 1906 earthquake and fire, little remained on the hill but the memory of golden days, and it seems fitting that the city's grandest hotels occupy the summit today. The Fairmont stands on the foundations of the old Fair estate. Across the street, the Mark Hopkins occupies the site of the Hopkins mansion, with the elegant Stanford Court behind it. Cross Powell Street, walking west on California alongside the brass fence of the lone survivor: James Flood's brownstone mansion, now the home of the Pacific Union Club.

Cross Taylor Street and ascend the steps to Grace Cathedral, the city's major Episcopal church, built on the site of the Crocker estate. Pause to examine the marvelous Ghiberti doors cast from Florentine originals, then enter to tour the Gothic interiors.

When you are ready, exit the cathedral, turn left on Taylor and walk two blocks to Washington; turn left again and proceed down Nob Hill westward on Washington Street for the next half mile.

While the great 1906 fire raged over Nob Hill, the Army dynamited Van Ness Avenue to deter the course of the conflagration westward. As a result, when you cross Van Ness, you enter what is virtually an architectural preserve. The streets of Pacific Heights, which extend steeply before you, bloom with exquisite specimens of Victorian design. Cross Franklin Street, turn right and walk to number 2007 Franklin, one of the loveliest examples of the genre. The Haas-Lilienthal House is now the headquarters of the San Francisco Architectural Foundation. It is open to the public for inspection, with tours at specified hours.

Upon departure, turn left on Jackson and pause before the Queen Anne Victorian, circa 1880, at 1819 Jackson. Another vintage mansion, from the Classic Revival style of the early 1900s, awaits you one block west at 1901 Jackson.

Continue to the corner and turn left up Octavia Street to Washington to discover the opulent Spreckles Mansion at 2080 Washington. Built in 1912 for the heir of the sugar fortune, the great estate was designed by George Applegarth, architect of the California Palace of the Legion of Honor, in Lincoln Park.

Proceed one block to the corner of Washington and Laguna streets. Here, guests of the Mansion Hotel and Hermitage House turn left for a two-block walk to Sacramento Street; guests of Jackson Court turn right for a one-block walk to Jackson.

Journey's End

Pacific Heights

Because what little remained of San Francisco after the 1906 fire lay to the west of Van Ness Avenue, any walk through Pacific Heights or its westernmost limit, Presidio Heights is a treat for admirers of Victorian architecture. Many fine specimens of nineteenth-century design can be found here. The grand mansions, lofty views and sculptured gardens support Pacific Height's claim to being San Francisco's most elegant neighborhood.

The Inns

Hermitage House, 2224 Sacramento Street, San Francisco 94115; (415) 921-5515. An inn, with continental breakfast included; moderately expensive to expensive.

A four-story mansion in Greek Revival style, built in 1900. Each of ten rooms has antique furnishings and custom accessories.

Jackson Court, 2198 Jackson Street, San Francisco 94115; (415) 929-7670. An inn, with continental breakfast included; expensive.

The Callahan mansion dates from 1900 and conveys an aura of old San Francisco with its high ceilings and marble-faced fireplaces. Ten rooms, each distinctively decorated.

The Mansion Hotel, 2220 Sacramento Street, San Francisco 94115; (415) 929-9444. An inn, with full breakfast included and a restaurant on the premises; expensive.

A Queen Anne-style Victorian, built in 1887 high on a landscaped knoll. The 19 rooms are imaginatively decorated; antiques, tapestries and paintings abound. Nightly concerts in the Music Parlour, pool in the Billiard Room.

The Way Back

By Public Transportation: Take Muni bus 41 from Sacramento Street to Clay and Kearny streets; then take the 15 to Washington Square. Alternatively, walk north on Laguna five to eight blocks for the 41 to Washington Square. (Call (415) 673-6864 for schedule.)

By Foot: Union Street extends 1½ miles back to Washington Square; pass along its level strip of boutiques, then continue steeply up and over Russian Hill. Alternatively, from your inn walk a few blocks east and take Laguna north, down to Bay Street; cross the Great Meadow at Fort Mason and follow the paved road at the meadow's northeast corner east along the Bay bluffs. Continue along the Bay, passing Aquatic Park and picking up Beach Street for a half block. Turn south on Columbus to Washington Square — 2½ miles, in all.

Chapter 3
Pacific-Presidio Heights to Cow Hollow

A 5½- to 7-mile walk around the shores
of San Francisco between inns and guest houses.

The Night Before

Getting There

By Public Transportation: Take Muni bus 1, 2, 3, 4, 22 or 24. (Call
(415) 673-6864 for schedule.)

By Car: From Highway 101 along Van Ness Avenue, for Casa
Arguello turn west on Jackson Street to its end at Arguello
Boulevard. For the El Drisco Hotel turn west from 101 onto Pacific
Avenue to Broderick Street.

Pacific Heights

See the preceding chapter for description.

The Inns

Casa Arguello, 225 Arguello Boulevard, San Francisco 94118; (415)
752-9482. A guest house, with full breakfast included; inexpensive
to moderately expensive.

Five spacious guest bedrooms with homey ambiance in a fine
residential neighborhood.

El Drisco Hotel, 2901 Pacific Avenue, San Francisco 94115; (415)
346-2880. An inn, with a restaurant on the premises in a fine
residential neighborhood.

A survivor of the 1906 quake, atop Pacific Heights; many of the comfortable rooms have panoramic Bay and city views.

Your choice of inn will determine the length of your route, so you may want to consult the distance table that follows before making reservations.

A Look at the Day's Walk

The Presidio of San Francisco has functioned as a military installation for the past 200 years. From the environmental point of view, its government ownership has been a happy circumstance, preserving the choice real estate on the San Francisco headlands as a green belt.

This walk rims three sides of the Presidio's 6½-mile perimeter (from the entry point at the height of Pacific Avenue). Alongside the southern wall, you pass between rows of fine turn-of-the-century homes on the one side and groves of Monterey cypress on the other, and pause to enjoy Mountain Lake. On the west, you negotiate the dunes of Baker Beach, with its sparkling vistas of the Marin headlands and the Golden Gate Bridge. Rounding Fort Point, you walk the northern shore along the Golden Gate Promenade with the skyline of the city stretched before you. Then, continuing past the yacht harbor, you follow Marina Boulevard until the cross street for your inns presents itself.

The Route

Distance: 5½ to 7 miles (depending on your choice of inns, see below).
Walking Time: 3 to 4 hours.
Grade: Level.

From	To	Miles
Casa Arguello	Union Street Inn	6
	Stewart-Grinsell House	6
	Bed and Breakfast Inn	6
	Hotel Edward II	5½
El Drisco	Union Street Inn	7
	Stewart-Grinsell House	7
	Bed and Breakfast Inn	7
	Hotel Edward II	6½

From the El Drisco Hotel, walk left on Pacific Avenue and turn right on Baker Street to Broadway. Walk left on Broadway, past the elegant old mansions overlooking the Marina and Fisherman's Wharf, through the stone pillars at Lyon Street. Walk on the paved path across Presidio Boulevard and continue on West Pacific Avenue, through the groves of eucalyptus and cypress, as it swings around and runs parallel to Pacific Avenue.

From Casa Arguello, walk north on Arguello Street four blocks into the Presidio. Turn left on West Pacific Avenue. From either inn continue walking on West Pacific, past the golf course. Where West Pacific veers right (circled number 1 on the map), go left on the dirt road along the edge of Mountain Lake (the first campsite of the Anza Expedition, which founded San Francisco in 1776). Proceed up the path, pick up Lake Street, and cross Park Presidio Boulevard. At 14th Avenue turn right and pass through the gates of the former U.S. Public Health Service Hospital.

As you walk up the paved road of the hospital, veer left through the parking lot to the cyclone fence bordering the hospital area. At this point, leave the paved area and pick your way up to the top of the ridge through the iceplant and the forest of cypress and pine trees. At the top of the hill, notice a grassy path leading downhill (2). Follow this, veering to the left where the path splits and continuing down into the open meadow at the bottom. The path you want next is across the meadow, running alongside the fence straight ahead. Take that dirt path to the right.

After a bit, the broad dirt road of the U.S. Army Reserve Center appears on the right, running along your path. That is Howard Road; cross over to pick up, and continue walking in the same direction. Cross Lincoln Boulevard; turn immediately right on Bowley Street, then left on Gibson Road to Baker Beach.

Baker Beach is named for Col. Edward Dickinson Baker, who commanded the first regiment of California volunteers in the Civil War. It was a glorious walking beach and has a view of the western face of the Golden Gate, the side seen first by the great ships entering the harbor from faraway ports. If it is lunchtime, this is a wonderful spot for a picnic.

Walk north along the beach toward the bridge. After passing Battery Chamberlin, climb up the sand dunes to the right where a white handrail marks the path (3), and take the broad dirt road up and to the left to Lincoln Boulevard. Here, continue walking left on the narrow path running along the boulevard, with dramatic views of the Pacific and Helmet Rock below.

As you draw close to the bridge, take Merchant Road, left; it winds toward the toll plaza. Follow the Pacific Coast Bicentennial Bicycle Route signs to the left and through the tunnel to the right. Cross the little plaza with the statue of Joseph Strauss, the builder of the Golden Gate, and go down the path behind the statue. Veer to the right, through the fence, and then left toward Fort Point.

At the Fort Point National Historic Site viewpoint, with a unique perspective on the massive underpinnings of the bridge, you might wish to rest or enjoy a late lunch before heading down the path and into the fort for a tour of this nineteenth-century landmark.

After spending some time in the fort, walk out along Marine Drive, where crashing waves send sea spray high in the air above the seawall, scattering unwary pedestrians. When you arrive at the little white house marked Fort Point National Historic Site, veer left along the seawall toward the pier, following the blue-and-white Golden Gate Promenade signs. Walk the wide dirt path along the water, through the Fort Point Coast Guard Station parking lot. (A Golden Gate Promenade marker appears on the fence straight ahead.)

Walk the length of the promenade, a popular jogging path, enjoying the skyline of San Francisco with the dome of the Palace of Fine Arts in the foreground and the Transamerica Pyramid and the dark Bank of America rectangle looming behind it. At the end, where the San Francisco Yacht Club fronts the Bay, turn to the right up the stone steps and cross the Marina Green to Marina Boulevard. Walk left along the boulevard past the rows of sailboats and huge yachts bobbing in the harbor.

If your hotel is the Edward II, turn right at Scott Street and walk seven blocks to Lombard Street and your inn.

For the Union Street Inn, turn right at Fillmore Street and walk eight blocks to Union. Turn right; your inn is halfway down the street on the left side.

Stewart-Grinsell House patrons turn right on Laguna (at the end of Marina Boulevard) and walk seven blocks to Filbert Street.

For the Bed and Breakfast Inn, walk right on Laguna eight blocks to Union Street, where a right turn takes you to the little Charlton Court on the left side.

Journey's End

Cow Hollow

Cow Hollow was named for the dairy ranches that thrived here during the last half of the nineteenth century. Its proximity to the mansions of Pacific Heights has made its hopping corridors a center of fine art, antiques, designer clothing, and gourmet dining.

The Inns

Hotel Edward II, 3155 Scott Street, San Francisco 94123; (415) 921-9776. An inn, with continental breakfast included; inexpensive.

European style, providing "a modest room at a reasonable price" on the busy motel strip in the Marina. Decor is English country style.

Union Street Inn, 2229 Union Street, San Francisco 94123; (415) 346-0424. An inn, with continental breakfast included; expensive to very expensive.

One of the oldest bed-and-breakfast inns in San Francisco, with a tranquil garden setting. Nineteenth-century Edwardian decor in six elegantly fitted guest bedrooms.

Stewart-Grinsell House, 2963 Laguna Street, San Francisco 94123; (415) 563-3314. An inn, with continental breakfast included; expensive.

A lovely Victorian, circa 1880, situated one block off Union. Five comfortable rooms with antiques appropriate to the Italianate interiors.

Bed and Breakfast Inn, 4 Charlton Court, San Francisco 94123; (415) 921-9784. Continental breakfast included; expensive to very expensive.

Every detail of a country inn is transplanted to a quiet courtyard off one of the most fashionable shopping areas in San Francisco. Library, garden and nine guest rooms.

The Way Back

By Public Transportation: Take Muni bus 22; transfer at Jackson Street to the 3, westbound. (Call (415) 673-6864 for schedule.)

By Foot: Climb the steep hill to Pacific Heights from Lombard (eight blocks) or Union (five blocks).

Chapter 4
The Panhandle to Sutro Heights

A 4½-mile exploration of Golden Gate Park,
from Victorian inns to an ocean-view motel.

The Night Before

Getting There

By Public Transportation: Take Muni bus 5, 7, 21, 43, 71, 72 or 78.
(Call (415) 673-7864.)

By Car: From the Highway 101 Fell Street exit, take Fell Street west
(toward Highway 1) to Panhandle of Golden Gate Park.

The Panhandle

This long strip of land attached to the eastern end of Golden
Gate Park does indeed resemble a pan handle. In the 1960s this
green mall and the Haight Ashbury district to the south were
swarming with "flower children," dreaming psychedelic visions of
peace and love, who in the 1970s were largely replaced by
derelicts. Now the area is enjoying a dramatic rebirth, and among
the old Victorian mansions being restored are some of the most
delightful inns in the city.

The Inns

Victorian Inn on the Park, 301 Lyon Street, San Francisco 94117;
(415) 931-1830. Continental breakfast included; expensive.

Six guest rooms in a beautifully refurbished Victorian mansion. Oak paneling and antique furnishings authentically reflect its nineteenth-century origins.

Spreckels Mansion, 737 Buena Vista West, San Francisco 94117; (415) 861-3008. An inn, with continental breakfast included; expensive to very expensive.

An elegant Victorian built in 1887 — the former residence of such literary luminaries as Ambrose Bierce and Jack London. One of the top inns in the city, but requires a two-night stay on weekends.

Red Victorian Hotel, 1665 Haight Street, San Francisco 94117; (415) 864-1978. Includes continental breakfast; inexpensive.

A turn-of-the-century inn that appeals to students and young people — rather funky but full of personality.

A Look at the Day's Walk

In 1870, most people scoffed at the plan to turn 1,000 acres of windswept sand dunes on the outskirts of San Francisco into a sylvan retreat. But under the loving hand of John McLaren, a Scottish gardener, the dream became verdant Golden Gate Park.

If you started from the eastern end of the Panhandle and followed the curves of John F. Kennedy Drive all the way to the ocean, the four-mile tour of the park would take about two hours to complete. Your route today, however, includes numerous forays off the main road around serene lakes and past lily ponds, tree ferns and exotic flowers. To do justice to every detour possible would require much more time than a one-day walk allows. You must, therefore, reserve some of them for a return walk, or choose to see some and forego others. To make some preliminary choices, take an advance look at the route description that follows and especially for the Conservatory, the Japanese Tea Garden and the Arboretum, which are chock full of botanical wonders and will tempt you to linger.

The Route

Distance: 4½ miles or more.
Walking Time: A half to a full day, depending on detours.
Grade: Mostly level through park; an uphill walk of ¾ mile along the Great Highway to the Seal Rock Inn.

The imposing Statue of Justice on Baker Street marks the start of your day's ramble through Golden Gate Park. From here, in the shade of pine, cypress and eucalyptus, stroll the eight-block length of the Panhandle until meeting the Stanyan Street entrance to the park proper, the park headquarters in McLaren Lodge at the right. Stop here at the headquarters to pick up maps or detailed guide books.

Continuing west now on Kennedy Drive, take the second right turn on the footpath toward the Fuchsia Garden, turning left through the dell — at its brightest in August — and out to the east side of the Conservatory (circled number 1 on the map). This lovely late-Victorian greenhouse boasts an extensive collection of tropical blooms and well warrants a small detour. Upon departure, proceed down the front steps, across Conservatory Valley with its colorful floral plaques, and through the tunnel underpass below Kennedy Drive. Take the first right turn along the footpath, then the left on the dirt path through the tree ferns to the lily pond. From here, veer uphill to the right, and you will shortly find yourself in John McLaren Rhododendron Dell (2). If you visit in spring, there is no mistaking the place, since the concentrated blaze of color — there is nothing subtle about rhododendrons — is extraordinary.

Follow the path out to the east side of the Academy of Sciences and continue on the sidewalk in front of this great building that houses a planetarium, aquarium, African Hall and countless scientific displays. Across the music concourse, where Sunday afternoon concerts fill the amphitheater, is the Mission-style facade of the de Young Museum, an all-day detour for fine art enthusiasts.

At the end of the concourse, cross South Drive, turn left, and follow the Botanical Garden gate until you arrive at the main entrance of Strybing Arboretum (3). Here, you may purchase a garden guide for $1, wait for a docent-led tour or simply wander on your own through the 70 acres of remarkable plant specimens, exotic and native, that qualify the Arboretum as a horticultural paradise.

Leave the Arboretum via the Tea Garden Drive exit, and recrossing South Drive, you will find yourself outside the Japanese Tea Garden (4). From where you stand, observe the path veering uphill to the left; upon exiting the garden, you will need to retrace your steps to this point, which begins your path to Stow Lake. In the meantime, follow the garden wall around to the front entrance and, for a small admission charge, enter a world rarely seen this side of the Pacific. Here, a serene Kyoto garden awaits you, complete with reflecting pools, greenery, wooden bridges and stone lanterns. Be sure to relax and imbibe in the tea house before you leave.

Retracing your steps to the point opposite the Arboretum exit, follow the path uphill to the left and up the flight of steps to Stow Lake. Turn right at the path around the lake, following the loop until a sign at your left directs you to Golden Gate Pavilion. Cross to the small island of Strawberry Hill (5). When ready to proceed, return to this spot. You may enjoy the circular lakeside stroll, around the base of the hill, or the panoramic views from the top, which can be reached by the flight of steps directly ahead of you. In either case, upon returning, proceed left, past the boathouse, then down to the Redwood Memorial Grove at Kennedy Drive.

For the next mile and a half, your walk west on Kennedy Drive takes you past a succession of favorite park attractions, all clearly signposted and each to be passed quickly or perused at length according to your pleasure. Rainbow Falls, Lloyd Lake with its Portals of the Past or Spreckels Lake with its model yachts could be sufficient reason for a sojourn in the park, or, depending on the hour, a congenial setting for a picnic lunch.

At Chain of Lakes Drive, just after the Buffalo Paddock, turn right, following the footpath to the right that loops North Lake. Once you have rounded the northern edge and are heading south, back to Kennedy Drive, be alert for a dirt road to your right. Follow it west past the pitch-and-putt course until you are once again on Kennedy Drive. Turn right here, and walk past the Dutch Windmill to the Great Highway. Turn right again, and walk up the Great Highway about ¾ mile (toward Sutro Heights), rounding Point Lobos Avenue to the Seal Rock Inn.

Journey's End

Sutro Heights

Sutro Heights, on the cliffs at the southern border of Land's End, was named for Adolf Sutro, Comstock Lode millionaire. His home was named for Adolf Sutro, Comstock Lode millionaire. His home was located in Sutro Heights Park on 48th Avenue, just south of your motel. You may wish to visit the park, which has a garden setting and expansive views of the northern end of Ocean Beach. This beach's windy stretch of sand, flanked by the Great Highway, is thronged with visitors on sunny days. If you are here on a more typically foggy day, however, you can bundle up and enjoy a solitary stroll along the water's edge.

Below the heights, the Cliff House, a third generation descendant of the original one built in 1863, sits high on its promontory with views of Seal Rock and the broad Pacific beyond.

The Inn

Seal Rock Inn, 48th and Point Lobos avenues, San Francisco 94121; (415) 752-8000. A motel, with a restaurant on the premises; moderately expensive.

Overlooking the ocean, 27 units, some with fireplaces; clean and quite pleasant.

The Way Back

By Public Transportation: Muni bus 5 runs on Fulton Street the entire length of the park. (Call (415) 673-6864 for schedule.)

By Foot: If you have the time and energy to walk back to the Panhandle, you may choose Kennedy Drive again, taking those detours that you missed earlier. If you wish to vary the walk a bit more, you might turn off onto South Drive which will take you east through the park but along the southern route. This leads directly into the Arboretum and might be preferable if you missed that botanical highlight before.

Chapter 5
Sutro Heights to Fisherman's Wharf

A 7½-mile hike around Land's End
between city motels.

The Night Before

Getting There

By Public Transportation: Take Muni bus 38 west on Geary. (Call
(415) 673-6864 for schedule.)

By Car: From Highway 101 North, take the Fell Street exit; turn
right on Masonic Avenue and left on Geary, which leads into Point
Lobos Avenue. From Highway 101 South into the city, take the
19th Avenue exit and turn right on Geary, continuing to Point
Lobos Avenue.

Sutro Heights and the Inn

See the preceding chapter for description of Sutro Heights Park
and the Seal Rock Inn.

A Look at the Day's Walk

For the city hiker, the experience closest to sailing into San Francisco Bay is walking the cliffs and beaches of the Golden Gate National Recreation Area on the northern perimeter of the city. The
walk begins at Sutro Heights on the rocky ridge of Land's End that
guards the southern entry into the natural harbor and affords

unparalleled views of the ocean, the Bay and the Marin coastline. From here you watch the great ocean liners making the turn past Baker Beach and under the Golden Gate, and your route follows their path. Fort Point welcomes you to the harbor; you then continue your walk past the sailboats and yachts in the Marina to your lodging at Fisherman's Wharf.

The Route

Distance: 7½ miles.
Walking Time: 3½ hours.
Grade: Mostly level.

Walk seaward from the Seal Rock Inn, down Point Lobos Avenue to the parking lot above the ruins of the old Sutro Baths. Turn right (circled number 1 on the map) and follow the dirt path that leads out the north end of the lot, through a low-branched grove of Monterey cypress. This path continues a mile or so around Land's End, and if you remember to keep the Pacific to your left, you can't go too far wrong. At major junctions, bear left, but otherwise ignore offshoots from the main trail; the posted signs announcing the dangers of the precipitous cliffs should be warning enough to all but the most intrepid. The vistas from the tried-and-true path are sufficiently awesome — Mile Rock light and the Marin headlands seem close enough to touch, and halfway along, the Golden Gate Bridge swings fully into view. Shortly after the Baker Beach and Seacliff areas open before you, the trail joins a green of the Lincoln Park Golf Course and ends at El Camino Del Mar.

Walk down El Camino Del Mar and enter the rarified atmosphere of Seacliff — the exclusive neighborhood of Mediterranean-style mansions overlooking Phelan Beach. Development here, although initiated in 1912, proceeded later according to a code of exacting construction standards, resulting in the high quality of the individual homes as well as the aesthetic harmony of the community as a whole. Continue down El Camino Del Mar, then turn right on Seacliff Avenue (2) for a sidewalk stroll alongside a characteristically luxurious street. At the end of Seacliff (3), turn right on 25th, then left on El Camino Del Mar — which becomes Lincoln Boulevard upon entering the Presidio.

Turn left (4) on Bowley Street, then left (5) again on Gibson Road to Baker Beach.

Baker Beach was named for Colonel Baker, the commander of the first California volunteer regiment of the Civil War. It is a perfect place for a picnic lunch with its unobstructed view of the western face of the Golden Gate Bridge.

After resting here, walk north along the beach past Battery Chamberlin, a 1906 military installation. At the northern perimeter of the installation, notice a handrail at the top of the sand dune on the right (6). Climb up and take this path as it follows the cyclone fence around the installation, then continue on the wide road curving to the right and up to Lincoln Boulevard above the beach.

Turn left on the convenient footpath alongside Lincoln Boulevard. As you walk this stretch of road above the beach, you can see the green hills of Land's End to the south and, to the north, the rugged Marin County headlands with Point Bonita lighthouse at its tip.

At the end of the footpath, continue along the edge of Lincoln Boulevard to Merchant Road, where you turn left. Battery Boutelle is straight ahead, but you stay on Merchant Road as it curves to the right toward the tollgate of the bridge.

In the parking lot, notice the white Pacific Coast Bicycle Route signs. Follow them to the left down the ramp and then to the right under the freeway and out to the little park dedicated to Joseph Strauss, the builder of the bridge. Take the path leading from the back of the statue, curving down to the right, then through the fence and to the left toward Fort Point, seen below straddled by the mighty southern foundation of the Golden Gate.

When you reach the bottom of the path, you may choose to spend some time exploring this nineteenth-century fort built by the U.S. Army Engineers. The route, however, continues to the right along Marine Drive. As you walk here, beware of the seaspray that douses unwary pedestrians when the waves crash the seawall.

Continue along the path to the left of the white administrative office of the Fort Point National Historic Site, taking note of the blue Golden Gate Promenade sign straight ahead. Follow this and the bike signs, which lead you along the Bay and through the Fort Point Coast Guard Station.

The Golden Gate Promenade, a favorite of joggers and walkers, affords clear views of the San Francisco skyline ahead. You can see the dome of the Palace of Fine Arts in the foreground, the Transamerica Pyramid behind it, Nob Hill to the east and Russian Hill to the west. In the Bay on the left are Angel Island and Alcatraz.

Proceed along the Bay toward the Saint Francis Yacht Club at the end of the promenade. Take the broad stone steps to the right and the path through the Marina Green to Marina Boulevard. Walk left along the boulevard, past the rows of sailboats berthed in the harbor. Swing left, around the harbor, to follow the bay-side path along the east end of the Marina Green.

Circle Gas House Cove and enter Fort Mason via the small pedestrian ramp at the water's edge. Fort Mason, once the Western headquarters of the U.S. Army (McDowall Hall dates back to 1855) now houses the headquarters of the Golden Gate National Recreation Area. From the parking lot of Fort Mason Center, scan the signs on the piers, then check the bulletin boards inside them and perhaps amble through the open galleries to investigate the array of cultural, educational and recreational programs that now inhabit the old military installation.

When you are ready, head for the great Bufano sculpture at the far end of the lot, and ascend the stairs close by. Turn left at the top and proceed eastward, following the road through the lovely cypress grove overlooking the Bay. At the top of the hill you will get your first glimpse of Fisherman's Wharf — a welcome sight, if you are beginning to slow down about now. Continue to Aquatic Park, passing the World War II liberty ship *Jeremiah O'Brien*, now anchored here, then following the shoreline route around the curve of the beach below the Maritime Museum. For sea buffs, an hour or two here is irresistable; for window-shoppers and pleasure seekers, the time can be happily whiled away across Beach Street at Ghirardelli Square.

If you wish first to fortify yourself after the long walk, stop next one block east on Beach at the Buena Vista Cafe, renowned for its Irish coffee. To find any of the inns on Beach, or on Columbus or Mason streets, which are cross streets nearby, continue east on Beach. Bay Street, on which you'll find the Ramada Inn, is two blocks south.

Journey's End

Fisherman's Wharf

This area was once the domain of the Italian commercial fishermen, whose fleets started operating here in the midnineteenth-century. Now, though few fishermen are based here, every visitor to San Francisco eventually makes his way to the wharf. Attracted by fresh sea breezes and fish restaurants, the visitors throng the gift shops and souvenir stores and sample such local delicacies as Dungeness crab cocktails in sidewalk vendors' paper cups. Of special interest, at Pier 43, is the *Balclutha*, a restored late-nineteenth-century steel-hulled ship.

The Inns

Since the following motels belong to chains you are probably familiar with, their descriptions are minimal.

Howard Johnson's Motor Lodge, 580 Beach Street, San Francisco 94133; (415) 775-3800. Expensive. Very comfortable.

Holiday Inn, 1300 Columbus Avenue, San Francisco 94133; (415) 771-9000. With a restaurant on the premises; expensive to very expensive. Very comfortable.

Ramada Inn, 590 Bay Street, San Francisco 94133; (415) 885-4700. With a restaurant on the premises; expensive. Very comfortable.

Sheraton, 2500 Mason Street, San Francisco 94133; (415) 362-5500. With a restaurant on the premises; expensive to very expensive. Luxurious.

Travelodge, 250 Beach Street, San Francisco 94133; (415) 392-6700. Expensive to very expensive. Comfortable.

Wharf Motel, (A Thunderbird Motel), 2601 Mason Street, San Francisco 94133; (415) 673-7411. With a restaurant on the premises; moderately expensive. Very comfortable.

The Way Back

Public Transportation: Take Muni bus 42 to Geary Street, then transfer to the 38 bus west on Geary to the end. (Call (415) 673-6864 for a schedule.)

By Foot: There are as many routes back to Ocean Beach as your imagination and interest can conjure, so you need not retrace your steps. A walk south to Jackson, then west to Arguello will give you an opportunity to see Pacific Heights. From Arguello, you can walk south to Clement Street or Geary and continue west along those neighborhood shopping streets all the way to Sutro Heights Park. This 6¾-mile alternate route back should take about 3½ hours walking time.

The North Bay

From the redwood forests of Mount Tamalpais to the wind-swept beaches of the Point Reyes National Seashore, there are no more beautiful trails than those in the North Bay. Hikers long have been drawn here from all over the Bay area, and now, with the proliferation of fine inns and guest houses in and around the Golden Gate National Recreation Area, the ideal combination for weekend trekking has been created. Indeed, it is possible to head north from the Golden Gate and, by combining contiguous treks, take a spectacular seven-day walking tour over 60 trail-miles to Inverness (see Appendix C).

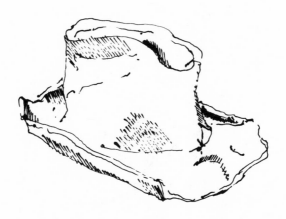

Chapter 6
Cow Hollow (San Francisco) to Sausalito

A 9-mile hike across the Golden Gate
from city inns to bay-view hotels.

The Night Before

Getting There

By Public Transportation: Muni buses 41 and 45 run down Union Street; Golden Gate Transit buses from the North Bay run down Lombard Street. (Call (415) 673-6864 for Muni and 332-6600 or 453-2100 for Golden Gate Transit schedules.)

By Car: The hotels are easily reached from the Lombard Street section of Highway 101.

Cow Hollow and the Inns

See chapter 3 for description of the neighborhood and the Hotel Edward II, Union Street Inn, Stewart-Grinsell House and Bed and Breakfast Inn.

A Look at the Day's Walk

According to Indian legend, the Sun God, attempting to abduct a beautiful maiden, fell and caused a rift in the mountains through which the ocean poured, creating San Francisco Bay. In 1937 Joseph B. Strauss, poet, engineer and visionary, completed the bridge that many had thought impossible to construct, and which in spanning the Golden Gate became a modern legend.

Both these legends inspire this hike, which follows the edge of the Bay in San Francisco and Marin and, in between, crosses the graceful orange-red span. You begin with a stroll along the Marina and the Golden Gate Promenade toward a horizon dominated by the graceful towers and cables of the bridge. From the rocky headlands of Fort Point, guarding the southern entrance to the harbor, it is just a short climb to the toll plaza above. Here you begin a nearly two-mile walk north across the bridge, which, at a 235-foot height above the water, affords unmatched views of San Francisco and the East Bay.

Arriving at Vista Point on the Marin side of the gate, you continue the walk with a crossing under the mammoth pillars of the bridge, through Fort Baker nestled at its northern foot, and into the bustling bayside town of Sausalito.

The Route

Distance: 9 miles.
Walking Time: 5 hours.
Grade: Mostly level except for a gentle descent to and climb from Fort Baker.

From Stewart-Grinsell House, walk up to Union Street and turn right; or, from the Bed and Breakfast Inn or Union Street Inn, turn left on Union. Walk north to Scott Street. Turn right on Scott, where Hotel Edward II guests join the walk at the corner of Lombard Street. Proceed down Scott toward the Bay until you reach Marina Boulevard. From here turn left (circled number 1 on the map) and walk the length of the yacht harbor, turning right (2) on Yacht Drive and following it to the Bay. A left turn (3) at the stone steps puts you on the Golden Gate Promenade — the paved footpath marked by blue-and-white Golden Gate Promenade Markers that runs along the water's edge. Follow the promenade for the next two miles to Fort Point, a brick Civil War military fortress. You might like to explore the arched casement chambers on the upper floors where once great guns were poised to defend San Francisco's harbor.

Take the path uphill from the Fort Point green (4), climbing the slope from below the bridge to the top. Here, bear left, walking through the gates toward the small circular structure that houses the Equal Employment Opportunity (EEO) office. Turn right and walk north, using the pedestrian lane on the east (city) side of the bridge. As you stroll across the Golden Gate Bridge, the remarkable vista of San Francisco Bay opens about you.

Arriving at Vista Point, 1¾ miles north of the toll plaza, follow the weekend-and-holiday bike-route signs, using the westbound walkway underneath the bridge. At the construction area, take the low road (5), following the bike-route signs that direct you down and under the bridge, and arrive finally at Fort Baker. This fort was established in 1897 as yet another link in the Army's coastal defense system.

Staying on the main road, turn right at Murray Circle and then continue straight along East Road (6) where it diverges from the circular drive. Signs to Sausalito will direct your path along the paved road, which crosses Yellow Bluff, until, veering right at the overpass, you join Alexander Avenue (7), the main southern access road into Sausalito. Be alert to car traffic at this dangerous turn, but once arrived at the safety of the sidewalk take a moment to enjoy your first sweeping view of Sausalito.

Continue down Second Street until reaching the Chart House, formerly Sally Stanford's Valhalla, where until her death in 1982 Sausalito's colorful former madam and sometime mayor presided. Here, at the corner of Main, a right turn takes you to a delightful boardwalk along the edge of the Bay. The boardwalk meets Bridgeway Boulevard at the turreted Castle-by-the-Sea where Jack London is reputed to have written *The Sea Wolf.* Proceed north along the Bay side of Bridgeway, passing the sculptured seal and then Sausalito's bastion of haute cuisine – Ondine's.

At Princess Street, Alta Mira guests should turn left and proceed uphill, veering to the right on Bulkley Avenue, where, almost immediately, the beautiful inn rises to your left. Guests of the Sausalito Inn should continue on Bridgeway to El Portal, where a right turn will lead you to the front door. If Casa Madrona is your destination, continue down Bridgeway to Bay Street, where, on your left just past the Village Fair complex, you'll find the newly remodeled hotel.

Journey's End

Sausalito

Mediterranean visitors have debated Sausalito's resemblance to one or another Riviera resort: Portofino, Santa Margherita Rapallo. But at second glance they come to agree with the natives that, obvious comparisons aside, Sausalito, like all enchanting places, is truly one of a kind.

Named "Saucelito" — little willow — by eighteenth-century Spanish explorers, it remained little until 100 years later, when the town began to push out across the three sections that define it today — hillside, waterfront and downtown. In the late 1800s, San Francisco "aristocracy" began to establish gracious country homes on the central hillsides, while at the same time immigrant Portuguese families took up residence on the flatlands close to their sources of livelihood — fishing, boat building and dairying. By 1893 when the city was incorporated, the downtown, a railhead for the North Pacific Coast Railroad, was already a tourist center of sorts, boasting a rollicking life of its own complete with saloons and gambling halls.

Today downtown gambling palaces have been replaced by boutiques, galleries and trendy watering spots, the passenger train, by bumper-to-bumper tourist traffic. Even so, in its picturesque waterfront and spectacular natural setting enough of a "Saucelito" remains to delight each new generation of visitors afresh.

The Inns

Alta Mira Hotel, 125 Bulkley Avenue, Sausalito 94965; (415) 332-1350. An inn, with a restaurant on the premises; moderately expensive to expensive.

A tourist mecca, perched on a hillside above the busy town center. This magnificent Victorian landmark has a variety of guest rooms with sweeping bay and city views, as well as separate cottage accommodations.

Casa Madrona, 802 Bridgeway, Sausalito 94965; (415) 332-0502. An inn, with continental breakfast included and a restaurant on the premises; moderately expensive to very expensive.

Newly refurbished inn with lovely bay views and an intimate European *pensione* atmosphere. Thirty-two guest rooms each imaginatively decorated by a different Bay Area designer.

Sausalito Hotel, 16 El Portal, Sausalito 94965; (415) 332-4155. An inn, with continental breakfast included and a restaurant on the premises; moderately expensive.

A Spanish-style hotel in the heart of downtown Sausalito. Fourteen guest bedrooms decorated with Victorian antiques retain the flavor of days gone by.

The Way Back

By Public Transportation: After a late night on the town, you may prefer the easiest return to San Francisco via Golden Gate Transit bus 10, which leaves regularly from Anchor Street on Bridgeway. If the day is fine, you may choose to return by ferry. (Call (415) 332-6600 for Golden Gate Transit bus and ferry schedules.) It will leave you at the Ferry Building at the end of Market Street in San Francisco, from which you can take a Muni bus (673-6864) or walk back to your hotel.

By Foot: Retrace the described route.

Chapter 7
Sausalito to Muir Beach

An 8½-mile hike from Sausalito bay-view hotels
to a Muir Beach seaside inn.

The Night Before

Getting There

By Public Transportation: Take Golden Gate Transit bus 10 or 20 to
Bridgeway in Sausalito. Golden Gate Ferries run to Sausalito from
the San Francisco Embarcadero. (Call (415) 332-6600 or 453-2100 for
both Golden Gate Transit and Golden Gate Ferry schedules.)

By Car: From Highway 101 north of the Golden Gate Bridge, take
the Sausalito exit.

Sausalito and the Inns

See the preceding chapter for description of the town and the
Alta Mira Hotel, Casa Madrona and the Sausalito Hotel. (That
chapter's section on The Route ends with directions to the inns
from Bridgeway.)

You begin by climbing the Sausalito slope via a series of hidden
pedestrian footpaths — a close-up look at the bright mosaic of
hillside homes and gardens. Leaving the houses behind, you pick
up Morning Sun Trail, which completes the 900-foot ascent of
Wolfback Ridge. You walk north along the spine of Wolfback,

enjoying spectacular vistas of the Bay to the east, the ocean to the west and Mount Tamalpais ahead, before descending to the green shelter of Tennessee Valley. Here, the pristine crescent of beach at Tennessee Cove is an ideal setting for a picnic lunch.

From Tennessee Valley, the Coast Trail takes you the rest of the way, climbing steeply from the valley floor and following the crest of the high bluffs directly above the sea. After three miles the trail drops gently to Muir Beach, delivering you to the door of the Pelican Inn.

An alternative, bayside route to Tennessee Valley, easier because it is completely level, is described after the main route guide. This alternative also affords a closer look at the Sausalito waterfront: the yacht harbors, houseboats and Bay Model Visitor's Center.

The Route

Distance: 8½ miles.

Walking Time: 5 hours.

Grade: A moderately steep climb and descent, 2 miles each, plus 4½ miles of mostly level terrain.

Start at the picture-postcard center of downtown Sausalito — Vina Del Mar Plaza. With the plaza's fountain at your back, position yourself on the steps between the elephant sentinels and you will see Excelsior Lane, a long flight of stone steps across the street and to the left of Wells Fargo Bank, directly in front of you. Cross Bridgeway (using the crosswalk at the corner of El Portal) and walk up this first flight to Bulkley Avenue. Here, the Alta Mira Hotel rises above you, and the Casa Madrona signpost is visible to your right further down the street. If you are staying at either hotel, you can start your walk here.

Climb the second level of Excelsior Lane directly ahead and at the top, cross the street (Harrison Street, unmarked here), continue up the third and last flight. This brings you to San Carlos Avenue. Turn right, and walk along San Carlos until it meets Santa Rosa Avenue at the Christ Church intersection.

Veer left on Santa Rosa. You are now looking for a long straight flight of steps, unmarked, that serves as a public easement

between 137 and 139 Santa Rosa. Climb these steps to the street
above, which is Spencer Avenue. Turn right on Spencer and proceed up the hill, past the fire station on your right, to the large
freeway sign at the top. Turn right again, and walk along the frontage road that parallels Highway 101 North.

Here you will see the small brown-and-white trail markers that
direct you to the trailhead. Following these signs, turn left under
the freeway overpass. Straight ahead is a small parking lot and the
sign that marks the Morning Sun Trailhead. Your mile climb above
the boutiques has now delivered you to the threshold of the
Marin County coastland.

Starting from the trailhead (circled number 1 on the map), walk
up the steps and continue to follow the switchbacks of Morning
Sun Trail to its end. Arriving at the top, turn right on Ridge Road
(unmarked here and further on called Alta Avenue, number 2 on
the map) through the eucalyptus grove. Proceed straight ahead
about half mile to the crossroads (also unmarked). Turn left at the
crossroads (3), then take a sharp, immediate right on the Bobcat
Trail (unmarked). If the day is clear, you can observe at the crest of
a ridge ahead the white inverted funnel of a United States air-
navigational-aid station. The trail to follow leads directly to it, so
use it as your own navigational guide.

Proceed straight along the Bobcat Trail, ignoring a turnoff to
Hawk Camp (4), until you reach a V junction (5). Take the left fork
here, and continue straight to the perimeter of the navigation station, where there are two trails a few yards apart. Both are marked
"Miwok" (6). The first of the two, the more easterly, is the one
you want, so turn right here and follow the Miwok as it descends
the ridge down into Tennessee Valley. At the bottom of the hill,
turn right at the stable. Walk through the parking lot and turn left
on the paved road. At the wood gates you have arrived at the next
trailhead (7).

Go through the gates and follow the road (Tennessee Valley
Trail) to the V junction. Take the lower fork, on your left, and proceed to the intersection marked Pacific Coast Trail (8). A right turn
here will take you to your journey's end at Muir Beach. However,

if you follow the Tennessee Valley Trail ahead of you to its end, you will arrive at Tennessee Cove in time for lunch; when you've had your fill of picnicking and beachcombing, return to the Pacific Coast Trail marker.

The Pacific Coast Trail, one of the most dramatic in the Bay area, starts at the Golden Gate headlands, climbs halfway up Mount Tamalpais, then stretches north above the sea to Point Reyes. The afternoon hike follows a three-mile stretch from Tennessee Valley to Muir Beach.

From the trail marker (8), cross the small meadow as directed and turn left to follow the trail uphill. Make your way to the crest, where you will see an intersection (9). Do not turn right, but continue straight ahead on the grassier of the two paths, the Pacific Coast Trail, which continues along the bluffs directly above the ocean. From here, the trail drops steeply toward the sea. At its lowest point, you might take a detour to the pristine beach below — Pirate's Cove. The trail, however, veers right, steeply uphill, and this is the way to Muir Beach. At the top it flattens out, and you again stroll the ridge above the breakers. Farther on, be sure to follow the wooden steps that extend up to the right (10). Continue on the trail where it veers uphill to the right. (It meets the Coyote Ridge Trail at the crest.)

At the crest, the Muir Beach community is plainly visible ahead. Stay on the Pacific Coast Trail; in a short time, the gabled rooftop and whitewashed walls of the Pelican Inn, your destination, appear in the valley at the foot of the ridge. After descending to Muir Beach, continue toward the white gate, ignoring the Green Gulch Trail to the right. Go through the white gates and proceed right, to the doors of the Pelican Inn.

Alternative Route to the Tennessee Valley Trailhead

Beginning from Vina Del Mar Plaza, walk north on Bridgeway Boulevard for one block. At Anchor Street, turn right toward the Bay, then left on Humboldt, and proceed north along the Bay side of Humboldt. This small diversion off Bridgeway allows you a stroll along the yacht harbor; take the boardwalk that begins at Sausalito Yacht Sales and Chandlery.

At the end of the boardwalk, turn left at Flynn's Landing on Johnson Street (unmarked here) and right on Bridgeway again where the marked bike route begins. It will lead you all the way to Tennessee Valley Road.

Walk north on the bike path, passing Zack's, considered by many singles Sausalito's most attractive waterfront refuge. You may prefer the green shade of Dunphy Park, which begins two blocks further north on Litho Street. At Napa Street, where Dunphy Park ends, continue north along the sidewalk of Bridgeway until a Bay Model Visitor's Center sign on Easterby Street directs you down to the right. The center houses a huge hydraulic working model of San Francisco Bay — an important resource for local engineers, scientists and sailors as well as a major tourist attraction. We urge you to spend some time here, but bear in mind that you still have a four-mile walk ahead before you arrive at Tennessee Cove for lunch.

Proceed along the street between the Visitor's Center and Bridgeway, following the old railroad tracks. As you continue north, you pass tennis courts to your right, with Bridgeway above on your left. At Marinship Way and Harbor Drive, return to the paved bike path running alongside Bridgeway.

At the freeway entrance veer to the right, where the bike path, marked by a cyclone fence, continues alongside the northbound freeway. Strolling along the edge of the Bay gives you a close-up glimpse of the colorful houseboat communities alongside Sausalito's northernmost shores. Directly ahead, enjoy your first unobstructed view of Mount Tamalpais, which more than any other natural feature emphasizes the physical landscape of Marin County.

At the freeway overpass, a cyclone fence once again marks the bike path. Proceed north under the freeway, continuing through the marshlands, to the bike-route crossroads just past the Howard Johnson's Motor Lodge. Take the left fork here, and follow the path through the marshland nearby to where it meets Shoreline Highway at a small wooden footbridge. Just before the bridge, take the wooden steps down and under the highway. Then follow the streamside path until it meets Tennessee Valley Road, where you turn right. This country road will take you the rest of the way

(1¾ miles) to the Tennessee Valley Trailhead. On the map, the trailhead is marked number 7. You can now pick up the route followed in the preceding description.

Journey's End

Muir Beach

Muir Beach was originally settled by Portuguese fishermen and dairy farmers. It wasn't until the 1950s and 1960s that poets and artists, escaping city development, discovered this idyllic spot between the Pacific and the giant redwoods. Since then, professionals and executives, too, have built homes on the hills above the beach, but the area has maintained a sense of peace and isolation quite unusual for a bedroom community so close to a large city. In fact, the Pelican Inn is the only commercial enterprise that has been allowed in fiercely private Muir Beach.

The Inn

Pelican Inn, Muir Beach 94965; (415) 383-6000. Full breakfast included, with a restaurant on the premises; expensive.

Built in the architectural style of sixteenth-century England, with a Tudor-paneled bar complete with dart board, whitewashed cottage walls, beamed ceilings and a huge brick fireplace in the dining room. Each of the six guest bedrooms has antique high canopied beds and oriental carpets. Dinner and breakfast menus offer the traditional specialties of English country fare.

The Way Back

By Public Transportation: None available.

By Foot: The Green Gulch Trail, which is passed on the route to Muir Beach just before the white-gate entrance to the beach, is a lovely alternative route as far as Tennessee Valley. You can follow this trail inland through Green Gulch Ranch, the serene Zen retreat, then up the ridge to join the Miwok Trail, which takes you back to the Tennessee Valley Trail.

At the trailhead (on the map the trailhead is marked number 7) turn left, and enjoy the wooded length of Tennessee Valley Road about 1¾ miles, out to Shoreline Highway (Highway 1). If you prefer, from this point, you can take a Golden Gate Transit bus, which stops at Tam Junction (one block to the left), back to Sausalito. If you choose to walk the rest of the way, take the steps down and under the highway and join the bike route across the marshlands, veering right at the Howard Johnson's Motor Lodge. From here, you can follow the bike route all the way, passing the colorful houseboat communities, then strolling the length of Sausalito's waterfront before returning to Vina Del Mar Plaza.

Chapter 8
Muir Beach to Stinson Beach

A 9-mile hike through Muir Woods
and Mount Tamalpais State Park
from a country inn to a seaside motel.

The Night Before

Getting There

By Public Transportation: None available.

By Car: From Highway 101, take the Stinson Beach exit following
the signs for Highway 1 (Shoreline Highway) to Muir Beach.

Muir Beach and Its Inns

See the preceding chapter for description of the community and
the Pelican Inn.

A Look At the Day's Walk

Mount Tamalpais, which shapes your route, remains a magic
place for those who know it today, just as it was for the Tamal Indians who lived in its shadow centuries ago. They are said to have
named it to honor the beautiful maiden Temelpa, whose self-
sacrifice turned her to stone. We descern her form, still, in the
graceful curve of the mountain against the sky. For the past 100
years, hikers have explored its redwood groves, precipitous

waterfalls, and high meadows via an ever-increasing network of sensitively engineered trails. While it may have been Temelpa's fate to become a part of the mountain, the reverse is also said to be true; the mountain becomes a part of anyone who hikes it.

From Muir Beach, a three-mile walk through quiet Frank Valley brings you to Muir Woods, the 425-acre redwood forest established as a national monument in 1908. Here you stroll through the shade of the giant trees before ascending some 1,000 feet of mountain trail to Tamalpais's western flank. Then, with the Pacific in view below, you descend the meadows of the Dipsea Trail to Stinson Beach.

The Route

Distance: 9 miles.
Walking Time: 5½ hours.
Grade: Level for 5 miles; the rest, a moderately steep 2 miles uphill and 2 miles downhill.

Leaving the Pelican Inn, turn left on Shoreline Highway for about 500 feet to the intersection with Muir Woods Road. Proceed a few steps on Muir Woods Road to the Redwood Creek Trail on the right. The Redwood Creek Trail runs parallel to Muir Woods Road as far as the entrance to Muir Woods itself, where it meets the Deer Park Fire Trail toward which the signposts so kindly direct you. At this intersection, turn right on Muir Woods Road (1) and follow it about a half mile to Muir Woods. Starting in the first parking lot on the left, the Redwood Grove walk takes you past the restrooms and through the park entrance.

You have now walked about three miles from Muir Beach, and you may be ready for lunch or a coffee break in the cafeteria, as well as some exploration of the information center area to learn the history and biology of this virgin redwood forest preserve.

When you are ready, continue your walk the entire length of Muir Woods along the main pathway to the end of the park, where you cross the final bridge on the left and take the Ben Johnson Trail (2). Here begins a steep, two-mile climb up the heavily forested slopes of Mount Tamalpais. This ruggedly beautiful ascent is typical of the kind of hiking that attracts people here from all over the Bay Area.

Where the Ben Johnson Trail splits (3) take the left fork toward the Dipsea Trail, which you meet after a series of switchbacks up to the top of the ridge. Take the Dipsea to the right, toward Stinson Beach. (This is the last portion of the route followed by runners who come here from all over the country to compete in the nearly seven-mile race from Mill Valley to the sea.)

The Dipsea Trail leaves the broad fire road a bit farther on; here take the trail to the right, to the crest of the hill. Cross the fire road at the signpost and continue on the narrow Dipsea Trail toward Stinson Beach. Where the trail meets the broad fire road, again pick up the road, ignoring the narrow trails that branch off from time to time.

At the marker, continue on the Dipsea toward Stinson Beach, 1¾ miles downhill through groves of giant trees. Here again the route follows switchbacks, this time down the fern-lined steps of Steep Ravine.

At the bottom, take the Dipsea Trail with half-buried pipe on a slight uphill course, ignoring the Steep Ravine Trail to Highway 1. Walk left at the large Golden Gate National Recreation Area sign marked "Dipsea Trail." At the top of the rise, cross the wide fire road and continue on the narrow trail across the meadows ahead.

At Panoramic Highway (4), turn left and then immediately right on Highway 1 toward town. At Arenal Avenue, turn left for the two motels: the Sandpiper on the left and the Ocean Court on the right.

Journey's End

Stinson Beach

This sparkling sea town at the foot of Mount Tamalpais boasts the finest swimming beach in the Bay Area. Crowds flock here every summer weekend to enjoy the swimming and picnicking facilities at Stinson Beach State Park. Originally called Willow Camp, the community was renamed for Nathan H. Stinson, creator of its first subdivision in 1906.

The Inns

Ocean Court Motel, 18 Arenal Avenue, Stinson Beach 94970; (415) 868-0212. Moderately expensive.

Most of the spacious suites with kitchens are rented out on a long-term basis. Overnight guests are welcome as vacancies occur in these comfortably appointed rooms.

Sandpiper Motel, Marine Way, Stinson Beach 94970; (415) 868-1632. Inexpensive.

A clean, quiet stop after a long day's hike. Some of the nine units include kitchens.

The Way Back

By Public Transportation: None available.

By Foot: The 5½-mile route along the Dipsea-Coast trails will return you to Muir Beach in superb style. From Arenal Avenue turn right on Shoreline Highway, then left on Panoramic Highway. Walk uphill until you see the stile that marks the trailhead. Follow the Dipsea for 3⅓ miles as it crosses the meadows above the sea, then climbs Steep Ravine through the woods to the top of the ridge, where it joins the Coast Trail. Veer right on the Coast Trail, heading south about two miles to Shoreline Highway, which takes you the rest of the way back to Muir Beach.

Chapter 9
Stinson Beach to Bolinas

A 10⅓-mile hike on Bolinas Ridge
between beach-town motels and guest houses.

The Night Before

Getting There

By Public Transportation: Take Golden Gate Transit buses 10 or 20 to Sausalito, then 61 to Stinson Beach. (Call (415) 332-6600 or 453-2100 for schedule.)

By Car: From Highway 101, take the Stinson Beach exit, then follow the signs for Highway 1 (Shoreline Highway) to Stinson Beach.

Stinson Beach and the Inns

See the preceding chapter for description of the community and the Ocean Court and Sandpiper motels.

A Look at the Day's Walk

The mountain ridge rising dramatically behind the white sand crescent of Stinson Beach is the locale of this hike. The top of the ridge is a strenuous two-mile climb above the town, but as you catch your breath at the height you will enjoy a panoramic vista of sea, sky and shoreline that on a clear day includes the tip of the Point Reyes peninsula and, 30 miles offshore, the tiny Farallone

Islands. On the ridge you join the magnificent Pacific Coast Trail for three miles, heading north.

A descent through heavily forested slopes of redwood, fir and bay laurel trees into the Audubon Canyon Ranch, a wildlife sanctuary on the Bolinas Lagoon, affords a restful interlude of bird watching before the three-mile walk into the colorful town of Bolinas.

The Route

Distance: 10⅓ miles.
Walking Time: 5½ hours.
Grade: A 2-mile climb and subsequent 2-mile descent with vertical gain and loss of 1,500 feet; 6⅓ miles, mostly level.

Starting at the hub of Stinson Beach, where Shoreline Highway meets Calle Del Mar at Ed's Superette, walk directly uphill on Calle Del Mar. Turn left on Buena Vista Avenue, right on Lincoln Avenue, left on Belvedere Avenue, and immediately right on Avenida Farralone, your pathway to the Willow Camp Fire Trail. Shortly after the trailhead marker, ignoring the first trail to the right (which leads to the water tank), take the second right (circled number 1 on the map) uphill. Now you can follow the Willow Camp Fire Trail as it wends its way aggressively up the western slope of Mount Tamalpais for the next two miles, then joins the Coast Trail some 1,500 feet above the Pacific.

The Coast Trail (unmarked here, except for a "no horses" symbol) is a narrow footpath meeting the Willow Camp Fire Trail at right angles. Turn left (2) and you will be on your way. If you meet the paved Ridgecrest Boulevard, you've come too far uphill; turn back and find the Coast Trail. After a few minutes on the Coast Trail you come to the Bob Cook memorial bench, where, depending on the hour, you might want to linger to enjoy the view along with a picnic lunch, before continuing with the remainder of your three-mile stroll along the wooded side of Mount Tamalpais.

About a mile past the Bob Cook bench, you meet Ridgecrest Boulevard. Proceed through the white gate, taking a sharp right on the Coast Trail again (3). (Ignore the McKennon Gulch Fire Trail that leads downhill to the left.)

Another mile farther along, the trail veers to the left (4) off Ridgecrest Boulevard through the spicy fragrance of deep woods. Ignore the grassy trail that descends to the left (5) and proceed the rest of the way, paralleling Ridgecrest Boulevard closely now, to where the Coast Trail ends, just past the junction of Ridgecrest with the Bolinas-Fairfax Road.

Continue for a short way north on the Bolinas-Fairfax Road (6) until you notice the Audubon Canyon ranch gate (7) at your left. Walk through the gate and follow the Bourne Trail, a wide fire trail, downhill. If you stay on the Bourne all the way down to the Ranch Headquarters, your journey will be quite scenic, and shorter by at least a half mile than the alternative. During the May-July nesting season, however, we recommend that at a point about ¾ mile down the Bourne Trail you veer to the right (8) on the Canyon Loop Trail; this will bring you eventually to the Henderson Overlook. Follow the overlook signs (9) to your left for an amazing grandstand view of the nesting birds, before proceeding down the switchback to the Ranch Headquarters.

Once back on Shoreline, continue one mile north along Bolinas Lagoon, until meeting the crossroads. Take the first left turn, and turn left again on the Olema-Bolinas Road; from here it is a two-mile country walk to Wharf Road, the village center of Bolinas. Two of the inns are on Wharf Road itself, and the third is a few houses down Brighton Avenue from its intersection with Wharf.

Journey's End

Bolinas

There is no road sign on Shoreline Highway to direct the traveler into Bolinas. Though this was once just another beach resort for San Francisco vacationers, it has in recent years developed into a real town with a unique identity staunchly protected by its citizenry.

Like Main Street, U.S.A., Wharf Road is always busy with people greeting friends, lounging in Smiley's saloon and lunching in Scowley's restaurant. Though here the men sometimes sport pony tails and earrings and the women often favor long skirts and sandals, the feeling is still pure small town, and Bolinas is a very pleasant place to end the long day's hike.

The Inns

Wharf Road Bed and Breakfast, 11 Wharf Road, Bolinas 94924; (415) 868-1430. A guest house, with a restaurant on the premises; moderately expensive.

Two newly refurbished pretty rooms above the Wild Rose Cafe — definitely the nicest in town.

Bolinas Motel, 41 Wharf Road, Bolinas 94924; (415) 868-1311. Inexpensive.

Three units in the center of town — clean and quite adequate.

Grand Hotel, 15 Brighton Avenue, Bolinas 94924; (415) 868-1757. A guest house; inexpensive.

Funky rooms above an antique store — very basic accommodations.

The Way Back

By Public Transportation: Golden Gate Transit bus 62 runs from Bolinas to Stinson Beach. (Call (415) 332-6600 or 453-2100 for schedule.)

By Foot: If you choose to hike back, an alternative to the route in is a walk along Shoreline Highway to Stinson Beach. Though this is a main road and you will be forced to be wary of cars, it has serene views of Bolinas Lagoon and some of the harbor seals and many species of wetland birds that make their homes there.

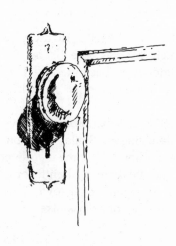

Chapter 10
Bolinas to Olema

A 12-mile walk through Olema Valley
from a Bolinas guest house or motel
to a historic country inn.

The Night Before

Getting There

By Public Transportation: Take Golden Gate Transit bus 61 or 63 to
Bolinas. (Call (415) 332-6600 or 453-2100 for schedule.)

By Car: From Highway 101, take the Stinson Beach exit, then
Highway 1 (Shoreline Highway) to Panoramic Highway over
Mount Tamalpais. Pick up Shoreline again and proceed to the
Olema-Bolinas Road turnoff; take the Olema-Bolinas Road left,
and follow it to the junction of Wharf Road and Brighton Avenue.
For Wharf Road Bed and Breakfast, veer left on Wharf Road to
number 11 on the left, or for the Bolinas Motel continue on Wharf
Road for the short distance to number 41, also on the left. For the
Grand Hotel, at the intersection of Wharf Road and Brighton
Avenue, turn right on Brighton; the hotel is a few houses down on
the left side.

Bolinas and the Inns

See the preceding chapter for description of the community and
the Wharf Road Bed and Breakfast, Bolinas Motel and Grand Hotel.

A Look at the Day's Walk

This walk traces the San Andreas faultline through Olema Valley, the epicenter of the great quake of 1906 that moved the entire Point Reyes Peninsula some 16 feet northward in a single shake. A trained geologist's eye can discern telling evidence everywhere about; if you lack that facility you might enjoy visiting the self-guided Earthquake Trail at the Bear Valley Visitor's Center at the end of the day.

From Bolinas, 2½ miles of country road brings you to the Olema Valley Trailhead; once you are within the boundaries of the Point Reyes National Seashore, a level path leads through fragrant meadow and marshland for the five miles to Five Brooks. You might enjoy a picnic lunch here by the duck pond before resuming your walk. From Five Brooks, the trail climbs gently through groves of bay, laurel, oak and conifer, leveling out again almost immediately. You stroll the last four miles of grassy valley trail through the Vedanta Retreat, arriving at Shoreline Highway. The Olema Inn welcome mat is just ahead.

The Route

Distance: 12 miles.
Walking Time: 6 hours.
Grade: Level.

From the town of Bolinas, walk along Olema-Bolinas Road about ¾ mile to Horsehill Road (circled number 1 on the map) which will take you 1½ miles to Shoreline Highway (2). Turn left on this main road and walk about a half mile to the Olema Valley Trail (3), which you will see on the lefthand side of the road just after reaching Dogtown Pottery in Woodville. (Across the street from this trail you can see the McCurdy Trail, which goes uphill to the Bolinas Ridge Trail and is an alternate route back to Bolinas, described under The Way Back.)

Take the level Olema Valley Trail, which is a gentle ramble through meadow and woods toward Five Brooks. Ignore the sign to Pablo Point (4) that appears after the first of many streams' crossings. (During summer and fall, fording of streams is less of a problem than at other times.) After the third stream, at crossroads take the wider path veering uphill to the right (see hiker sign). At the next crossroads continue straight ahead (see hiker sign ahead). You have now come 2½ miles from Woodville, where you entered the trail, and you have another 2½ miles to go to reach Five Brooks.

At the Olema Valley Trail Marker, take the trail uphill to the right toward Five Brooks. (Do not go through the wooden gate.) About a half mile on, at the crossroads with the hiker sign on the right, take the left fork; this is a serene fern-lined path shaded by graceful trees. Exit from the trail at a crossroads. Behind you the trail marker says Bolema Trail, indicating that for the last bit of your walk the Olema Valley Trail had merged with the Bolema Trail. Veer right here (there is a small lake to your left: (5)), and follow the "P" sign toward the parking lot and into the picnic area of the Five Brooks Trailhead, for lunch and a well-deserved rest. You have another four miles to walk before your arrival in Olema.

To proceed: with your back to the picnic tables turn left on the wide road heading toward the Rift Zone Trail. Take this trail, which leads eventually through the Vedanta Retreat and then to the Bear Valley Trailhead and Olema. The Rift Zone Trail, named for the San Andreas Fault that runs through this area, is actually a public trail through private property. (The Vedanta Society, which owns extensive acreage here, attempts to reconcile Eastern and Western thought through the teachings of Swami Vivekenanda.) At the signpost indicating directions, make sure you veer right on the narrow trail, though the sign's placement may make its meaning a bit confusing. Following the signs toward the Bear Valley Trailhead, take the wooded path out into a large clearing and picnic site. In the center of the clearing, notice a sign attached to a spigot that says "No Open Fires"; to the right of this sign and right across the meadow is the trail sign directing you out of the clearing and into the woods. Farther on, cross the stream and mount the steps for a small climb on the Rift Zone Trail to the Retreat.

After the final gate, veer slightly right across the field toward the road and out the green gate (6). The white Retreat building is on your left. Turn right to Shoreline Highway; then walk left to the Olema Inn, just ahead on your right.

Journey's End

Olema

Once a bustling town on its way up, boasting two hotels, a well-stocked grocery, a dry goods store and a reputation for drunken and rowdy behavior, Olema's star began to set in 1975, when it was bypassed as a railroad depot in favor of Point Reyes Station. Now the town is a handful of vintage buildings at the intersection of Sir Francis Drake Boulevard and Shoreline Highway. Though its dimensions are small, however, Olema's position at the threshold of the Point Reyes National Seashore ensures its survival as a tourist stop.

The Inn

Olema Inn, P. O. Box 10, 10001 Sir Francis Drake Boulevard, 94950; (415) 663-8441. Full breakfast included with a restaurant on the premises; moderately expensive.

Lovingly restored to its original 100-year-old charm, the Olema Inn offers fine cuisine in high-ceilinged dining rooms. Furnished with antiques and country iron and brass, the three spacious guest bedrooms also maintain the flavor of days gone by.

The Way Back

By Public Transportation: Golden Gate Transit bus 61 runs Monday through Friday in early morning. (Call (415) 332-6600 or 453-2100 for schedules.)

By Foot: The Bolinas Ridge Trail, about 14 miles in all, offers a strenuous but glorious alternative to retracing the rift zone route back to Bolinas. From the Olema Inn, walk a little more than one mile uphill on Sir Francis Drake Boulevard, until you spot the Bolinas Ridge Trail marker on your right. Once en route, the trail climbs along a 7¾-mile section of the ridge through redwood groves and past open sea vistas, then meets the McCurdy Trail marker to Bolinas, your path down to Shoreline Highway. When you reach the highway, turn left; look for Horseshoe Hill Road, turn right on it and follow it back to the Olema-Bolinas Road route into Bolinas.

Chapter 11
Olema to Inverness Park

A 9- to 9½-mile hike over
Mount Wittenberg between country inns.

The Night Before

Getting There

By Public Transportation: Take Golden Gate Transit bus 64. (Call (415) 332-6600 or 453-2100 for schedule.)

By Car: From Highway 101, take the Sir Francis Drake Boulevard exit, continuing west on Sir Francis Drake to Olema.

Point Reyes National Seashore

Point Reyes, the focus of the hikes in this chapter and chapter 18, was first inhabited by the Coast Miwok Indians. It is believed that in 1579 the English explorer Francis Drake arrived at the wind-swept peninsula in his ship the *Golden Hinde*, and called the land Nova Albion (New England). It was later claimed for Spain by Don Sebastian Vizcaino and named La Punte de Los Reyes (The Point of the Kings).

The peninsula was declared a national seashore in 1962 and is one of the most beautiful recreational areas in California. It is also of great geological interest, because the peninsula is actually part of an island on the eastern edge of the earth's Pacific plate, moving separately from the rest of the continent, which is part of the North American plate. The resulting area of friction between the two plates is the San Andreas Rift Zone.

Olema and the Inn

See the preceding chapter for description of the community and the Olema Inn.

A Look at the Day's Walk

This walk in the Point Reyes National Seashore begins with an exploration of the Earthquake Trail, a vivid reminder of the great quake of 1906. You will see signs along the trail to describe the San Andreas fault and the displacement of earth by about 16 feet that took place here on that historic occasion.

From the grassland area of the Earthquake Trail area, the Bear Valley Trail begins a gentle ascent through dense growths of fir, alder, oaks and ferns, following the creek that eventually empties into the sea. You leave this broad road at Divide Meadow to make a steeper climb up Old Pine Trail, a lovely fir-shaded path lined with huckleberry bushes, and continue on toward Mount Wittenberg.

Here, 1,407 feet above the ocean with a magnificent view of the Point Reyes Peninsula and Drake's Bay, you can enjoy a picnic lunch and a well-deserved rest.

Your descent is through forests of Douglas fir and Bishop pine into an area called Inverness Park, which borders the national seashore.

The Route

Distance: 9- to 9½ miles.
Time: 5 hours.
Grade: The half-mile approach and return from Mount Wittenberg are somewhat steep; the ascent and descent of Inverness Ridge gentle.

A short walk south on Shoreline Highway (Highway 1) from the Shoreline Highway — Sir Francis Drake Boulevard crossroads — a left turn on Shoreline from the Olema Inn — brings you to the Vedanta Retreat signpost. Turn right (circled number 1 on the map) on the dirt road and you will see the Point Reyes sign to the Bear Valley Trail on your right. Follow the path through the gate, across the meadow, and then along the self-guiding Earthquake Trail to the Bear Valley Trailhead (2), about ¾ mile in all. The Bear Valley Trail, a broad fire road, runs alongside a stream through a ferny grove of bay, laurel, oak and fir. Keep following signs to the coast, and in about 1½ miles Divide Meadow opens before you. The first turn (3) puts you on Old Pine Trail. This narrow, fir-shaded path — a treasure trove for huckleberry pickers in the fall — climbs gently for the next two miles. Veer right onto the Sky Trail at the first junction (4), and follow it for a mile or so in the direction of Sky Camp and Mount Wittenberg. The Wittenberg Trail veers uphill to the right (5); make this short, steep climb up the trail and beyond to the grassy summit to reach the perfect setting for a picnic lunch. On a clear day, the panoramic view of Point Reyes, its long beach and the wide seascape is splendid.

When you are ready to tear yourself away, descend till you rejoin the Wittenberg Trail, just above Sky Camp; it proceeds northwest along the ridge, descending slightly. At the first junction, turn left (6) towards Sky Camp; at the second, veer right (7) on the Sky Trail to Limantour Road, ignoring the narrow path at your left, which returns to Sky Camp. In about ¾ mile, Sky Trail ends at a gate onto Limantour Road. Just a few feet before the gate, turn left (8) on the Bayview Trail, which parallels Limantour Road closely. After a half mile or so, turn right up the log post stairs to Limantour Road (9), cross Limantour and proceed straight ahead through the gate and onto Drake's Summit Road. Take Drake's Summit down the ridge, turning left on Balboa Avenue. When Balboa intersects Portola Road, Hollytree Inn guests turn right, and right again on Sir Francis Drake Boulevard to the inn sign, less than a quarter mile all told. Blackthorne Inn guests have a mile walk, turning left on Portola and then right on Vallejo Avenue through the glade; the inn is above the road to the right.

Journey's End

The Inns

Holly Tree Inn, Box 642, 3 Silverhills Road, Point Reyes Station 94956; (415) 663-1554. A guest house, with full breakfast included; moderately expensive.

A 19-acre estate of well-manicured lawn and holly trees, with four delightfully decorated guest rooms. A one-mile walk to restaurants for dinner.

Blackthorne Inn, P. O. Box 712, 266 Vallejo Avenue, Inverness 94937; (415) 663-8621. A guest house, with continental breakfast included; inexpensive to moderately expensive.

A ferny canyon is the setting for this California-modern woodsy, redwood house complete with hot tub. Four charming guest rooms. A two-mile walk to restaurants for dinner.

The Way Back

By Public Transportation: Take Golden Gate Transit bus 65. (Call (415) 332-6600 or 453-2100 for schedule.)

By Foot: To try a different hike back, you could retrace your steps toward Mount Wittenberg but turn off on the Meadow Trail to reach the Bear Valley Trailhead. This alternate will shorten the return hike, as well as display new aspects of this beautiful seashore preserve.

Chapter 12
Inverness Park to Inverness

An 8½- to 9-mile hike on Inverness Ridge
between country guest houses and inns.

The Night Before

Getting There

By Public Transportation: Take Golden Gate Transit bus 64 or 65 to
the Inverness Park stop at Balboa Avenue and Sir Francis Drake
Boulevard. (Call (415) 332-6600 or 453-2100 for schedule.)

For the Holly Tree Inn, walk a quarter mile south on Sir Francis
Drake. At the junction, continue straight ahead on Bear Valley Road
(unmarked) just a few steps to the inn sign at your right. For the
Blackthorne Inn, from the bus stop, walk north about ¾ mile on Sir
Francis Drake. Turn left on Vallejo Road and proceed another half
mile or so to the inn, which is above the road to your right.

By Car: From Highway 101, take the Greenbrae — Sir Francis Drake
Boulevard exit, and follow Sir Francis Drake Boulevard west to
Olema. For the Holly Tree Inn, follow signs to Point Reyes Na-
tional Seashore, but take Bear Valley Road beyond the park head-
quarters about one mile; from Olema continue on Sir Francis
Drake Boulevard through its junction with Bear Valley Road.
About ¾ mile past the junction, turn left on Vallejo Road; follow it
about a half mile to the inn, above the road on the right.

A Look at the Day's Walk

The first two miles, up Balboa Avenue and Drake's Summit Road to the crest of Inverness Ridge, is the only real climb of the day. From here, for about five miles, the trail traces the spine of the ridge past hilltop homes, pine woods and grassy meadows. Glimpses of the Point Reyes Seashore to the west and the coastal range to the east tease the eye until landscape and seascape begin to open about you at the foot of Point Reyes Hill. Finally, at the Mount Vision overlook 1,282 feet above sea level, the view lies unobstructed before you — ocean, bay, valley and mountain. The 1½- to 2-mile descent via Vision Road brings you to Inverness and the inn of your choice.

The Route

Distance: 8½ to 9 miles.

Walking Time: 5 hours.

Grade: 2-mile moderately steep ascent, and similar 1½- to 2-mile descent; 5 miles level terrain.

Leaving the Holly Tree Inn, turn left on Sir Francis Drake Highway and walk a quarter mile to Balboa. Turn left (circled number 1 on the map).

From the Blackthorne Inn, turn right on Portola Road and walk about one mile to Balboa. Turn right (1).

Climb up Balboa and Drake's Summit Road 1½ miles — to the top — and there meet unmarked Limantour Road (2). Continue straight through the gate and veer right on the road. Proceed about half a mile to a clearing on the right (3). The first blue-and-white sign identifies the Bayview Trailhead. Do *not* take this trail. Instead, take the fire road on the far right.

Walk on this fairly level fire road lined with pine and fir trees for about one mile. Pass through a gate and meet Tamalpais Road leading off the right (4); do not veer off on Tamalpais or any of the intersecting roads, but continue straight ahead, uphill, on the broad fire road. This becomes Sunnyside Drive.

Farther on, Sunnyside Drive (marked by a street sign, for the first time) meets a broad road leading off to the left (5). Here, take the left turn, which veers uphill, until you come to a crossroads; turn left on Drake's View Drive. You are now walking through the Inverness Ridge area and among some spectacular examples of modern California architecture. Your destination is Point Reyes Hill.

At another intersection, notice three roads ahead; the left-hand one is identified as Reyes Ridge and the right-hand one is marked 420 Drake's View Drive. Take the narrow road in the middle, which continues straight ahead, walking past the posted "private road" sign to the blue-and-white trail sign on the left.

Immediately upon starting along this new trail, veer to the right on the broader trail. At the trail marker pointing in both directions, take the right fork. Now the path becomes a lovely, rustic trail winding through fir, pine and oak trees and then out into a large meadow. From the clearing, begin climbing up the trail ahead to the top of Point Reyes Hill, 1,336 feet above the sea. (Do not take the narrow trails going off to the left; stay on the main path.)

Pass the white navigational-aid station at the crest of the hill to your left and continue on the main paved road, enjoying the view of the Point Reyes Peninsula to the west and the Sonoma and Napa County hills stretching to the north. Continue along the windswept ridge top past the chain in the road to a large parking area on the right. You have now come about five miles from Inverness Park and may be ready for a picnic lunch on the grassy area to the right. Find your way to a spot — perhaps on one of the many hillocks from which you can enjoy a sweeping view from Tomales Bay to the ocean.

When you are ready, return to the paved road and continue about another half mile to a large open area on your right. Here you will see a blue sign to the far right and a gate in the center. Take the trail to the left of the gate, heading left in the same direction as the road, toward the top of the ridge with Tomales Bay stretching ahead on the right. This narrow trail through dense shrubbery and trees eventually meets the paved road again at Mount Vision. Where the trail splits you can take either fork. During winter and early spring the less muddy left fork is recommended.

When you reach the paved road (Inverness Ridge Trail) again, you are at Mount Vision overlook (6), 1,282 feet above the sea, where a visitor's guide is posted to help you identify the magnificent stretch of Drake's Bay below.

From the overlook, continue on the main road a short way to a gate on the right marked "Fire Lane," take this lane (which is Vision Road, unmarked here) downhill 1½ miles, past Madrone Avenue (where Vision is marked) and on down to Aberdeen Way.

If you are heading to Inverness Lodge, turn left on Aberdeen Way and right on Callendar Way to the lodge on the corner. For other accommodations, continue down Vision Road to Sir Francis Drake. For the Golden Hinde Boatel, walk left a half mile to the inn.

For 10 Inverness Way (and MacLean House), walk right a half mile to Inverness Way. To get to MacLean House, continue up Inverness Way past the firehouse and turn right on Hawthorne Way to 122.

Journey's End

Inverness

The 1889 real estate prospectus touted Inverness as the "Brighton of the Pacific Coast possessing all the picturesque beauties of the Highlands of Scotland." Fortunately, large-scale development of this lovely hamlet on the shores of Tomales Bay never came to pass — only the Scottish place names and many fine old homes remain to remind us of its grandiose beginning. Inverness exists today as the perfect resort for those who prefer the quiet beauty of woods and water to package-plan vacationing.

The Inns

Golden Hinde Boatel, 12938 Sir Francis Drake Boulevard, Inverness 94937; (415) 669-1398, 669-1128. An inn, with a restaurant on the premises; moderately expensive.

Fronting Tomales Bay, with private beach, complete boating facilities and swimming pool. Most of the 26 units have fireplaces and some, kitchens.

Inverness Lodge, Callendar Way and Argyle, Inverness 94937; (415) 669-1034. An inn, with a restaurant on the premises; inexpensive.

Grand old rustic inn situated on a wooded hillside overlooking Tomales Bay. Nine units.

MacLean House, P. O. Box 651, 122 Hawthornden Way, Inverness 94937; (415) 669-7392. A guest house, with continental breakfast included; moderately priced.

Small with Scottish motif; two guest bedrooms. Open Thursday, Friday and Saturday.

Ten Inverness Way, 10 Inverness Way, Inverness 94937; (415) 669-1648. A guest house, with full breakfast included; moderately expensive.

Built in 1904 and decorated throughout with antiques, handmade rugs and quilts; five guest bedrooms.

The Way Back

By Public Transportation: Take Golden Gate Transit bus 64 or 65. (Call (415) 332-6600 or 453-2100 for schedule.)

By Foot: Retrace the described route.

Chapter 13
Mill Valley to Corte Madera

An 8¼-mile hike through Baltimore Canyon
between a guest house and a suburban motel.

The Night Before

Getting There

By Public Transportation: Take Golden Gate Transit bus 10 down East Blithedale Avenue. For Sycamore House, get off at Sycamore Avenue. For Cutter's Guest House, get off at Elm Avenue and walk east to Del Casa Drive. (Call (415) 332-6600 or 453-2100 for schedule.)

By Car: From Highway 101, take the Mill Valley exit for East Blithedale Avenue. For Sycamore House, turn left at Sycamore Avenue. For Cutter's Guest House, turn right at Elm Avenue and continue to Del Casa Drive.

Mill Valley

Once a summer haven for San Franciscans, the Mill Valley area has grown from its origins as the site of a midnineteenth-century sawmill to a community of 30,000, populated by professionals and executives as well as artists, writers, musicians and filmmakers. Above the Spanish- and Tudor-style village, redwood and glass homes cling to the heavily wooded southern slopes of Mount Tamalpais, the majestic 2,571-foot-high heart of Marin.

The Inns

Cutter's Guest House, 220 Del Casa Drive, Mill Valley 94941; (415) 388-5475. A guest house with continental breakfast included; inexpensive.

A large, thoughtfully furnished guest room in a rustic hillside home with terraced garden and pool — very private.

Sycamore House, 99 Sycamore Avenue, Mill Valley 94941; (415) 383-0612, 383-0614. A guest house with continental breakfast included; moderately expensive.

Two large, comfortable rooms in a 1911 brown-shingled Mill Valley classic.

A Look at the Day's Walk

The walk up and over Blithedale Ridge is beautiful any time of the year, but it's most likely to be fully appreciated on a warm summer day, when the cool redwood canyons on either side provide shade. This is an ideal hiking area all summer long. From your hillside perch in Mill Valley you descend to the valley floor, then climb up and around Warner Canyon to the spine of Blithedale Ridge. Along the ridge top, you enjoy limitless vistas on all sides before descending to Larkspur through the redwood glades of Baltimore Canyon and on to Corte Madera.

The Route

Distance: 8¼ miles.

Time: 4½ hours.

Grade: 4 miles, gentle to moderate uphill climb; 3 miles, gentle to moderate descent, 1¼ miles level.

From Cutter's Guest House, turn left and follow the sylvan turns of Del Casa Drive, downhill for a half mile. Turn right on Manor Drive, past the Mill Valley Tennis Club, then left on Buena Vista Avenue.

Or, from Sycamore House, turn right, following Sycamore Avenue out to its end at East Blithedale Avenue. Turn right on East Blithedale, and, after half a block, cross, taking the first left turn on

Carmelita Avenue. Follow Carmelita till it meets Buena Vista Avenue, where a left turn leads you to Oakdale Avenue.

With a right turn on Oakdale Avenue, begin your mile climb upward through Mill Valley's hillside lanes to the beginning of the trail. A left turn on Circle Avenue brings you to Elinor Avenue, which will deliver you to the trailhead. Turn right on Elinor and follow it as it winds steeply uphill. Shortly after Via Van Dyke branches uphill to the left, follow the dirt path that veers to the right off the final paved section of Elinor Avenue.

Walk through the gate and begin your easy ascent up the unnamed Warner Canyon trail and around the southern side of Warner Canyon. Dense redwood groves that shade the beginning of the walk eventually open up to allow vistas across the canyon, and as you approach its mouth you can enjoy some fine views of the Bay, the Golden Gate Bridge and San Francisco. The trail rounds the canyon's mouth and, shortly after, begins to head back toward Mill Valley and San Francisco; be alert for a trail that makes a hairpin turn upward to the left (circled number 1 on the map). Follow it, turning left at the T junction (2) on the crest of Corte Madera Ridge. Take in more city views as you swing around Blithedale Knoll. Turn right on Blithedale ridge Road (3), striding to the ridge top. Mount Tam looms above to your left, San Quentin is below to your right, and the Richmond-San Rafael Bridge reaching to the East Bay is also in view.

Continue walking Blithedale Ridge Road at the next junction, by taking the second trail to the left (4), which climbs steadily toward the Mount Tam summit. Take the Hoo-Koo-E-Koo Trail to the right (5), following its gentle descent through Madrone and Oak, with views of the Larkspur hillsides on the other side of the canyon. After ¾ mile or so, look for a narrow trail that entends steeply downhill to the right (6). This is Dawn Falls Trail. If you reach the waterfall in the bend of the canyon, you have passed it; turn back some 25 yards and look again. Descend the steep wooded slope on Dawn Falls Trail, cross the fire road, and continue to follow this trail past the waterfall. Then take the Baltimore Canyon Trail along Larkspur Creek, through the redwood glades.

As the path reaches the canyon floor, houses appear high on the bank opposite. Pass through the open cyclone fence; soon you see the trail that runs parallel to the creek and on the other side. The wooden footbridge that appears shortly leads you right to it and your exit route to Larkspur. After crossing, turn right on Madrone Avenue, and follow its wooded length all the way out to Magnolia Avenue. Turn right on Magnolia to its end at Redwood Avenue. Turn left and follow Tamalpais Drive through the tiny town of Corte Madera, then east for a half mile along this main thoroughfare to your motel at the corner of Madera Boulevard.

Journey's End

Corte Madera and its Inn

See Chapter 17.

The Way Back

By Public Transportation: Take Golden Gate Transit bus 70, 80, 50 or 60 to Tiburon. At the freeway overpass, change to 10 going down East Blithedale.

By Foot: The most direct route back is west on Tamalpais Drive, south up Corte Madera Avenue and down Camino Alto, etc.

Chapter 14
Mill Valley to San Rafael

A 10½-mile hike along Blithedale Ridge
from a vintage suburban guest house
to a funky town hotel.

The Night Before

Getting There

See the preceding chapter.

Mill Valley and Its Inns

See the preceding chapter for description of the town and of Cutter's Guest House and Sycamore House.

A Look at the Day's Walk

One of the joys of living in Marin County is the easy access to the very best hiking that the Bay region has to offer. Walking from Mill Valley to San Rafael by way of the slopes of Mount Tamalpais is a perfect way to experience this for yourself.

This hike is fairly demanding because it requires a serious climb at the outset and another — though this one is more gradual — at the end. In between, however, you will enjoy a glorious walk along the spine of Blithedale Ridge under the brooding eye of the East Peak of Mount Tam, followed by a pleasant stroll around Phoenix Lake.

The Route

Distance: 10½ miles.

Walking Time: 6 hours.

Grade: Two moderate-to-steep climbs and descents of 4-mile stretches; between, about 2½ mostly level miles.

From the Sycamore House, turn right and follow Sycamore Avenue (ignoring the left fork on Park) out to East Blithedale Avenue. Turn right on East Blithedale, then take the first left on Carmelita Avenue, swinging left again where it joins Buena Vista Avenue.

From Cutter's Guest House, turn left and follow the sylvan turns of Del Casa — downhill for a half mile. Turn right on Manor Drive, past the Mill Valley Tennis Club, then left on Buena Vista.

Next, from either inn, take a right turn on Oakdale Avenue. Here begins the mile climb up Mill Valley's hillside lanes — followed on the walk to the beginning of the Blithedale Ridge Road trail. A left turn on Circle leads to Elinor Avenue. Turn right on Elinor and follow it steeply uphill to its junction with Via Van Dyke. Turn left, uphill, on the Via Van Dyke fork, and continue through the locked gate to the water tank. Here, pick up a narrow dirt path that takes you up to Blithedale Ridge Road (circled number 1 on the map). Turn right, and enjoy the view ahead of the Mount Tamalpais summit. A backward glance rewards you with a panoramic vista of San Francisco and the Bay.

Follow Blithedale Ridge Road northwest along the ridge top, with the summit looming above to your left. Just past the turnoff to Corte Madera Ridge, you can view the progress of the trail clear to Marin's Knob Hill, a mile or so ahead. Views of San Quentin, the Richmond — San Rafael Bridge and the East Bay open to your right. You lose your unobstructed view a bit farther on, as the trail descends for a short distance.

At the next junction, continue walking Blithedale Ridge by taking the second trail from the left (2), which climbs steadily toward the East Peak. Stay on it past the Hoo-Koo-E-Koo Trail intersection as it swings uphill to the right around Knob Hill. Turn right at the junction with the Hoo-Koo-E-Koo Fire Road (3), then right again, proceeding downhill on the Indian Fire Trail (4).

Follow the Indian Fire Trail (ignoring the Kent Trail that forks off at the right) all the way down past the water tank to the paved road. Turn left here — on Phoenix Road — and walk a short way to where it intersects with Crown Road. Just opposite the street sign, on the left side of the road, is the Tucker Cut-off Trail (5); take this narrow, steep path that cuts downhill through the brush, then contours the slope of a lovely wooded canyon. Turn left (6) at the first intersection, then right (7) at the next downhill fork.

Cross the stream, and follow the Tucker Trail straight ahead, ignoring the right fork (which simply drops down to the stream you just forded). The trail soon crosses a second creek, then swings right, cleaving to the canyon side above the water. Follow the trail as it once more drops down to the stream, then continues on the opposite side, along the water's edge.

Soon, you arrive at a dam and cross a footbridge; continue on Tucker Trail, as it parallels Ben Williams Creek all the way to Phoenix Lake.

At the intersection with Gertrude Ord Trail (8), turn left up the steps. Or, if you wish to shorten the circle of the lake, you can make a right turn here on the Harry Allen Trail and shave a half-mile off your route. In any event, do enjoy a lakeside rest whenever the clearing seems most inviting, especially since another climb awaits you after leaving Phoenix Lake.

Follow the Gertrude Ord Trail around the lake, taking the steps down and across the southwest corner. Just past the northwest corner the trail joins the broader fire road, which leads down past the fishing area and restrooms to the parking lot.

At the parking lot, turn left; follow the park road out through the gates to Lagunitas Road. Continue straight on past Lagunitas Tennis Club and Ross School and out to Sir Francis Drake Boulevard, just opposite the Marin Art and Garden Center. Cross Sir Francis Drake, turn left, then take the first right turn on Laurel Grove Avenue. Climb Laurel Grove through the cloistered neighborhoods of Ross and Kentfield to its junction with Poplar Road. Turn left on Poplar, which ends a way farther up at Wolfe Grade. Cross Wolfe Grade and turn left, using the pedestrian sidewalk. Soon you will see the city of San Rafael below, and the road merges into D Street. Walk straight downhill on D Street, turning right on Bayview Street. A two-block walk brings you to the head of B Street on the left, and the Panama Hotel.

Journey's End

San Rafael

Mission San Rafael Arcangel was founded here in 1817 by Father Vicente Sarria, but little remains of the original building. During the 1850s the town grew into a thriving business center for the surrounding ranches, and in the area north of Fifth Street some of the original houses remain. San Rafael is now the sprawling county seat of Marin, whose bustling main drag, Fourth Street, was a frequently photographed setting in the film *American Graffiti*.

The Inn

Panama Hotel, 4 Bayview Street, San Rafael 94901; (415) 457-3993. Full breakfast included, with a restaurant on the premises; moderately expensive.

Seventeen homey rooms in a hotel with a distinctly Mexican flavor, well situated on a quiet street near the town center.

The Way Back

By Public Transportation: From the San Rafael bus depot at Fourth and Hetherton take Golden Gate Transit bus 1 to the Strawberry Shopping Center and bus 10 down East Blithedale to Sycamore. (Call (415) 332-6600 or 453-2100 for schedule.)

By Foot: The fastest route back is via back roads, avoiding the freeway. Take D Street and Wolfe Grade over the hill to Sir Francis Drake Boulevard. Turn left to Bon Air Road and right to Magnolia; stay on Magnolia to its end. Then take Corte Madera Avenue and Camino Alto over the grade to East Blithedale, and turn right to Sycamore.

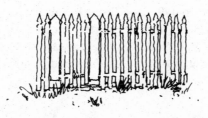

Chapter 15
Fort Mason to Fort Barry

A 9½-mile hike through the Golden Gate
National Recreation Area from hostel to hostel.

The Night Before

Getting There

By Public Transportation: Take Muni bus 42, 27 or 30 and stop at
Van Ness Avenue and Bay Street. (Call (415) 673-6864 for schedule.)
Enter Fort Mason across the street, and angle northwest to find the
hostel.

By Car: Take Highway 101 to Van Ness Avenue and Lombard
Street. Here, northbound travelers continue straight ahead on Van
Ness, and those southbound turn left onto it; proceed three blocks
north to the Fort Mason entrance gate near the corner of Bay Street
and Van Ness. Once inside, follow the signs to the hostel. (Hostel
personnel suggest you check in and they will direct you to overnight parking.)

Fort Mason

Originally built in 1797 as a Spanish military fortification, and
used during the Civil War to quarter United States troops, Fort
Mason served during World War II as the largest Army port on the
Pacific Coast. Now its historic buildings and picturesque lawns are

the bay-side setting for the headquarters of the Golden Gate National Recreational Area, as well as for the host of cultural and educational programs at Fort Mason Center.

The Inn

San Francisco International Hostel, Building 240, Fort Mason, San Francisco 94123; (415) 771-7277. Inexpensive.

A completely refitted Civil War barracks on a bluff overlooking San Francisco Bay. Kitchens and dining room for guest use; accommodations for 130 guests.

A Look at the Day's Walk

The Golden Gate National Recreation Area (GGNRA) has been a much appreciated, much utilized parkland for Bay area residents since it was established by act of Congress in 1972. At that time some 25,000 acres, spanning the San Francisco shoreline and extending up the Marin coast to Point Reyes, was set aside for public use, connecting already existing parks. Largely through the incorporation of additional public lands into its jurisdiction, the park land has been growing ever since.

This walk between hostels allows you a small sample of the countless recreational possibilities brought to being with the creation of the GGNRA. Leaving the headquarters at Fort Mason, you stroll beside the yacht harbors of the San Francisco shoreline, then follow the Golden Gate Promenade along the beach to Fort Point. From here, you begin the ultimate San Francisco experience: a trek across the Golden Gate Bridge itself. Once arrived on the Marin side you navigate the high bluffs of the headlands surrounded by Bay, sea and city vistas, then descend to Fort Barry and, beside Rodeo Lagoon, Golden Gate Hostel.

The Route

Distance: 9½ miles.
Walking time: 5½ hours.
Grade: Some gradual uphill climbs and descents.

Find the path from the back of the hostel that leads west; descend the steps into the parking lot of Fort Mason Center.

Continue out of the fort by means of the small pedestrian ramp at the water's edge, and circle Gashouse Cove to the right around the harbor.

Follow the bayside path along the Marina Green (circled number 1 on the map) past the harbor master's office, where the route turns left and meets Marina Boulevard (2). Proceed west along the harbor past the rows of bobbing sailboats and yachts and, at the end, turn right on Yacht Drive, following it to the Bay. A left turn at the stone steps puts you on the Golden Gate Promenade (3) — the paved footpath that runs along the water's edge. Here you have an unobstructed view of the Golden Gate Bridge; take it as your signpost, along with the blue-and-white Golden Gate Promenade markers, which direct you the next two miles to Fort Point. This Civil War military fortress is always worth an exploratory detour.

From the Fort Point green, take the path uphill, climbing the slope below the bridge. At the top of the slope bear left, walking through the gates toward the small, circular structure that houses the office marked "EEO." Turn right and, using the pedestrian lane on the east (city) side of the bridge, walk north, to the Marin County end.

From Vista Point, 1¾ miles north of the bridge's toll plaza, follow the weekend-and-holiday bike-route signs, using the westbound walkway undernearth the bridge. At the cyclone fence, turn right, following the high road uphill as it curves to the left. At the top you can rest on the conveniently placed benches near Battery Spencer, a maze of turn-of-the-century military bunkers updated for each major war since.

After you have enjoyed a respite from the climb, continue on Conzelman Road past the turnoff to Kirby Cove (4). (A bit farther on, you can spot the cove's idyllic little beach far below, at the base of the cliffs.) As you walk these high bluffs you are treated to views of the city framed by the graceful spires and cables of the Golden Gate. The straight rows of "the avenues" are bounded at the western edge by the green hills of Land's End.

Eventually you arrive at a junction where Conzelman Road, which is paved, veers off to the left; McCullough Road, also paved, veers to the right; and a dirt road extends away between the two (5). Take this middle path, which is the Pacific Coast Trail, through the white gate. To the north you can see the sweep of Wolfback Ridge and the top of Mount Tamalpais beyond. The ocean stretches ahead to the west, and on a clear day you might see the Farallone Islands on the southwest horizon.

At the next junction, ignore the sharp right turn and continue straight ahead toward the ocean; finally walk downhill to Bunker Road (6). Veer left on Bunker and walk past the stables, ignoring the first paved road to the left. Take the second paved road to the left, which is beyond the "Do Not Enter" sign (7). As you walk this portion of the route, you may see hang gliders practicing their graceful sport from the top of the hill across the road.

As the road veers to the left, many white buildings come into view. Continue walking until you see a tennis court ahead on the right. The hostel is on the left just before the court. If you arrive at Rosenstock Road you have gone too far and should turn left on Rosenstock to return to the hostel.

Journey's End

Fort Barry

In 1904, the U.S. Army carved an 893-acre chunk out of Fort Baker in the Marin headlands and renamed it Fort Barry, in honor of a Civil War general. Although the Army continues to house military personnel in many of the existing buildings, most of the reserve is now part of the GGNRA.

The Inn

Golden Gate Hostel, Building 941 Fort Barry, Sausalito 94965; (415) 331-2777. Inexpensive.

A historic landmark nestled in the Marin headlands, a short walk from Rodeo Beach. Kitchen and recreation rooms for guest use; accommodations for 60 guests.

The Way Back

By Public Transportation: On Sundays and holidays only, Muni bus 76 departs from Field Road, ⅓ mile from the Fort Barry hostel, and runs down Lombard Street to Van Ness Avenue, only three blocks south of Fort Mason. (Call (415) 673-6864 for schedule.)

By Foot: Consider hiking over to Sausalito, then taking the bus or ferry from there back to San Francisco. To do so, follow the route to Fort Barry in reverse to the Golden Gate Bridge underpass. See chapter 6 for the hiking route from the underpass to Sausalito and directions from Sausalito to San Francisco.

Chapter 16
Mount Tamalpais to Muir Beach

A 6-mile hike through Muir Woods
from a mountaintop inn to a Tudor-style country inn.

The Night Before

Getting There

By Public Transportation: Take Golden Gate bus 10, 20, 50 or 60 to
Marin City, then bus 63 (Saturdays, Sundays and holidays; on
weekdays, bus 61) to Mountain Home Inn. (Call (415) 332-6600 or
453-2100 for schedule.)

By Car: From Highway 101, take the Stinson Beach exit, then
follow the signs for Highway 1 (Shoreline Highway) to Panoramic
Highway, and take Panoramic to Mount Tamalpais.

Mount Tamalpais State Park

This park, 960 acres, comprises most of the southern and western
slopes of majestic 2,571-foot Mount Tamalpais. One report has it
named for the Tamal Indians; another, for an Indian maiden
named Temelpa. According to Indian legend, evil spirits lived on
the mountaintop, and, to put this belief to rest, sometime in the
1800s surveyor Jacob Leese climbed it and planted a cross at the
summit.

At the turn of the century, an eight-mile track known as the
"Crookedest Railroad in the World" brought tourists to the top to

marvel at views extending from San Jose to the Sierra. Today, visitors use scenic Panoramic Highway to reach the park's riches: Mountain Theatre, a natural amphitheater with stone seats where the *Mountain Play* is annually presented, and beautiful camping grounds and hiking trails, including a popular East Peak loop walk around the top.

The Inn

The Mountain Home Inn, 810 Panoramic Highway, Mill Valley 94941; (415) 381-9000. Full breakfast included, with a restaurant on the premises; expensive.

The spanking new, luxurious Mountain Home Inn, perched nearly at the top of Mount Tamalpais, replaces a 74-year-old Bavarian chalet of that name. The ten spacious guest rooms, some with jacuzzis, fireplaces, skylights and private decks, combine with elegant "California cuisine" dining and panoramic bay views to provide incomparable lodging.

A Look at the Day's Walk

It would be impossible to find a more perfect Marin County weekend trek than this particular combination of inns and walk. You leave the mountaintop eyrie and descend ferny canyon trails to Muir Woods, a 485-acre preserve of virgin coast redwoods spared the woodsman's axe in part because of its isolated location. Leaving the preserve you continue the walk along wildflower-strewn ridge tops overlooking the Pacific, then descend to the remote beauty of Muir Beach.

The Route

Distance: 6 miles.
Walking Time: 3 hours.
Grade: 3½ miles, moderate downhill; 1½ miles level terrain; 1 mile moderate uphill.

From Mountain Home, turn left and walk to the trailhead junction, about 100 yards down the right side of Panoramic Highway. At the junction, turn left onto the Panoramic Trail (circled number 1 on the map); a short distance further, turn right toward Muir

Woods, onto the Ocean View Trail (2). Both trails, aptly named, afford fine Pacific vistas from the lofty slope above Redwood Canyon.

At the next junction, turn right on Lost Trail (3), toward Fern Creek. This lovely trail, rediscovered and reestablished a short time ago, continues downhill through forests of bay, oak and mixed evergreen. Soon redwoods begin to predominate and you arrive at the creek that shaped this enchanting canyon. Turn left on the Fern Creek Trail (4), which runs alongside the water's edge through groves of first-growth redwood the rest of the way to Muir Woods National Monument.

When you arrive at the narrow, paved path (5), turn left on it and stroll either side of Redwood Creek through the park proper. Understandably, the park is likely to become congested with tourist traffic on weekends and holidays, but even so the grandeur of the great trees tends to prevail here. Continue past Cathedral Grove to the Visitor Center, where you can stop for park information or refreshment.

When you are ready to exit the park, walk through the parking lots, following the path beside the creek. At the end of the second lot, turn right on Frank Valley Road (6) and follow it a scant quarter mile, to the next trail junction. A broad fire road climbs uphill to the right, but your route is on the narrower Miwok Trail at the left (7). This grassy path gets overgrown from time to time but can always be discerned by close scrutiny. It leads down to the creek once more. After the first crossing the trail continues on the left side of the creek, then jumps back to the right. A few more crossings follow. The season will determine whether your feet get wet and how easily the trail is discerned on the opposite bank.

Eventually, the Miwok Trail runs up the left bank and out to a junction clearing. Continue left, uphill, on the Miwok (8), climbing high above bucolic Frank Valley to the top of Dias Ridge, enjoying splendid views of Mount Tam and the Pacific along the way. At the top, turn right on the broad Dias Ridge Trail (9), then, at the next junction, left towards Muir Beach (10), which you begin to sight below. The trail comes down through the local riding stables and out onto Shoreline Highway (Highway 1), just opposite the Pelican Inn.

Journey's End

Muir Beach and the Inn

See chapter 7 for description of the community and the Pelican Inn.

The Way Back

By Public Transportation: None available.

By Foot: Follow the Muir Beach-to-Stinson Beach route (see chapter 8) as far as Muir Woods. In the park, take the first right after the Visitor Center — Ocean View — to Panoramic, which returns you to the Mountain Home Inn.

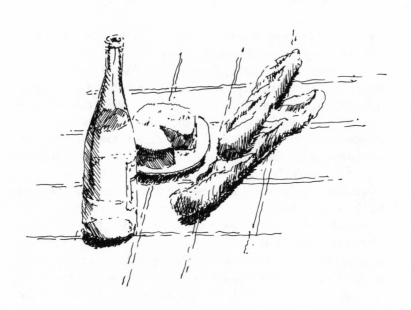

Chapter 17
Corte Madera to Tiburon

An 8½-mile hike over Ring Mountain Preserve
between two suburban motor lodges.

The Night Before

Getting There

By Public Transportation: Take Golden Gate Transit buses 1, 18 or
20 to the Corte Madera exit at Madera Avenue and Tamalpais
Drive. (Call (415) 332-6600 or 453-2100 for schedule.) Walk the one
long block north on Madera Avenue, around the shopping center,
to the Corte Madera Inn.

By Car: From Highway 101, take the Corte Madera exit. Turn right
at the corner of Tamalpais Drive and Madera Avenue, and proceed
one long block around the shopping center on Madera to the Corte
Madera Inn.

Corte Madera

Passersby tend to think of Corte Madera as the utilitarian
shopping center sprawled between Highway 101 offramps in central Marin. However, once headed west on Tamalpais Drive one
finds the town itself — an old, gracious community nestled in the
eastern foothills of Mount Tam. It was here that, almost 150 years
ago, pioneer John Reed logged great redwood forests. Later, in

1885, well-known San Francisco editor, banker and attorney Frank Pixley fixed his title to Owlswood, the 160-acre country estate on which the town park and village center stand today.

The Inn

Corte Madera Inn, 1815 Redwood Highway, Corte Madera 94925; (415) 924-1502 or (800) 528-1234. A motel, with a restaurant on the premises; moderately expensive.

A large, well-equipped complex in a park setting with 86 spacious, comfortably furnished rooms. Spa, playground and Olympic-size pool.

A Look at the Day's Walk

The Tiburon Peninsula, the locale of this walk, is a 1½-mile wide strip of hilly land bounded on three sides by San Francisco Bay, Richardson Bay and Raccoon Straits. The hike begins at the northern border with an exploration of 602-foot Ring Mountain, a so-called biological island whose serpentine-rock soil nurtures several rare plants.

After enjoying 360-degree views from the top of the mountain you descend its southern slope and walk the three-mile length of the peninsula along Richardson Bay, where sea breezes and broad vistas of the Sausalito waterfront, the Golden Gate and the San Francisco skyline heighten your senses.

The Route

Distance: 8½ miles.
Walking Time: 4½ hours.
Grade: ¾ mile each moderately steep uphill climb and descent; 7 miles, level terrain.

Leaving the motel, turn right on Madera Boulevard and, remaining on Madera, veer left. At Tamalpais Drive, turn left. The route crosses the freeway overpass with a spiral pedestrian ramp on each end.

After you have safely crossed to the eastern side of the freeway, look for the bike route; you will see it at the junction of Paradise

Drive and San Clemente. Take San Clemente Drive straight ahead to its end. Here, take Paradise Drive as it veers left through the small suburban community clustered around San Clemente Creek.

Just past Westward Drive on your right, about ¾ mile along Paradise Drive, find the entrance to the Ring Mountain Preserve (circled number 1 on the map). Go over the bridge and follow the trail signs up the moderately steep slopes of the mountain.

The trail winds gradually up; follow the trail signs carefully to avoid getting detoured on any of the side paths. If you are fortunate enough to be here in the spring you will find these slopes a mass of wildflowers, including some that grow only in this type of soil. The Tiburon mariposa lily, which appears in June, can be found only on this mountain.

Upon reaching the junction with another wide fire road (2), either take the left path or, if you wish to detour briefly to the large Petroglyph Rock, continue a few paces straight ahead and to the right of the trail. On the rock's southern side are circular markings chipped into the rock by Indians, perhaps 2,000 years ago. Returning to the junction, the turn is to the right.

From the junction the route winds north and then east toward Turtle Rock. If you prefer, you can take the shortcut uphill that proceeds more directly east. In either case, you may wish to stop for a rest or a picnic lunch on Turtle Rock, at the top of the hill just off the trail to the right. Here, enjoy the views to the south and behind you, of Belvedere Island, Sausalito and the city, and, to the northwest, the lovely silhouette of Mount Tamalpais.

At the junction with the old paved road (3), pause to notice the long sweep of the Richmond — San Rafael Bridge, extending from San Quentin to the East Bay. Take the old paved road veering south.

Take the first wide fire road going off to the right (4) winding downhill toward Tiburon and Richardson Bay. When you come to the preserve exit (marked on the outside by a yellow Ring Mountain Preserve sign), make an immediate right turn on the unmarked Reed Ranch Fire Road (5), which heads down into the Reed Ranch community. Continue on Reed Ranch Road all the way to Tiburon Boulevard.

Turn left on the pedestrian walkway of Tiburon Boulevard, and, at the crosswalk, walk across it and through the parking lot to the bicycle and walking paths. Follow this popular route along Richardson Bay, perhaps pausing for a rest in the open meadow.

At San Rafael Avenue turn right along the Bay and through the nautical Belvedere Lagoon community. At Belvedere Community Center, remain on San Rafael Avenue as it veers to the left; at the San Francisco Yacht Club, turn left on Beach Street. Walk past the yacht harbor, a central part of this water-oriented community, noticing the arc of Corinthian Island and its Yacht Club at the southeast end of Belvedere Cove.

At Tiburon Boulevard, cross the street and turn right to your motel.

Journey's End

Tiburon

On a flawless day in Tiburon, you take a seat at an open air cafe, order a crab Louis and watch a ketch thread the yacht harbor below. Just beyond, across Raccoon Strait, looms the green slope of Angel Island and, beyond that, the grand expanse of the Bay and the San Francisco skyline. Later, you amble along Tiburon's picture-postcard Main Street, with its enticing specialty shops. This village center originally sprouted up around the railroad-ferry depot established in 1884, and it has attracted browsers and sybarites ever since.

The Inn

Tiburon Lodge, 1651 Tiburon Boulevard, Tiburon 94920; (415) 435-3133. A motel, with a restaurant on the premises; moderately expensive to expensive.

Secluded and close by the picturesque waterfront; 98 spacious, attractive rooms, with private balconies or alcoves. Pool.

The Way Back

By Public Transportation: Take Golden Gate Transit bus 9 or 10 from Tiburon. Transfer at Strawberry Shopping Center for bus 1 to Corte Madera. (Call (415) 332-6600 or 453-2100 for schedule.)

By Foot: An easier walk for the return to Corte Madera follows the bike path along Tiburon Boulevard all the way out to the Highway 101 overpass. Just after the overpass, a bike-route sign directs you to North Marin. Accordingly, turn right here on Tower Drive; then turn right on Plaza Drive and right on Lomita Drive, which delivers you to the bike route to Corte Madera. Once over the grade, follow Meadowsweet Drive or Casa Buena Drive to Madera Boulevard.

Chapter 18
Olema to Point Reyes Hostel

A 9½-mile hike through the Point Reyes National Seashore from a country inn to a seashore hostel.

The Night Before

Getting There

See chapter 11 for directions.

Olema and the Inn.

See chapter 10 for description of the town and the Olema Inn.

A Look at the Day's Walk

There is no more beautiful open-space preserve in the Bay Area than the Point Reyes National Seashore, and this hike provides a rare opportunity for a weekend exploration of its cliffs, coves and pristine beaches.

Beginning with a walk along the Earthquake Trail, one senses an isolation on this peninsula that is a reminder of its geological location on the Pacific plate, as opposed to that of the rest of the continent, which is supported by the North American plate. After a climb to scenic Mount Wittenberg, you descend the western slope and walk the magnificent expanse of beach to the hostel, tucked away in the hills.

The Route

Distance: 9½ miles.

Walking Time: 5 hours.

Grade: A 1½-mile moderate-to-steep ascent of Mount Wittenberg and a 3½-mile gentle descent to the shore; the rest mostly level terrain.

A short walk south on Shoreline Highway (Highway 1) from Olema Inn and the Shoreline Highway-Sir Francis Drake Boulevard crossroads brings you to the Vedanta Retreat signpost. Turn right at the Vedanta Retreat (circled number 1 on the map) on the dirt road, and you will see the Point Reyes sign to the Bear Valley Trail on your right. Follow the path through the gate, across the meadow, then along the self-guilding Earthquake Trail to the Bear Valley trailhead (2), about ¾ mile in all.

Follow the Bear Valley Trail and then, only about a quarter mile along it, turn right onto the Sky Trail (3), which climbs toward Mount Wittenberg through forests of oak and fir. Just short of a mile up the trail, pass through a clearing, then reenter the forest for another steep ascent. Take the Wittenberg trail where it veers uphill to the right (4), and, after the last short haul, the 1,407-foot summit rewards you with a panoramic vista of Point Reyes and its long beaches.

When you are ready, descend until you rejoin the Wittenberg trail, just above Sky Camp. This trail proceeds northwest along the ridge, dropping slightly. At the first junction, veer left toward Sky Camp (5); at the second, left onto the Fire Lane Trail (6). This is your route to the coast, some 3⅓ miles below. The trail descends gently through fir forest again, then through open shrub, where the spectacular Point Reyes seascape begins to emerge once more.

About two miles along, ignore the grassy Laguna Trail, which forks off at the right, and continue straight ahead on the Fire Lane Trail. It contours the last of the coastal hillsides and drops down toward the sea, ending at a junction with a graveled path.

At this junction, turn right onto the Coast Trail (7), paralleling the shore for the next mile or so. Access to the pristine beach below is possible here and at a few other spots along the way. It is possible to walk this mile stretch westward on the beach, continuing westward onto the glorious beach at Limantour Spit, as long as you remember that the tide tends to come up most rapidly when the least attention is paid to it, and it can be lethal.

When you've had your fill of sand and surf, return to the Coast Trail, which heads north through marshland and then follows the valley turns of a small stream the rest of the way to the hostel.

Journey's End

Point Reyes National Seashore

See chapter 11 for description.

The Inn

Point Reyes Hostel, P. O. Box 247, Point Reyes Station 94956; (415) 669-7414. Inexpensive.

A former ranch house located deep in the coastal hills, with accommodations for 40 guests. The hostel features a wood-paneled common room, patio with outdoor barbecue, kitchen and dining room. Bring your own food.

The Way Back

By Public Transportation: None available.

By Foot: The shortest return route, without too much retracing of the route in, begins at the Education Center, located just east of the hostel. From the hostel turn left and continue along the road past the sign pointing to the Environmental Education Center. Go through the gate leading to the Point Reyes Center; turn right, pass the center building and find the sign picturing a hiker that points left. That indicates the Laguna Trail, which you take 1¾ miles uphill to a three-way junction. The Bayview Trail (unmarked) is the one extending to the right and left (and the trail straight ahead ends shortly); take the Bayview Trail to the right. After ¾ mile, the Bayview Trail meets the Sky Trail and Limantour Road. Take the Sky Trail 2¾ miles back to the Bear Valley Trailhead, and then continue back to the inn.

The East Bay

Each of the excursions in this section cashes in on a small part of the great open-space legacy bequeathed Bay Area residents in 1934, when by popular mandate citizens of Alameda County established the East Bay Regional Parks District. The 10,000 acres then set aside as parkland, a pioneering investment in the environment, was further augmented 30 years later when Contra Costa joined its fortunes with the district.

In this section, six of the treks scramble up, along or over glorious Skyline Ridge, which faces westward to San Francisco Bay and eastward to the lush inland valleys of Contra Costa. Two of the treks explore the oak-dappled hillsides of Briones Regional Park, a bucolic landscape particularly inviting during the green seasons of winter and spring. Whatever your route, you'll find the inns along the way as wide-ranging a selection as any in this book, reflecting the wonderful diversity of the East Bay community itself.

Chapter 19
Kensington Loop

A 4½-mile loop hike through Wildcat and
Tilden parks from a hillside guest house.

The Night Before

Getting There

Ask for directions when making your room reservation.

Kensington

Just north of Berkeley and south of El Cerrito the unincorporated
community of Kensington climbs the hillside high above San Francisco Bay. Here, oblivious to the clamor of traffic on San Pablo
Avenue a mile below, one discovers winding, tree-lined streets
and the single row of neighborhood shops on Arlington, the small
town center, where everyone seems to know each other by name.
The residents of Kensington enjoy their separateness and point
with pride to the prevailing volunteer ethic that has sustained
their small-town independence since the first gathering of the
Kensington Improvement Club more than 60 years ago.

The Inn

Kensington Bed and Breakfast International, contact Bed and
Breakfast International, 151 Ardmore Road, Kensington 94707;
(415) 525-4569 or 527-8836.

Bed and Breakfast International will arrange your lodging in one of their carefully selected Kensington guest homes; cost, location and ambiance to suite your taste.

A Look at the Day's Walk

Kensington's Shangri-la identity is much enhanced by the presence of the East Bay Regional Parklands along its eastern border: Wildcat Canyon to the north and Tilden Park to the south. This walk explores the rolling hills and wooded valleys of both territories. A hike uphill through Kensington's tranquil lanes brings you to the Laurel Canyon Trailhead in Tilden Park. The trail climbs gently through woods and brushland, then continues up the grassy slope, making a final short, steep ascent of Wildcat Peak. From the Peace Grove Lookout, 1,230 feet above sea level, you enjoy the kind of top-of-the-world view that well rewards the uphill effort. If you wish to make a short day of it, you can follow the Wilcat Peak Trail directly down from the summit, retracing your steps to Amherst Avenue. The wider loop described swings north through Wildcat Canyon and along the wide, open ridge top with its wonderful vistas, then south beside Wildcat Creek, past Jewel Lake, and back to the Laurel Canyon Trailhead, less than a mile from Kensington.

The Route

Distance: 7 miles or 4½ miles.

Walking Time: 4½ hours or 3½ hours, depending on your choice of the regular route or the shorter alternative.

Grade: Fairly level terrain except for 1½-mile moderately steep uphill and downhill climbs.

Ask your innkeeper for walking directions to the intersection of Grizzly Peak Boulevard and Canon Drive.

Proceed straight ahead on Canon (past the "Road closed" sign) to Tilden Regional Park. At Central Park Drive, head left to the nature study area, where you may wish to rest and examine some of the information available in the Environmental Education Center.

From the back door of the Environmental Center, take the Laurel Canyon Trail, which is on the right, marked with a bay laurel leaf. The trail climbs through forests of eucalyptus to a broad dirt road; walk left on it a few paces to where Laurel Canyon Trail continues on the right (circled number 1 on the map). Here the trail narrows, heading uphill through bay laurel trees, then downhill to cross the creek. Across the creek, the trail continues steeply uphill; at a fork, take the left path (2), which becomes a very narrow trail all the way to Laurel Canyon Road (3).

From the meeting with the broad road, take it to the right a short way to a trail marker on the left that indicates a mountain peak (4). Head left on this trail, which climbs steeply up the grassy flanks of Wildcat Peak, to the junction with Wildcat Peak Trail (5).

For the ascent to Wildcat Peak, turn right on Wildcat Peak Trail and continue uphill. At the broad road, stay on Wildcat Peak Trail; continue up to the circular stone benches of the Peace Grove Lookout. This is a wonderful lunch spot, with a 360-degree view of San Francisco, the Golden Gate and Marin to the west; the San Pablo reservoir, beyond the young Sequoia Peace Grove, to the east; and Mount Diablo in the distance.

After lunch, position yourself with your back to the Peace Grove plaque. The direction you take on Wildcat Peak Trail determines whether you take the shorter or longer route.

Wildcat Peak Trail to the left is the return path for those who wish to shorten the hike. Follow this trail as it winds down the ridge. Where it meets the Wildcat Creek Trail at Jewel Lake, turn left to rejoin the regular route. (For further directions, skip to the last paragraph.)

For the regular hike, take the trail on the right (6) through the break in the barbed wire fence and into Wildcat Canyon Regional Park. At the meeting with the broad Conlon Trail (7), turn left.

Conlon Trail is a windswept, level road along the top of the San Pablo Ridge, with extensive views of hills, open meadows, grazing cows and wildflowers. At its end, Conlon meets the Wildcat Creek Trail (8) coming from the northern end of the park; turn left to follow the trail alongside Wildcat Creek back into Tilden Park.

Pass the Jewel Lake Trail marker (with a picture of a duck) on the right, continue to the second marker (not the path immediately over a bridge) on the right, and take the trail it indicates on bridges over and around the shrubbery- and willow-festooned lake to its southern end, where it meets the main road back to the Environmental Center. You may choose to take a final rest at the center retracing the route up to Grizzly Peak Boulevard and on back to Kensington.

Chapter 20
Kensington to Lafayette

A nearly 15-mile hike over Skyline Ridge
from a hilltop guest house to a suburban motel.

The Night Before

Getting There

Ask for directions when making your room reservation.

Kensington

See the preceding chapter.

The Inn

Kensington House, Contact Visitor's Advisory Service, 1516 Oak
Street, Suite 327, Alameda 94501; (415) 521-9366. A guest house,
with continental breakfast included; moderately expensive.

A contemporary rustic-style home in the Kensington Hills. Two
guest bedrooms, one with view deck.

A Look at the Day's Walk

What better way to pass a bright spring day than to walk over
San Pablo Ridge and follow the reservoir trails to Lafayette? In the
spring the East Bay hills are resplendent with wildflowers, and the
route, lengthy enough to challenge the young of limb, is also gentle enough to accommodate any hiker in reasonably good shape.

From Kensington, a two-mile climb brings you to Inspiration Point, the entrance to East Bay Municipal Utility District (EBMUD). You will need a trail use permit to hike here, obtainable for a nominal fee by contacting EBMUD, at P. O. Box 24055, Oakland, 94623; (415) 835-3000.

The Inspiration Trail descends the green slope of San Pablo Ridge to the eastern tip of San Pablo Reservoir. From here, you follow the wooded southern shore of Briones Reservoir all the way to Happy Valley Road, your route to the journey's end in Lafayette.

The Route

Distance: Nearly 15 miles.
Walking Time: 8 hours.
Grade: Rolling hills; ascents and descents are gradual.

Ask the innkeeper for directions to Spruce Street. Turn left on Spruce and proceed to Canon Drive, then take the paved road that veers left down to Tilden Regional Park. At Central Park Drive, turn right (circled number 1 on the map).

At the first left turn (2), take the paved road toward Wildcat View. A short distance along, you come upon the Lone Oak Picnic Area. Here, take Seaview Trail to the right, following as it winds uphill (3).

At the meeting with the broad trail, turn left and walk a short way to Inspiration Point. You may wish to walk over to the view area, but be sure to return to this spot for the continuation of the route.

With your back to the stone gates of Nimitz Way, take the fire road to the left marked Inspiration Trail (4). As you walk the San Pablo Ridge you can see San Pablo Reservoir, which is your destination for this part of the hike. The upper lake is Briones Reservoir, which you will follow along during the afternoon.

After about half a mile, just before you reach a gate and paved road, the trail makes a hairpin turn to the right (5). A small white post with an arrow directs you to follow this U-turn as you proceed, winding downhill, toward the reservoir.

At another junction, a bit farther on, take the right turn indicated by the white marker and walk up a small knoll in the direction of the southeastern end of the reservoir. Then proceed downhill to a small pond on the right (6). Keeping the pond on your right, follow the trail up the wildflower-strewn hillock and down again to San Pablo Dam Road.

Head through the gate to the right and across the highway. Heeding the white trail marker, pass through a narrow opening to the dirt trail that winds through tall grass to the paved Old San Pablo Trail (7). Take this road to the right as it meanders along the serene shore of the San Pablo Reservoir.

Walk a short way past the Headquarters of the Forestry Division of EBMUD, and take the Oursan Trail on the left (8). The trail winds through shady groves of pine and oak, crosses San Pablo Creek, and forms a U to return downstream on the opposite side. Across the pipeline and at the bottom of Briones Dam, Bear Creek Trail takes off to the right (9).

Here you may wish to rest before beginning the 4½-mile hike along the Bear Creek Trail. Starting at the southern end of the Briones Reservoir, the trail winds along the shore in a gradual climb toward the Briones Overlook Staging Area. Pass the staging area and continue north on the Bear Creek Trail, which climbs steadily to the top of the ridge where the reservoir bends to the east. Walk along the ridge, where the trail roughly parallels Bear Creek Road, before heading downhill through the trees to the end of the reservoir.

From the meeting with Bear Creek Road (10), walk east on Happy Valley Road for about two miles to Upper Happy Valley Road (11). Take this pretty suburban street to its end at El Nido Ranch Road and turn left to Highway 24, where you cross under the freeway, then take Mount Diablo Road left to the motel.

Journey's End

Lafayette

In 1848, Elam Brown purchased the entire Acalanes Rancho — site of present-day Lafayette — for $900, not enough to pay the yearly taxes on a homesite in this attractive residential community today. Housing construction boomed here after World War II, transforming what was a tranquil farming village into a commuter suburb. Residents have fought to preserve something of the rural quality of the past. Their success is evident in Lafayette's tree-shaded lanes and rolling green hillsides.

The Inn

Hillside Motel, 3748 Mount Diablo Boulevard, Lafayette 94549; (415) 283-8200. Inexpensive.

Sixty comfortable units, some with kitchens, surround a swimming pool. On a quiet hillside.

The Way Back

By Public Transportation: From the motel, turn left on Mount Diablo Boulevard and left again on Happy Valley Road to the Lafayette BART Station. Take BART to the Berkeley Station and transfer to AC Transit bus 7 or 67 to Kensington. (Call (415) 933-BART for BART and 839-2882 for AC Transit schedules.)

By Foot: Retrace the described route.

Chapter 21
Berkeley: The French Hotel to Gramma's

A 6-mile hike through the East Bay hills
from one Berkeley inn to another.

The Night Before

Getting There

By Public Transportation: Take AC Transit bus F or 33. Or, from
the BART Berkeley Station, walk north on Shattuck Avenue to
Cedar Street. (Call (415) 839-2882 for AC Transit and 465-BART for
BART schedules.)

By Car: From Highway 80, take the University Avenue exit; drive
east on University, then north on Shattuck to Cedar.

Berkeley

The human factor is so overwhelming an ingredient in the rich
Berkeley brew that one may fail to notice the city's splendid
natural setting. It does, after all, front on San Francisco Bay below
a high ridge of wooded, westward-looking hills; Berkeley's peaks
command some of the grandest vistas in the Bay Area. Much of
Tilden Park, which bounds Berkeley to the east, has been set aside
as a natural preserve, where hikers and bikers can explore the
unspoiled landscape of eucalyptus groves, gemlike lakes and
grassy hillsides.

Still, to visit Berkeley without sampling the diverse flavors and textures of its cultural environment is to miss the point completely. With the possible exception of San Francisco itself, no city in the Bay area offers quite so many exciting things to do, places to visit or people to gawk at. You might choose to take in the latest exhibit at the University Art Museum or the Judah Magnes Museum, or maybe check whether your favorite symphony orchestra or ballet company is performing at Zellerbach Auditorium. There are cinemas of every variety, little theaters, big theaters and night spots just for music. For window-shoppers and people watchers, a stroll down Telegraph Avenue between the street stalls and boutiques should suffice. Take the opportunity, too, to rest awhile in any one of a dozen coffeehouses here, where the price of a cappuccino can buy you an afternoon of good company. When the dinner hour arrives, you'll be hard put to choose among the plentiful and varied culinary offerings featured at Berkeley's innovative eating establishments — some of the finest in the Bay Area.

Of course, the heart of the city, its life source, is the great university. Founded in 1868 with 10 faculty members and 40 students, the University of California at Berkeley currently educates some 31,000 students in 300 separate degree programs on its campus of more than 900 acres. Whether you amble through the political marketplace of Sproul Plaza, attend a public lecture at Wheeler Auditorium or cheer on the Cal team at Memorial Stadium, the vitality of the institution is everywhere abundantly in evidence. It is this energy that sets Berkeley apart, rendering it as stimulating a site as you could wish for a weekend or a lifetime.

The Inn

The French Hotel, 1583 Shattuck Avenue, Berkeley 94709; (415) 548-9930. An inn; expensive.

Contemporary, urban and European in feeling. Many of the 19 rooms feature view patios and decks. Situated in an attractive shopping area with the award-winning restaurant Chez Panisse directly opposite.

A Look at the Day's Walk

When you've dallied long enough with the pleasures of Shattuck Avenue — the specialty shops, charcuteries and cafes — you climb upward through a residential neighborhood for 1½ miles. At the top, you enter the scenic preserve of the University of California Ecological Study Area, picking up a dirt fire road that runs two miles south along the crest of the ridge through pine, cypress and eucalyptus. Along the way, there are many glimpses of San Francisco Bay to the west and the San Pablo Ridge lands to the east. The view west expands to a full vista as you descend the hill between Strawberry and Claremont canyons; then, with the university's campanile directly ahead, you drop down to the south side of the campus. A short walk straight down Derby Street and a left turn on Telegraph brings you to your night's lodgings.

The Route

Distance: 6 miles.

Walking Time: 4 hours.

Grade: A moderately steep 2-mile uphill and a moderate half mile downhill climb; 3½ miles level terrain.

The most strenuous part of the day's walk comes at the beginning, with a two-mile climb up the Berkeley hills to Tilden Regional Park at the top of the ridge.

Leaving the French Hotel, turn right on Shattuck Avenue and left on Cedar; follow Cedar uphill all the way to its end at La Loma Avenue. Here, turn left, enjoying views of Berkeley and the Bay, then right on Buena Vista Way as it winds uphill past old mansions, dramatic contemporary estates and even a 1920s stone castle with a red mission tile roof.

At Delmar Avenue turn left, then make the first right on Parnassus Road (aptly named for the Greek home of the gods). Continue uphill and turn left on Campus Road and right on Avenida Drive; from Avenida make the first right onto Harding Circle. (The street sign is missing.) Turn left on Fairlawn Drive, right on Senior Avenue and, at the top of the ridge, right on Grizzly Peak Boulevard. Here you will need to catch your breath; enjoy the vast Bay area views in all directions.

Stay on Grizzly Peak Boulevard past the junction with Golf Course Road and Centennial Road (circled number 1 on the map).

The trail you are looking for leads off to the right (2) and is marked "UC Ecological Study Area." Stay on this trail as it winds through the university's preserve, past eucalyptus, pine and cypress trees and gradually broadening vistas of rolling hills. At a crossroads, take the left fork, continuing on the broad trail. Road marks along the way indicate the mileage.

About one mile along, arriving at a fork, take the broad road steeply uphill to the left (3). At the top, take the road to the right (4). You are now at the highest point of the trail and may wish to find a comfortable spot for a picnic lunch. Views here are spectacular — to the north, rolling hills; to the east, Mount Diablo and, on a clear day, the Sierra. San Francisco Bay and the peninsula stretch to the south, and the Golden Gate and Marin lie to the west.

After lunch the route heads downhill — through fields of wildflowers, if you are lucky enough to be here at the right time of year. Stay on the trail past the UC Ecological Study Area sign on the right (5), then head slightly uphill into the Berkeley Open Space Preserve (which is unmarked). At a junction, take either fork — they meet again up ahead.

At the end of the trail, take the paved road to the left and then at the fire trail to the left (6). This trail goes steeply downhill as it approaches the campus. Stay on the main fire trail (ignoring the road to the left marked "no admittance") as its switchbacks lead down to a paved road (7). Here, take the narrow easement immediately on the right which connects to Derby Street. Take Derby to College Avenue, then turn left and immediately right to continue on Derby to Telegraph Avenue. Walk left 1½ blocks to your inn, Gramma's, on the right.

Journey's End

The Inn

Gramma's Bed and Breakfast Inn, 2740 Telegraph Avenue, Berkeley 94705; (415) 549-2145. Full breakfast included; moderate to expensive.

A painting of Gramma greets you at the top of the stairs of this fully restored turn-of-the-century Tudor mansion. The 19 guest rooms are furnished with antiques; many have decks, fireplaces and access to the English country garden.

The Way Back

By Public Transportation: Take AC Transit bus F or 33. Or take BART from the Ashby Station to the Berkeley Station and walk north on Shattuck on Cedar. (Call (415) 839-2882 for AC Transit and 465-BART for BART information.)

By Foot: Stroll Telegraph or Shattuck north just over a mile to Cedar. Or, returning to the ridge, you can take the Grizzly Peak Trail as a longer alternative to retracing the original route.

Chapter 22
French Hotel to Gramma's: The Long Way

An 8½-mile hike through the East Bay hills
from one Berkeley inn to another.

The Night Before

Getting There

See the preceding chapter.

Berkeley and the Inn

See the preceding chapter for description of the city and the
French Hotel.

A Look at the Day's Walk

High above Berkeley, the Seaview Trail follows the top of San
Pablo Ridge for nearly two dazzling miles before it ends at Vollmer
Peak. From almost any point along the way, the city, bay and
mountain vistas are eyefilling.

To get to the ridge, you climb through North Berkeley's distinc-
tive hillside neighborhoods, passing through Shasta Gate and continuing uphill through Tilden Park to the trailhead. Leaving the
Seaview Trail at the foot of 1,905-foot Vollmer Peak, you descend
the curve of Claremont Canyon, with Berkeley and all of
downtown Oakland stretched out before you like an architect's
model.

The Route

Distance: 8½ miles.

Walking Time: 5½ hours.

Grade: 3¾ miles, moderate uphill climb; 1½ miles, level terrain; 3¼ miles, moderate descent.

Turn left on Shattuck, walk north two blocks, and right on Rose Street. Proceed uphill, curving left on Arch, then immediately right again on Rose. Swing left on Bayview Place, which curves uphill past some especially imposing Berkeley homes, to the junction with Euclid Avenue at Codornices Park. If you wish to explore the Berkeley Rose Gardens for a bit, detour on the left. The route to the ridge, however, continues right on Euclid and up Rose Walk, which extends up to the left just after the park. From Rose Walk, take Rose Street, veering left on Tamalpais a few steps to reach Shasta Road.

Turn right, up Shasta Road, following its turns all the way up, veering left at its junction with Campus Drive and then right again to stay on Shasta. A left turn on Grizzly Peak Boulevard delivers you to Shasta Gate; from here, continue to follow Shasta Road through Tilden Park.

At the second stone marker, veer left toward "all other facilities." At the crossroads where the Brazilian House can be seen on the left (circled number 1 on the map), either veer right on the paved path around to the main entrance to the Botanical Garden or cut across the lawn directly in front of you to the side entrance, then follow the fence right, around to the Botanical Gardens main gate. If you choose the latter, you will have a passing view of the beautifully landscaped gardens within.

Arriving at the main gate, notice the stone marker set in a triangle in the middle of South Park Drive. With your back to the gate, cross the street to the marker and take South Park Drive to the left, 40 paces beyond the marker triangle. At this point you will see a narrow, unmarked dirt trail heading up the slope (2). Take this steeply climbing path to where it meets the wider trail above (3).

Turn left and continue on this broad fire road which, in season, is ablaze with wildflowers. At the crossroads (4) continue straight ahead on the path climbing the ridge.

At the top, meet the Seaview Trail (5) and take it to the right for a nearly two-mile walk along the spine of San Pablo Ridge. This is a glorious trail, with unparalleled views from the Pacific to Mount Diablo. After an initial stretch of fairly level terrain the path climbs to its highest point, where a strategically located bench affords a perfect spot for a lunch break. Here, enjoy the 360-degree view of the Bay area, including the Richmond, Golden Gate and Bay bridges to the west, and, to the east, the San Pablo and Briones reservoirs, Carquinez Straits, the Delta and Mount Diablo.

After lunch, continue walking the Seaview Trail, ignoring the Big Springs Trail turnoff to the right (6). Eventually the trail becomes a paved road (7), then makes a U-turn; here, take it to the right, and, shortly thereafter, take the unmarked wide, grassy path straight ahead going south (8) rather than continuing on the paved path that heads uphill to Vollmer Peak.

The trail narrows as it skirts the perimeter of the peak, winding through a pine forest to its exit at a paved road (9). Turn right on this road, which winds downhill, through the gate and straight ahead on the National Skyline Trail.

At the junction with Lomas Cantadas Road (10) turn right, then immediately left on the main road, which is Grizzly Peak Boulevard (unmarked here). About a quarter mile down Grizzly Peak Boulevard you will see a fire road on the right marked "UC Ecological Study Area." Continue a few paces beyond it to a narrow unmarked trail going off to the right (11). You can further locate this trail by noting that it is directly across the road from a private road and gated fire trail. Take this narrow trail, which contours the side of the hill around and downhill, until you arrive at the crossroads (12).

Veer left on the broad fire road, which runs the ridge above Claremont Canyon and affords breathtaking views of downtown Oakland to the south, the campanile to the west, and, before long, the white turrets of the Claremont Resort below.

Turn left on the paved road and left again on the fire road as it descends steeply toward the campus. Stay on the main fire road, ignoring the road to the left marked "no admittance," until you reach the paved road.

For your lodging at Gramma's, take the narrow easement immediately to the right, which connects to Derby Street. Turn right on Derby, left on College, then immediately right to continue on Derby to Telegraph Avenue. Walk left 1½ blocks to Gramma's on the right.

If your destination is the Claremont Resort, swing right again upon reaching the paved road (the lower arm of Stonewall Road), following it until it joins Claremont Avenue at the back entrance of the hotel.

Journey's End

The Inns

See the preceding chapter for description of Gramma's.

The Claremont Resort, P. O. Box 23363, Ashby and Domingo avenues, Oakland 94623; (415) 843-3000. A hotel-resort, with a restaurant on the premises; moderately expensive to very expensive.

A much praised Bay area landmark, the Claremont has charmed its clientele since 1915. The white-turreted, castlelike structure is set in 20 gardened acres above Berkeley. An Olympic-size pool and 10 pro tennis courts are at guests' disposal. Most of the 235 rooms offer grand views. Check for special package plans.

The Way Back

By Public Transportation: AC Transit bus 43 runs along Shattuck. (Call (415) 839-2882 for schedule.)

By Foot: You may retrace your steps to this point or reverse the shorter version of this hike described in the preceding chapter.

Chapter 23
Berkeley: Gramma's to the Claremont Resort

A 7-mile hike to Vollmer Peak and back
from an inn to a grand resort.

The Night Before

Getting There

By Public Transportation: Take AC Transit bus 40. Or, by BART, from the Ashby Station walk east on Ashby Avenue, then north on Telegraph Avenue. (Call (415) 839-2882 for AC Transit and 465-BART for BART schedules.)

Alternatively, to begin the loop from the Claremont described under Berkeley and the Inns, take AC Transit bus 37, 65 or E to the Claremont Resort. By BART, take the train to the Rockridge Station and call the Claremont for limousine pick-up.

By Car: From Highway 80, take Berkeley's Ashby Avenue exit; drive east on Ashby Avenue, then north on Telegraph.

Alternatively, to begin the loop from the Claremont described under Berkeley and the Inns, from Highway 80 take Berkeley's Ashby Avenue exit; drive east on Ashby Avenue to the Claremont Resort on Domingo Avenue.

Berkeley and the Inns

See chapter 21 for description of the city and Gramma's; see chapter 22 for the Claremont Resort. Since Gramma's and the Claremont Resort are less than a mile apart, this route also could be taken as a loop from either.

A Look at the Day's Walk

Vollmer Peak, 1,905 feet above sea level, is the highest of the East Bay hills and, as such, provides a perfect vantage point for viewing the Bay area. From Gramma's, the route to Vollmer begins with a mile walk up Telegraph Avenue and Dwight Way to Panoramic Way, which climbs the rest of the hill to the ridge above Strawberry Canyon. You follow this delightful ridgetop trail around the south side of the canyon, then climb again to Grizzly Peak Boulevard, a half mile above. From here, a short walk and easy climb bring you to the panoramic vistas of Vollmer Peak. The way down follows the ridge above Claremont Canyon, then drops to the back door of the Claremont Resort.

The Route

Distance: 7 miles.
Walking Time: 5 hours.
Grade: 3 miles, gentle to steep uphill climb; 3 miles, gentle to steep descent; 1 mile, level terrain.

A five-block walk north on Telegraph Avenue and a right turn uphill on Dwight Way, past the People's Park, the University of California dormitories and the gracious hillside homes bring you to the UC School for the Blind and Deaf property, on the right side of the street. Dwight Way swings to the left, but your trail runs straight uphill along the property fence; walk through a eucalyptus grove, then around and up the curve of a grassy slope above the school. Toward the top, veer left to join the paved road above at the junction of Dwight and Panoramic ways. Continue uphill on Panoramic to the top of the ridge. Turn left on the road, (circled number 1 on the map); after some 200 yards, a fenced fire trail marks the entrance to the UC Ecological Study Area.

Proceed through the Study Area gate, turn right (2) and follow the broad fire road as it swings around the south side of

Strawberry Canyon. The botanical gardens are below. For the next 1¼ miles, as you follow the gentle uphill course of this trail, views of the UC campus, the Lawrence Berkeley laboratories and San Francisco Bay open before you.

As you approach the head of the canyon, past another Ecological Study Area sign, a broad dirt road branches steeply up to the right (3). Follow it up to the next junction, and turn left (4) for another steep climb, this time to the crest. The road descends a short way, then proceeds uphill once more. Here, ignore the numerous branch-trail options and continue on the main trail; it veers left, finally, then extends down to Grizzly Peak Boulevard.

Turn right (5) and walk along the highway for a short distance to where it meets Lomas Cantados at the Steam Train Area. Turn left (6) into the picnic area, following the Skyline Trail left (7) and uphill, then right (8) on the Vollmer Peak Trail to the summit. If you are graced with a clear day, the vistas are limitless — San Francisco Bay and the Golden Gate to the west and Mount Diablo and glimpses of the Sierra way off to the east, with the village of Orinda nearly below you.

When you are ready to leave, retrace your steps down to the Steam Train Area, and turn left (9) on Grizzly Peak Boulevard for a short way. Pass the Ecological Study Area sign and path to the right, and where a private road and fire trail converge at the left, turn right (10) on the narrow trail directly opposite, which contours the side of the hill around and down until you arrive once again at the crossroads.

Continue straight ahead on the broad fire road, which runs down the ridge above Claremont Canyon, offering breathtaking views of downtown Oakland to the south, the campanile to the west, and, before long, the white turrets of the Claremont Resort below. Turn left on the paved road and left again, entering the continuation of the fire road, which proceeds downhill through a eucalyptus grove. Veer left at the fork, and continue out to the paved road at the bottom of the ridge. Swing right on the lower arm of Stonewall Road, following it until it joins Claremont Avenue at the back entrance to your destination: the Claremont Resort.

Journey's End

The Inn

See the preceding chapter for description of the Claremont Resort.

The Way Back

By Public Transportation: Take AC Transit bus 65 from Ashby to Telegraph. (Call (415) 839-2882 for schedule.)

By Foot: Stroll less than a mile west on Ashby, then north on Telegraph, to Gramma's.

Chapter 24
Oakland Hills to Moraga

A 5¼-mile hike over Skyline Ridge from
one guest house to another.

The Night Before

Getting There

By Public Transportation: From the BART Oakland City Center station transfer to AC Transit bus 18 — the Piedmont Pines Route — and ride to the 5700 block of Chelton Drive. Walk west to Chelton Lane. (Call (415) 465-BART for BART and 653-3535 for AC Transit schedules.)

By Car: From Highway 13, take the Park Boulevard exit eastbound and turn left after the overpass, then immediately right up Scout Road. Turn left on Ascot Drive, left on Chelton Drive, and left again into Chelton Lane.

Oakland

Already a railroad center, port and thriving urban hub at the turn of the century, Oakland doubled its population as a result of the great earthquake of 1906. By 1907, thousands of refugees from the devastation of the San Francisco fire decided that they liked their new surroundings well enough to put down permanent roots. Now a sprawling metropolis of 345,000, Oakland points with pride to its symphony orchestra, ballet company, museum, zoo and great sports coliseum as evidence of its cultural vitality. In appealing counterpoints, no visit to Oakland is complete without strolling along the shores of Lake Merritt or amid the heady waterfront ambiance of Jack London Square.

The Inn

Taylor Bed and Breakfast, Jessie and Peter Taylor, 59 Chelton Lane, Oakland 94611; (415) 531-2345. A guest house, with continental breakfast included; inexpensive.

On a quiet lane high in the Oakland Hills; walking distance to Redwood Regional Park. Two guest bedrooms with views of the Bay, city and bridges.

A Look at the Day's Walk

It is little more than five miles from the fashionable homes clinging to the slopes of the Oakland Hills to the rustic suburbia of Moraga. The route follows the ridge top of Redwood Regional Park, a 2,000-acre preserve along the Alameda — Contra Costa county line. Here the giant coast redwoods grew to 30 feet in diameter before being commercially logged in the mid-1900s. You will pass through groves of second-growth redwoods on the Redwood Trail down the ridge to Moraga Valley.

Because this trail goes through East Bay Municipal Utility District land, it is necessary to get a permit in advance, from EBMUD, P. O. Box 24055, Oakland 94623; (415) 835-3000.

The Route

Distance: 5¼ miles.

Walking Time: 3¼ hours.

Grade: 1¼ miles uphill climb; 4 miles, level terrain and gentle descent.

Leaving the guest house, turn left on Chelton Lane, right on Bagshotte Drive and left on Chelton Drive. Proceed on a moderately steep ascent to Damby Drive, where you turn right and continue uphill to Carisbrook Drive.

Turn right on Carisbrook Drive and continue on this street until you reach the junction with Skyline Boulevard. Do *not* turn toward Redwood Regional Park. (The route to be followed enters the park at a different gate.) Instead, continue straight ahead to the Skyline Gate of the park, which you will see a bit farther on. Go through the parking lot to the far end, where the Eastridge Trail begins.

Take the broad, well-marked Eastridge Trail almost three miles along the top of the ridge. The tall pines bordering the path and the expansive views of the Contra Costa hills and Mount Diablo make this a very pleasant ramble.

When you reach the Redwood Trail turnoff on the left, (circled number 1 on the map), begin your descent along the ferny path through the redwoods. After crossing San Leandro Creek, cross Pinehurst Road (2) and continue on the Redwood Trail on the right.

Cross a creek and proceed uphill as the trail emerges above a bucolic valley with vistas of rolling hills and grazing cows. At a crossroads with the old King Canyon Loop Trail (unmarked), continue straight ahead, following the arrow on the trail marker.

The trail continues out the gate and into a parking lot. Cross Moraga Road and the Valle Vista Staging Area. Continue on the trail, veering right as it parallels the road, all the way to Moraga Creek where the trail ends on Moraga Road. Take Moraga Road to Constance Place and your guest house.

Journey's End

Moraga

Originally part of a Spanish land grant, green Moraga Valley was once the exclusive domain of grazing sheep. Then, in the years following the close of World War II, an affluent community of single-family residences took root, becoming Moraga. The town's most notable landowner is Saint Mary's College, whose 500-acre campus was established by the Christian Brothers in 1928. The attractiveness of its Mission-style architecture belies the serious business of educating some 2,000 students a year.

The Inn

Hallman Bed and Breakfast, Frank and Virginia Hallman, 309 Constance Place, Moraga 94566; (415) 376-4318. A guest house, with continental breakfast included; inexpensive.

A family home in a quiet cul-de-sac, with the San Pablo Ridge lands for a backyard. Two guest bedrooms, a hot tub and swimming pool.

The Way Back

By Public Transportation: Take C.C.C. Transit bus 106 to the Orinda BART Station and BART to Oakland City Center Station. Transfer to AC Transit bus 18 — the Piedmont Pines Route — and ride to the 5700 block of Chelton Drive. Walk to Chelton Lane. (Call (415) 930-8999 for C.C.C. Transit, 653-3535 for AC Transit and 465-BART for BART schedules.)

By Foot: The redwood-bordered Stream Trail provides a pleasant alternative route back to Skyline Gate. Start by retracing the original path up the Redwood Trail, but at the East Ridge Trail, turn left then right on the Canyon Trail, descending to the parking area below. From here, follow the Stream Trail along Redwood Creek all the way back to your entry point at Skyline. Retrace your steps to Chelton Lane.

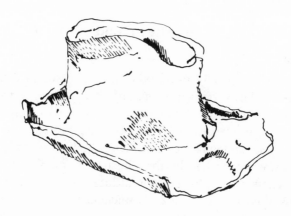

Chapter 25
Lafayette to Walnut Creek

An 8½-mile hike through Briones Regional Park
from one suburban motel to another.

The Night Before

Getting There

By Public Transportation: From the BART Lafayette Station, cross under the Highway 24 overpass, turn right on Mount Diablo Boulevard, and walk a half mile to the Hillside Motel. (Call (415) 933-BART for schedule.)

By Car: From Highway 24, take the Acalanes Road — Mount Diablo Boulevard exit. Follow Mount Diablo Boulevard one mile to the Hillside Motel, on the left.

Lafayette and the Inn

See chapter 20 for description of the town and the Hillside Motel.

A Look at the Day's Walk

The network of 106 trail miles linking the East Bay Regional Parks to each other is a tangible expression of a particularly characteristic Bay area concern: ready access to open space. These specially marked trails, meandering through parklands, town centers and over suburban hillsides, allow hikers and bikers a means of traveling from park to park untroubled by the press of automobile traffic.

From suburban Lafayette, you climb to 1,357-foot Russell Peak in the pastoral splendor of Briones Regional Park, then walk along the top of Lafayette Ridge, with panoramic views of valley, mountain and far-off Bay. You descend to Walnut Creek via the Briones — Mount Diablo interconnecting trail, which then curves up and over a quiet neighborhood hillside, delivering you to the top of San Luis Road. A mile walk downhill brings you to Main Street and Motel 6.

The Route

Distance: 8½ miles.
Walking Time: 5 hours.
Grade: 1½ miles, a fairly steep uphill climb; 7 miles, gently rolling hills and level terrain.

Leaving the motel, turn right on Mount Diablo Boulevard and walk to Happy Valley Road. Turn left under the freeway, continuing on Happy Valley Road about two miles, to just past the Happy Valley School, on the left. Turn right on Panorama Drive (circled number 1 on the map) and follow it steeply uphill for about half a mile, veering to the left at the hairpin turn. Pick up Panorama Trail, which leads into Briones Regional Park, at the end of the street through the gate.

Ignoring the turnoff to Mariposa Trail, continue on Panorama until the paved road ends. Here, look for the broad, grassy continuation of the trail, which veers to the left (at the trail, unmarked; on the map, 2). If you miss this turn you will find yourself at a water tank; retrace your steps.

The Panorama Trail heads steeply uphill, and as you walk it you may wish to pause now and then to catch your breath and note the widening vistas of San Pablo Ridge. Go through the gate and continue uphill to the junction with the Russell Peak Trail (3); take this new trail straight ahead, then follow it as it veers to the right past Russell Peak.

You have probably noticed that these hills and meadows are cow pastures and sometimes share the trails with those peaceful

They scatter when approached and watch curiously from a distance. In the early spring these meadows are aflame with wildflowers, which, along with the superb views, make this a particularly satisfying walk.

At the junction with the Lafayette Ridge Trail, turn right and head gradually downhill. At the bottom, a broad trail leads off downhill to the left; straight ahead are two hills. Look closely to discern a narrow trail contouring the left side of the hill ahead of you, as well as a broad trail going directly up and over. Your route is the narrow trail, which bypasses the top of the hill. When you come to the second hill, notice that a narrow path bypasses the need to climb it by contouring the right side of the hill. By means of these narrow bypasses continue to walk along Lafayette Ridge yet avoid the most strenuous climbs directly over the tops of the rolling hills. As you do so, you have immense views of Lafayette to the south and Walnut Creek to the north, as well as Mount Diablo ahead.

When you arrive at a gate, continue through, walking along the top of the ridge where the view broadens to include Suisun Bay and Marinez. The next gate marks the beginning of the Briones — Mount Diablo Regional Trail, which you follow for the rest of this hike. Shortly, follow the trail where it veers to the right. (If you continue straight ahead, mistakenly, you arrive at a water tank.) At a junction with a broad fire road, cross the road and continue downhill. At a point where the road forms a hairpin around a hill to the left, you will notice a trail going up the hill, appearing to lead to the houses at the top of the ridge. This is the trail you must take; if you miss it, you will find yourself heading downhill, eventually reaching Brown Avenue. In that case, you must retrace your steps and find this trail.

Take the trail uphill and, shortly, where it splits in two take the right-hand fork, rather than the steep uphill fork toward the houses. At the gate marked Briones — Mount Diablo Trail, follow the trail markers that lead you across the ridge tops, where you may again contour the hills on narrow trail bypasses.

As you head toward Walnut Creek following the trail markers, avoid confusion by using the junction of Highway 24 with Pleasant Hill Road, which you can see below, as your general directional guide.

After going through another gate, descend by switchbacks through a lovely oak grove. At the bottom, you parallel Pleasant Hill Road, which runs below, and finally reach the parking lot adjacent to a school. Exit at the intersection of Pleasant Hill Road and Springhill Road (4). Cross Pleasant Hill Road and find the trail marker directing you north for a bit and then, off to the right, steeply uphill on a paved path.

The path becomes a dirt trail as it climbs the wildflower-covered hill. Through another gate, continue straight ahead, then follow the trail sign to the right and the top of the ridge. Here, the Walnut Creek area and beyond to Suisun Bay spread before you.

Continue following the trail signs through another gate, past a water tower and down a paved road lined with fine old oaks. Follow this older, more developed part of the trail to the intersection with San Luis Road, where you exit and turn right.

Take San Luis Road about one mile to Main Street, turn right, and walk on the overpass across the freeway to your motel.

Journey's End

Walnut Creek

In 1849, William Slusher built his cabin at a crossroads called The Corners and eventually great orchards were planted. Today, few orchards remain to bring to mind the rural past. Instead, basking in a sunny valley between the Briones Hills and Mount Diablo, Walnut Creek might well be termed the quintessential East Bay suburb. Within easy commuting distance of Oakland and San Francisco, its 53,000 residents have the pleasures of year-round outdoor living, an active civic arts program and a fashionable downtown shopping area. The community's postwar flowering paralleled expansion of the sophisticated highway and rail networks that link it to the urban centers.

The Inn

Motel 6, 2389 North Main Street, Walnut Creek 94596; (415) 939-8181. Inexpensive.

The king of budget accommodations, offering 72 comfortable, spotlessly clean rooms at economy prices. Swimming pool.

The Way Back

By Public Transportation: Walk south on Main Street a quarter mile to the Walnut Creek BART Station. Take BART to the Lafayette Station. (Call (415) 933-BART for schedule.)

By Foot: Retrace the described route.

Chapter 26
Lafayette to Martinez

A 9-mile hike through Briones Regional Park
from a suburban motel to a country guest house.

The Night Before

Getting There

By Public Transportation: From the BART to Lafayette Station, cross under the Highway 24 overpass, turn right on Mount Diablo Boulevard and walk a half mile to the Hillside Motel. (Call (415) 933-BART for schedule.)

By Car: From Highway 24, take the Acalanes Road – Mount Diablo Boulevard exit. Follow Mount Diablo Boulevard one mile to the Hillside Motel, on the left.

LaFayette and the Inn

See chapter 20 for description of the town and the Hillside Motel.

A Look at the Day's Walk

Briones Regional Park, just east of San Pablo Ridge, is 5,086 unspoiled acres of high, oakstudded hilltops, rolling, green valleys and shady canyons. From its southern access gate in Lafayette, you climb the crest of the Briones Hills, walking north along the ridge

tops to 1,483-foot Briones Peak. All along the way the views of surrounding valleys, Bay and far-off mountains are dazzling and they
continue to fill the eye as you drop gently down the Old Briones
Road to Martinez. Just beyond the back gate of the park, Home
Acre, part of John Muir's original ranch, is your journey's
destination.

The Route

Distance: 9 miles.
Walking Time: 6 hours.
Grade: 2 miles, a moderately steep uphill climb; 7 miles, rolling
hills and level terrain.

Leaving the motel, turn right on Mount Diablo Boulevard to Happy Valley Road. Walk left, under the freeway, and take Happy
Valley Road about two miles as it climbs gradually uphill through
this agreeable residential area of Lafayette.

Just after you pass the Happy Valley School on your left, look for
Panorama Drive on the right (circled number 1 on the map). Take
Panorama for a half mile, winding up the hill and veering to the
left at the hairpin turn. The Panorama Trail into Briones Regional
Park begins at the end of the street through the gate; continue on
this trail.

Shortly after the turnoff to the Mariposa Trail (which you ignore), the paved road ends. Look for the broad, grassy unmarked
continuation of the Panorama Trail, which veers to the left (2). If,
by mistake, you continue straight ahead on the dirt road, you will
come to a water tank and know you have missed the turn. Take
the Panorama Trail steeply uphill; your effort is rewarded by views
of San Pablo Ridge. Go through the gate, continue uphill and meet
the Russell Peak Trail (3). Take it straight ahead, passing Russell
Peak, which is 1,357 feet high.

At the meeting with the Lafayette Ridge Trail (4), continue
straight ahead on Briones Crest Trail. To the east you can see
Mount Diablo rising 3,800 feet above the Contra Costa towns.

Proceed downhill through the gate on the Briones Crest Trail.
Follow the gently rolling terrain to the crest of the hill, where the
Crescent Ridge Trail comes in from the left (5). Continue on the

Briones Crest Trail as it traverses the ridge top, with broad vistas of meadows and hills.

Look for a junction where an unmarked trail comes in from the left (6). You can recognize it by some rectangular stone slabs marked by a gas-pipeline sign. You must take this high road to the left rather than continuing straight ahead on the unmarked Withers Trail, which goes toward Pleasant Hill.

Veer right at the turnoff to Table Top and Spengler Trails (7), continuing on the high road rather than the low road of the Briones Crest Trail. (The high road is the easier route.) At the top of the hill, go through the gate and take Table Top Trail to the left up toward Briones Peak.

Walk left through another gate (8), veering uphill and at the end of an oak grove notice the narrow trail leading off to the right, which you may use to climb to Briones Peak. The bench conveniently located at this junction is a good place to unpack a picnic lunch.

Briones Peak, 1,483 feet high, commands a superb view in all directions. Mount Tamalpais and Marin County can be seen to the west, and Mount Diablo rises from the foothills of Concord and Walnut Creek to the south. Directly ahead, to the north, are the hills of Sonoma and Napa counties, and to the northeast you can clearly see Suisan Bay, the Benecia — Martinez Bridge, and your destination, the town of Martinez.

After lunch, return to the trail and continue across the rolling Briones Hills. Turn right on Old Briones Road Trail (9) and take it all the way out of the park, ignore the turn off to the Withers Trail (10).

Emerging from the Park (11) stay on Briones Road; your lodging is two miles beyond. Where Briones Road ends, at Alhambra Valley Road, turn right and then, a bit further on, left, following Alhambra Valley Road through this pleasant suburban area of Martinez. Turn right at Wanda Way to your guest house.

Journey's End

Martinez

Any avid environmentalist can tell you what's special about Martinez: it's where John Muir lived. At the John Muir Historic Site, visitors can explore the spacious country house, with its acres of flowering orchards and vineyards, where the Sierra Club founder settled with his family in 1890. But Martinez was a bustling city long before John Muir's day, due largely to its position on the Carquinez Straits as an overnight ferry stop for returning gold miners en route to San Francisco. Although oil refineries dominate the downtown landscape today, enough of Martinez's past remains in evidence to permeate the community with its special flavor.

The Inn

Home Acre, 2 Wanda Way, Martinez 94553; (415) 228-0227. A guest house, with full breakfast included; inexpensive.

A country ranch house on a well-planted acre, once part of John Muir's property. Two comfortable guest rooms, and an outdoor swimming pool. Dinners furnished upon advance request.

The Way Back

By Public Transportation: From the nearest bus stop, a mile up Alhambra Avenue at Walnut, take the BART bus to the Concord BART Station. Take BART to the Lafayette Station and walk a quarter mile west on Mount Diablo Boulevard to the Hillside Motel. (Call (415) 933-BART for schedule.)

By Foot: An alternative to the original route, about half a mile longer, gives you a chance to see a bit of the western edge of Briones Regional Park. Instead of turning toward Briones Peak on the Crest Trail, stay on the Old Briones Road Trail south to its junction with the Homestead Valley Trail at Bear Creek. Follow Homestead Valley Trail south, turning right on the Russell Trail, past Russell Peak once again, then down the Panorama Trail to Lafayette.

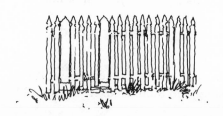

The South Bay

Weekend trekking in the South Bay can vary greatly, with settings ranging from deeply forested parks and open-space preserves amidst exclusive suburban enclaves, to small coastal communities at the Pacific shore. Most of the South Bay is best explored during the spring when wildflowers cover the open hills or during the pleasantly cool days of fall. Lodgings are generally reasonably priced, so these hikes are especially good choices for the budget-minded trekker.

Chapter 27
Pacifica: Sharp Park to Rockaway Beach

A 5½-mile hike to Sweeney Ridge
between beach town motels.

The Night Before

Getting There

By Public Transportation: Take SamTrans bus 1A, 1C, 1H or 1L
along Highway 1. Get off at Paloma Avenue and walk west to
Francisco Boulevard and north to the motel. (Call (415) 761-7000 for
schedule.)

By Car: From Highway 1, exit at Francisco Boulevard and continue
south to the motel.

Pacifica

This bedroom community for San Francisco commuters is the
result of the consolidation of nine towns, including Sharp Park and
Rockaway Beach, that stretch along the coast from Edgemar to
Pedro Point and encompasses about 12 square miles. The residents
here enjoy seven miles of beaches lined with rocky bluffs perfect
for trail riding and hiking.

The Inn

Marine View Motel, 2040 Francisco Boulevard, Pacifica 94044; (415)
355-2543. Inexpensive.

Very basic units with full kitchens and TV, two blocks from the
beach.

A Look at the Day's Walk

When the Spanish explorer Gaspar de Portola arrived in Pacifica on an overland expedition from Baja California, he had passed by Monterey Bay — the actual objective of his journey — because he had failed to recognize it. From an encampment on San Pedro Creek, Portola's scouting party climbed to Sweeney Ridge and discovered the immense bay now known for San Francisco.

This hike takes you to the very spot of Portola's momentous discovery. It is a rugged climb, requiring physical stamina and sturdy hiking shoes with good traction. The route takes you up the steep hills of the Sharp Park subdivision, through the Sweeney Ridge Skyline Reserve, now part of the Golden Gate National Recreation area, and to the granite marker where the Portola party stood.

Since you will be hiking on easements through private property, you must obtain a permit in advance, by applying to City of Pacifica, Park, Beach and Recreation Department, 170 Santa Maria Avenue, Pacifica 94044. On request, this department will also send you a certificate commemorating your re-creation of the Portola expedition.

The Route

Distance: 5½ miles.

Walking Time: 4 hours.

Grade: 2¾ miles, a moderate-to-steep uphill climb; ¾ mile, level terrain; 2 miles, a moderate-to-steep descent.

From the corner of Francisco Boulevard and San Jose Avenue in Sharp Park, use the pedestrian overpass to cross Highway 1. Turn right at the Eureka Square Shopping Center, left on Eureka Drive, and left again on Talbot Avenue which swings behind the shopping center and curves uphill for the next half mile.

At the end of Talbot, walk through the white fence auto-traffic barrier and continue steeply uphill on the dirt road that rises ahead. At the crest, cross Sharp Park Boulevard to the church directly opposite, and, walking through the church drive, pick up the dirt path that continues south along the edge of the ridge, keeping the sea vista to your right as a guide. After a small hillock, descend to the Skyline College parking lot, where the Sweeney Ridge Trail begins (1).

Climb the dirt path up from the parking lot to the water tank above. At the tank, turn right on the dirt road and continue the steep climb to the top of the hill. Here, a rest stop will give you a chance to take in the wide vistas; in any event, you'll need to catch your breath before the next pull. To the south, directly ahead, the radar site atop the next hill is your destination, and — barring the arrival of a friendly helicopter — you need to pick your way down the steep incline, then back up to the top of the ridge.

Walk through the entry gate to the radar site, then around the cyclone fence that surrounds it, to find the path continuing on — south from the other side. Walk south on the paved path for a short while, then bear right, following the dirt path up to the San Francisco Bay Discovery Site. Here, the vista is no less lofty than when the Portola party first glimpsed the Bay (if somewhat altered) on Nov. 4, 1769. Montara Mountain to the south, Tamalpais to the north, Diablo and the great Bay to the east, the Pacific to the west — these are the same natural guideposts that helped Portola fix his position for future explorers. Needless to say, the San Francisco Airport and surrounding urban sprawl to the east were later developments, as was the engineering of attractive San Andreas Reservoir below.

From the discovery site, cross the ranch road, and follow the trail that continues south along the ridge top for the next fifth of a mile before swinging west. To avoid mistakenly turning seaward too quickly, use the water tank visible to the southwest as your guidepost; it marks the trail you need to travel. At the junction (2), veer right, proceeding downhill till you reach the fence, and walk through the small metal gate on the left. The trail descends from here to the water tank, then drops more steeply to a second water tank farther below. Walk out through the gate and onto Fassler Avenue, following it all the way downhill to Donaldson Avenue, just above sea level. A right on Donaldson and a left on Rockaway Beach Avenue, crossing Highway 1, lead you to the beachfront Sea Breeze Motel.

Journey's End

The Inn

Sea Breeze Motel, 100 Rockaway Beach Avenue, Pacifica 94044;
(415) 359-3903. With a restaurant on the premises; inexpensive.

Comfortable units with TV. Situated 60 feet from the Pacific,
with vast ocean views and crashing surf to lull you to sleep.

The Way Back

By Public Transportation: SamTrans buses run along Highway 1
back to Sharp Park. (Call (415) 761-7000 for schedule.)

By Foot: Because the original hike was so strenuous, you might
prefer to return via the beaches and local streets.

Chapter 28
Half Moon Bay to Montara

A 9-mile Pacific Coast walk
between country inns.

The Night Before

Getting There

By Public Transportation: SamTrans buses run regularly along
Highway 1. (Call (415) 761-7000 for schedule.) From Highway 1,
turn east on Half Moon Bay Road to Main Street.

By Car: Take Highway 1 to Half Moon Bay, or take Highway 101 or
280 to Highway 92 and 92 west to Half Moon Bay. Then take Half
Moon Bay Road to Main Street.

Half Moon Bay

This small coastal community, once called Spanishtown, boasts
a long crescent beach protected by a two-mile submerged reef
breakwater. It is the center of Pilarcitos Valley, a region with cool
summers and mild winters that are perfect for the production of
the delicious globe artichoke.

The Inn

San Benito House, 356 Main Street, Half Moon Bay 94019; (415)
726-3425. An inn, with continental breakfast included and a
restaurant on the premises; inexpensive to moderately expensive.

This newly restored country inn is in the tradition of the comfortable European auberge, with 12 charming guest rooms furnished in antiques and decorative pieces.

A Look at the Day's Walk

Your day begins with a walk around the long arc of Half Moon Bay State Beach to its northern tip at Pillar Point Harbor. After stopping, perhaps, for a fresh crab cocktail at one of the dockside restaurants in Princeton, you climb Pillar Point and walk along the top of the cliffs overlooking the crashing surf of Fitzgerald Marine Reserve.

The cliffside community of Moss Beach, commanding breathtaking views of the Pacific, is your last stop before descending into the tiny beach town of Montara.

The Route

Distance: 9 miles.
Walking Time: 5 hours.
Grade: Mostly level.

From the San Benito House, walk south on Main Street to Kelly Avenue. Turn right on Kelly, and follow it half a mile through the artichoke fields and across Highway 1 out nearly to the shore. Just before the entrance to Half Moon Bay State Beach, notice a horse-trail sign to your right (circled number 1 on the map). Take this designated trail, which parallels the beach for the next two miles north and provides a more walkable, if less thrilling, alternative than negotiating the tides and dunes.

Just past the entrance to Roosevelt Beach at Miramar, turn right on Washington or Roosevelt Boulevard, then left on Alameda Avenue, and left again on Mirada Road, which continues northward to the Miramar Beach Inn. At the inn, take the steps down to the beach and then up to the inviting path along the bluffs above the sea; follow this path for the next mile or so, until it ends at the Half Moon Bay RV Park. The small path that leads out the northern end of the RV park takes you along the beach to the Pillar Point Yacht Harbor.

After exploring the harbor and its piscatory delights, return to the entrance and follow Capistrano Road through picturesque Princeton to the Princeton Inn. Turn left here on Prospect

Way, left on Broadway, then right on Princeton Avenue to its end at West Point Avenue, where another right turn begins your approach to Pillar Point. At the juncture where West Point Avenue curves left, uphill, to the Air Force Station, take the gated road to the right (2) and follow it up to the towers. From here, work your way over to the edge of the bluffs — any path heading north above the sea will do. From this vantage point, the mountain views and seascapes are breathtaking.

Eventually, your path drops down into the community of Moss Beach; take the access closest to the sea once more, following Ocean Boulevard, then Beach Way north to its end. Swing right on Cypress Avenue, then left just after the private fenced property, where a small dirt road leads north across the meadow, through a grove of cypress and eucalyptus, then over a small hillock to the James T. Fitzgerald Marine Reserve.

From the reserve, when you are ready to end your beachcombing, follow Nevada Avenue, turn left on California Street and left again on Wienke Way, right on Juliana Avenue, and left on Vallemar Street. Continue north on Vallemar to its end at the Montara Lighthouse Hostel, and follow Highway 1 about a half mile to the Farallone Hotel.

Journey's End

Montara

This tiny beach community was originally a station of the Ocean Shore Railroad called Farallone City. On a clear day one can see the Farallones, a chain of islands lying about 30 miles offshore.

The Inn

Farallone Hotel, 1410 Main Street, Montara 94037; (415) 728-7817. An inn; inexpensive to moderately expensive.

This is a beach establishment in the old style — six large, comfortable guest rooms with kitchens, decks and ocean views.

The Way Back

By Public Transportation: SamTrans buses run regularly along Highway 1 back to Half Moon Bay. (Call (415) 761-7000 for schedule.)

By Foot: Retrace the described route.

Chapter 29
Burlingame to Woodside

A 15-mile trek between two
suburban guest houses.

The Night Before

Getting There

Ask for directions when making your room reservation.

Burlingame

This suburban residential community is named for Anson Burlingam, a Massachusetts congressman who never actually resided here but owned a large tract of the oak-studded land. He became minister to China in 1861 and is remembered for negotiating the Burlingam Treaty with that country, one clause of which encouraged the immigration of Chinese to California.

The Inn

Burlingame Bed and Breakfast International: contact Bed and Breakfast International, 151 Ardmore Road, Kensington 94707; (415) 525-4569 or 527-8836. They will arrange your lodging in one of their carefully selected Burlingame guest houses; cost, location and ambiance to suit your taste. Minimum stay requirement (see A Look at the Day's Walk). Request directions from your guest house proprietors to the trailheads at the beginning and end of the hike.

A Look at the Day's Walk

San Andreas and Crystal Springs Lakes are the peaceful settings for this rather long walk through the huge expanse of San Francisco watershed lands. The journey begins on the old Sawyer Camp Road, named for Leander Sawyer, a horse trainer and innkeeper before the turn of the century. This six-mile trail is a very pleasant level stroll, with benches and picnic sites perfectly located for rest and contemplation of this Bay area version of the English lake country.

The balance of the hike borders Crystal Springs Lake, following the boundary fence between Canada Road and the watershed lands. This trail, though a bit less scenic because of its proximity to the road, has the added attraction of passing two South Bay landmarks — the Pulgas Water Temple and the Filoli estate. The Water Temple is a small building in classic Greek style, situated at a reflecting pool and surrounded by peaceful lawns for resting and picnicking. It was built as a tribute to the spot where waters from the Sierras end their long journey to the Crystal Springs Reservoir. The Filoli estate, originally owned by W. B. Bourn, president of the Spring Valley Water Company, is a magnificent mansion that can be visited only by arrangement with the Filoli Foundation. (Call (415) 366-4640 for information.)

The route leaves the watershed lands and enters the eastern edge of Huddart Park, with its towering redwoods and cool streams, then finally ends in Woodside.

Note that the guest houses at each end of this hike are under the auspices of Bed and Breakfast International, which requires a minimum two-night stay. For this reason, it is necessary to begin and end this hike at a guest house.

The Route

Distance: 15 miles.
Walking Time: 7 hours.
Grade: Mostly level terrain, with occasional rolling hills.

Ask your guest house proprietor for directions to Skyline and Hillcrest Boulevards. Proceed through the highway underpass to the Sawyer Camp Trail entrance on your left.

Walk through the trail gate (circled number 1 on the map) on the paved path, with the southern end of San Andreas Lake visible at your right. For the next six miles, take the Sawyer Camp Trail southward along the edge of the San Francisco watershed, passing through groves of oak, bay laurel and pine punctuated from time to time by small, sylvan picnic areas. Be sure to detour a bit off the road at the sign to the right to view the beautiful Jepson Laurel, reputedly the largest bay laurel in California. Just a short while after that point, the trail parallels the Crystal Springs Reservoir and you stroll through tranquil lakeside scenery.

At the end of Sawyer Camp Trail, turn right and walk uphill on Skyline Boulevard (2). Since the proposed trail to connect Sawyer Camp and Cañada Trail is not yet complete, walk along the shoulder of Skyline Boulevard southward for the next mile, to its intersection with Ralston Avenue. Turn left at the intersection (3), walk uphill, then continue paralleling the reservoir on the paved road until, at the beginning of Canada Road (4), the next section of the hiking trail begins.

The narrow dirt trail runs alongside Canada Road for the next four miles or so, passing the Pulgas Water Temple and the Filoli estate along the way. At the Woodside city limit sign (5), the trail turns right and climbs uphill through open pasture. At the top of the hill, after swinging left, the path descends through woods, past country houses and ends at Raymundo Drive. Turn right on Raymundo, following it to its end at a cul-de-sac, where three paths appear. The middle path is your entrance to Huddart Park; follow it as it descends by switchbacks into a redwood grove.

Cross the bridge at your left, over West Union Creek, and turn left on Richards Road (6), the broad, level dirt path that parallels the stream. Follow Richards Road out past the Meadow Walk-in Area, cross the bridge over Squealer Gulch Creek, and turn left to exit from Huddart Park.

Turn right on Greer Road (7), then left on Kings Mountain Road, which leads you to the Woodside Store, a welcome sight to travelers since 1854. You might like to take a moment to explore this historical landmark before following the proprietor's directions to your Woodside guest house.

Journey's End

Woodside

Rolling hills and large, rambling homes set well back on manicured lawns characterize the residential community known as Woodside. Three acres is the minimum lot size, and horseback riding is the preferred method of transportation. Though the architecture is California modern, the town dates back to the mid-nineteenth century when sawmills operated here, supplying lumber to the booming Bay area's cities.

The Inn

Woodside Bed and Breakfast International: contact Bed and Breakfast International, 151 Ardmore Road, Kensington 94707; (415) 525-4569 or 527-8836. They will arrange your lodging in one of their carefully selected Woodside guest homes; cost, location and ambiance to suite your taste. Minimum two-night stay at a Bed and Breakfast International Inn. Request directions from your guest house proprietor to the trailheads at the beginning and end of the hike.

The Way Back

By Public Transportation: There is no public transportation within the town of Woodside, so you must walk east on Woodside Road to Woodside Plaza. Ask your Woodside guest house proprietor for directions to your Burlingame guest house.

Chapter 30
Woodside: Loop into Huddart Park

A 7¾-mile forest hike from
a suburban guest house.

The Night Before

Getting There

By Public Transportation: Take SamTrans bus 5L or 7B to the Redwood City train station, then SamTrans bus 51C to Woodside
Plaza. (Call (415) 761-7000 for schedule.) Since there is no public
transportation within the town of Woodside, you must walk west
on Woodside Road. Ask for directions to your Woodside guest
house when making your room reservation.

By Car: Take Highway 280 to Highway 84; ask for directions to
your Woodside guest house when making your room reservation.

Woodside and the Inn

See the preceding chapter for description of the town and Woodside Bed and Breakfast International.

A Look at the Day's Walk

The pastoral village of Woodside is doubly blessed with two
county parks on its borders. Wunderlich Park, the locale of the
next chapter's hike, is the less developed of the two. Huddart

Park, to the northwest, is almost 1,000 acres of oak, fir and red-wood forest, with 15 miles of trails climbing some 2,000 feet to Skyline Boulevard.

You may choose many alternates to the route through Huddart Park described here, including longer, strenuous circles of the entire park or very short nature walks. Trail maps are available in the park office.

The route described takes you steeply up the center of the park through deeply forested canyons to the heights of Skyline Ridge. The loop back follows a nineteenth-century logging trail down to the town. On your return, you pass the old Woodside Store of Dr. Robert Orville Tripp, nineteenth-century dentist, postmaster and member of the first San Francisco Board of Supervisors.

The Route

Distance: 7¾ miles.

Time: 5½ hours.

Grade: Gentle-to-steep uphill climb of 4 miles; gentle-to-steep descent of 3¾ miles.

Follow the directions supplied by your guest house proprietor to the back gate of Huddart Park on Greer Road off Entrance Way.

Turn left, entering the park, then right (circled number 1 on the map) on Dean Trail, following it a short piece across Squealer Gulch Creek, then up to the paved road. Turn right (2) and proceed through the Meadow Walk-in Area — with meadow to your right and restrooms to your left — and on out, following signs to the Zwierlein Area. Here, follow the trail along West Union Creek up through redwoods, bay laurels and sword ferns until a buttonhook turn to the left (3) puts you on the Zwierlein Trail itself; follow the switchbacks up to the picnic area.

Turn right (4) to take the Dean Trail once more, which levels out, drops downhill, then climbs above and around the Werder, Madrone and Miwok picnic areas. Turn left at the fork just after the Miwok area (5), staying on the Dean Trail toward Skyline Boulevard, and continue on the Dean Trail at the next junction (6), ignoring the broad fire road that branches off to the left.

Shortly after you cross the bridge over McGarvey Gulch Creek, the Jackie Trail turns uphill to the left (7). This ¾-mile climb, the steepest part of the route, leads to a junction some 1,800 feet above sea level. At this junction, you've climbed about 1,200 feet since entering the park; the bench below the oak and redwood boughs is a welcome sight indeed.

From the rest bench at the end of the Jackie Trail, turn right (8), walk uphill, turn right again on the broad dirt path. At the junction that appears shortly, veer uphill to the left; then simply follow the Richard's Road Trail, an old logging road, downhill, enjoying the glimpses of San Francisco Bay and Woodside through fir, oak and madrone branches. A mile or so along, walk through the campground, picking up the Richard's Road Trail again between campsites 16 and 17, where it continues downhill. Follow it all the way back to the Meadow Walk-in Area, turning left after the bridge to exit from Huddart Park.

A right turn on Greer and a left on Kings Mountain Road brings you to Tripp Road, where the Woodside Store has provisioned passersby since 1854. When you have had a look there, follow the directions to your Woodside guest house supplied by the guest house proprietor.

Chapter 31
Woodside: Loop into Wunderlich Park

An 8½-mile ramble to the Meadows
from a suburban guest house.

The Night Before

Getting There

See the preceding chapter.

Woodside and Its Inn

See chapter 29 for description of the town and Woodside Bed and Breakfast International.

A Look at the Day's Walk

Of the two county parks on Woodside's borders, Wunderlich, to the south, certainly has the "road less traveled." Compared to Huddart Park's numerous picnic areas and recreational facilities, Wunderlich is a haven for the solitary hiker, with 942 acres of rolling hills, dense forests of oak and redwoods, and an enchanting open meadow halfway up the Skyline Ridge.

The expedition described here is perfect for the novice, because the climb is gentle and gradual, the trails are well marked, and plenty of time is allowed for a long, leisurely picnic on the wildflower-covered slopes of the area called the Meadow. However, the more ambitious hiker can extend the look to explore the heights of Skyline Ridge, which affords views extending to the San Francisco skyline and Mount Tamalpais. For that route, follow the excellent trail map available at the park office.

The Route

Distance: 8½ miles.

Walking Time: 4½ hours.

Grade: 4 miles, a gentle-to-moderate uphill climb; 4½ miles, a gentle-to-moderate descent.

Follow the directions to the entrance of Wunderlich Park supplied by your guest house proprietor.

Enter the gates and walk up the road to the Park Headquarters. Straight ahead, just left of the headquarters building, notice the Bear Gulch Trail sign. Follow this trail (circled number 1 on the map) across the bridge and up through giant oaks, bay laurels and redwoods for a quarter mile to its junction with the Loop Trail. Turn left (2) on the Loop Trail, and, from its junction with the Alambique Trail, continue forward for a few feet, taking instead the Meadow Trail that forks off to the right (3). Climb uphill through eucalyptus, veering left toward the Meadows, then taking the Oak Trail (4) straight ahead till it meets the Alambique once again with a hairpin turn to the right (5). Continue uphill a short way, staying left toward the Meadows, then right on the Bear Gulch Trail (6) to the high, grassy Meadows area, where all paths hereabouts seem to converge. If you are lucky enough to be graced with a fine day, this is as lovely a spot for a picnic lunch as you're likely to find anywhere. Climb any of the surrounding knolls and enjoy the views of Monte Bello Ridge off in the distance.

When you are ready to leave, head downhill on the Meadow Trail (7); then follow the Redwood Trail to the left (8) through a grand redwood forest. Stay left on the Redwood Trail to Salamander Flat, past the little reservoir, to Redwood Flat, where a circular grove of young redwoods surrounds the stumps of giants logged a century ago. Turn right on Bear Gulch Trail (9), which continues downhill for the last mile, affording glimpses of the South Bay skyline and Stanford University, until you arrive once more at Park Headquarters. Retrace your steps to your Woodside guest house.

Chapter 32
Saratoga to Sanborn-Skyline County Park

A 5-mile historic walking tour and hike
from a country motel to a forest hostel.

The Night Before

Getting There

By Public Transportation: Santa Clara County Transit buses 27 and
54 make frequent stops at Big Basin Way (Highway 9); Greyhound
runs three buses daily that make stops at Big Basin Way. (Call (415)
761-7000 for Santa Clara County Transit. In San Francisco, call (415)
433-1500 for Greyhound schedule or call the toll-free number for
your area.) Walk three blocks southwest on Big Basin Way to the
Saratoga Motel.

By Car: From Highway 280, take the exit for Highway 85 and
Sunnyvale-Saratoga Road. Turn right on Big Basin Way and drive
the few blocks to the Saratoga Motel.

If you wish to reverse this hike's route, spending your first night
at the Sanborn Park Hostel, turn right off Highway 85 onto Pierce
Road, then right again on Congress Springs Road, continuing for
about a half mile. Then turn left up Sanborn Road and follow the
signs to the hostel.

Saratoga

This especially verdant corner of the Santa Clara Valley, with
tree-lined lanes and sprawling homesteads, was once

rich orchard lands. Before the orchards, though, Saratoga was a lumber town, site of a water-powered sawmill, then a gristmill, built in 1853 at the upper end of Big Basin Way. The natural mineral springs, a mile above the town, were discovered at about the same time. In 1865 the waters provided the inspiration for the township's name, courtesy of Saratoga, New York, a popular mineral spa back East. Here and there an acre of flowering fruit trees remains in the local Saratoga, and many of the old buildings still stand as well, casting their historical shade in and around the quiet neighborhoods of the present day.

In addition to Saratoga's attraction as a historical landmark, it entices the passerby with the number and variety of its excellent restaurants and specialty shops. Time your visit to the summer season and you can catch a performance of the Music-in-the-Vineyards concert series or the Valley Shakespeare Festival under the stars at the Paul Masson Winery, just a mile or so above town off Pierce Road.

The Inn

Saratoga Motel, 14626 Big Basin Way, Saratoga 95070; (408) 867-3307. Inexpensive.

Twenty bright and cheerful units, some with kitchens, in a cloistered setting of giant oak trees. Steps away from Saratoga's fine restaurants and shops.

A Look at the Day's Walk

The walk begins with a short detour around historical Saratoga and a climb up to the Hakone Gardens at the western edge of town. You then follow Saratoga Creek westward, ascending Congress Springs Road for just over a mile before taking a final turn up wooded Sanborn Road into the park proper.

If you prefer a downhill hike the first day, or wish to have the pleasures of downtown Saratoga at the end, it is simple enough to reverse the route. (See the preceding directions under By Car for getting to the Sanborn Park Hostel.)

The Route

Distance: 5 miles.

Walking Time: 3 hours.

Grade: 3 miles, level terrain; 2 miles, a moderate uphill climb.

Since Saratoga is so interesting historically, the hike starts with a walking loop tour of the town before heading up Sanborn Park.

From the motel, turn left to Sixth Street; take it one block to the left, then take Saint Charles Street to its end at Oak Street and turn left. Walking along the right-hand side of the street, notice the site of the Sons of Temperance Hall at the far end of Saratoga School. (The original structure, built of hand-hewn redwood in 1854, has since been replaced by three successive schools.) Continuing on Oak Street, pass the old Saratoga Fire Department bell from the early 1900s, on the right.

At the intersection with Highway 9, where the old Saratoga Public Library is situated, turn right to see the two preserved buildings immediately adjacent. The first, the McWilliams House, was built in about 1865 and now serves as the Chamber of Commerce. The second, built in 1904, is a historical museum.

Retrace your steps to the intersection with Oak, noticing the memorial arch to World War I veterans across Highway 9. Continue on Highway 9 one block to Big Basin Way and, after crossing the street, turn left.

The route now takes you all the way up Big Basin Way, a charming main street that houses more fine restaurants per block than most major city centers. Notice numbers 14501 to 14503, currently a tea room and gift emporium. These buildings were built in the 1880s, and you can still see the original 10-inch-thick stone walls. Farther along, notice 14519, now a children's clothing store. This was built in the 1890s by a Mrs. McCarthy and was called The Green Store Building after its color. Farther up the street, number 14605, a former residence of E. T. King, co-owner of the Saratoga Paper Mill, was built of hand-hewn redwood in the early 1870s. Back at your starting point, you have completed the one-mile loop through the town center.

As you proceed up Big Basin Way toward Sanborn Park, take one more detour — into Hakone Gardens, a short distance ahead on the left.

This authentic Japanese estate was built in 1918 by Mrs. Isabel Stine, using Japanese craftsmen and a former gardener of the emperor. The main house and guest house are constructed in the Japanese fashion, entirely without nails, and the tea house and bamboo gate were brought from the 1915 San Francisco Panama Pacific International Exposition. The entire estate is now a city park, open to the public.

After enjoying the serenity of Hakone, continue up Big Basin Way, which now becomes Congress Springs Road. Notice Toll Gate Road, a reminder of the tollgate used by loggers bringing their lumber from the sawmill in the mountains.

Proceed up Congress Springs Road, using the convenient shoulder on the right-hand side to avoid occasional passing cars. About one mile beyond Hakone Gardens, Pierce Road enters from the right. This is the route to the Paul Masson Winery, which is not open to the public except for musical and theatrical perform-ances during the summer season. If you are here during that time, contact the winery for information about the programs.

Farther along Congress Springs Road are the Saratoga Mineral Springs, discovered in the 1850s and developed as a resort and health spa. Though the hotel burned down in 1903, the springs are open to the public. A rest and dip would be a restorative break before your final two-mile hike into the park.

When you are ready, continue the short distance to Sanborn Road; turn left onto it and follow the signs through the shade of the redwood forest to the Sanborn Park Hostel.

Journey's End

Sanborn-Skyline County Park

Located four miles west of Saratoga on the eastern slope of the Santa Cruz Mountains, the park's 2,856 acres are threaded by beautiful hiking trails. Redwood, oak and fir plus panoramic vistas of the Santa Clara Valley delight the eye.

The Inn

Sanborn Park Hostel, 15808 Sanborn Road, Saratoga 95070; (408) 867-3993 or 741-9555. Inexpensive.

Set in a redwood grove beside a duck pond, the hostel is a thoroughly enchanting forest retreat. The original Welch-Hurst House, built here of redwood logs in 1908, has been modernized to provide comfortable quarters for 25 guests, with hostel-style dormitories and fully equipped kitchens.

The Way Back

By Public Transportation: None available.

By Foot: Retrace the described route.

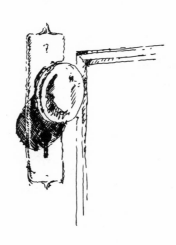

Chapter 33
Saratoga to La Hacienda Inn

A 4- to 4½-mile nature walk
through Villa Montalvo between
two suburban motor lodges.

The Night Before

Getting There

See the preceding chapter.

Saratoga and the Inn

See the preceding chapter for description of the town and the
Saratoga Motel.

A Look at the Day's Walk

Villa Montalvo is both a 170-acre arboretum and a 19-room
Mediterranean-style mansion, and its location, between the
historic town of Saratoga and gracious La Hacienda Inn, makes it
the perfect target for a day's trek.

It is a moderate climb out of Saratoga to the Villa Montalvo upper orchard that connects with the 1½-mile Nature Trail, a self-
guided walk through pleasant forests of pine, redwood, oak and
bay laurel, as well as other typical California flora. (Because this
walk uses a back entrance to the Villa Montalvo Arboretum where
the *Nature Trail Guide* isn't offered, we recommend that you

obtain a copy in advance of your trip, by writing to the Santa Clara Park and Recreation Department, 298 Garden Hill Drive, Los Gatos 95030.)

When you reach the end of the Nature Trail, at the villa, take a tour through this magnificent former summer home of U.S. senator and San Francisco mayor James D. Phelan. Built in 1912, it is named for the sixteenth-century Spanish author who called his fictional island California, which probably is the origin of the state's name. Today, in accordance with Phelan's bequest, the villa and its grounds are a public park and center for the arts.

The Route

Distance: 4 to 4½ miles.

Walking Time: 2½ hours.

Grade: 1½ miles, gentle-to-moderate uphill stretches; 1 mile, gentle-to-moderate descents; about 2 miles, level terrain.

Upon leaving the Saratoga Motel, turn left on Big Basin Way, left again on Sixth Street, then right on Oak Street toward Bohlmann Road. When you reach Norton Road, turn left and continue to climb, enjoying valley glimpses as you go. After passing Sigal Drive to your left, look for number 15381 Norton on your right. Directly opposite this house, on your left, are three mailboxes and, shortly after, seven log poles that mark the side entrance to Villa Montalvo Arboretum. If you arrive at the hairpin turn at the end of Norton, you've gone too far.

Walk through the entrance and proceed straight ahead, ignoring the trail that veers off to the right in the direction of the stream. Very shortly your trail angles downhill, skirting the edge of the upper orchard, which is resplendent with wildflowers in early spring. At the bottom of the orchard, the trail turns off to the right (circled number 1 on the map) alongside the creek. Cross the footbridge; then, taking the first right turn uphill (2), continue to climb steeply through lovely groves of bay laurel and oak.

Cross Wildcat Creek, and turn right, uphill (3), on the Nature Trail toward Lookout Point. Soon you pass numbered posts that identify the most important trees and shrubs growing in the arboretum — as representative a cross section of Bay region plant life as you'll find anywhere. The gentle uphill climb now continues through deep redwood groves, as you follow the Nature Trail up to the right (4) from its junction with the Redwood Trail.

The short detour to Lookout Point, via the direct high road or the more gentle switchback, is well worth the effort, especially if it is getting on to lunchtime. Here, you can pause for rest and refreshment with a sweeping view of the Santa Clara Valley from 1,160 feet above sea level.

When you are ready to resume your walk, turn right once more onto the Nature Trail. At Observation Point, some 350 yards farther on, stay on the trail along a sharp hairpin turn to the left, and follow it all the way down to Villa Montalvo. If possible, plan to spend time exploring the grounds and buildings of this magnificent estate. The art gallery, on the first floor of the main house, features monthly exhibits of the work of promising contemporary artists. It is open to the public Tuesday through Sunday from 1 – 4 p.m.

Upon leaving, follow the exit route (6) out past parking lot 4; when you reach the park boundary, continue straight on Piedmont Road to Mendelsohn Lane, where a right turn brings you to the Saratoga – Los Gatos Road, Highway 9.

The fastest way to your destination would be to turn right on this busy thoroughfare and follow it the 1¼ miles to La Hacienda Inn. An alternative back-road route adds an extra half mile to that but because it's quieter, it is more pleasant, if slightly meandering. If the latter is your pleasure, cross Highway 9 and continue on Three Oaks Avenue until it meets Fruitvale Avenue. Turn right on Fruitvale, then almost immediately turn left on Valle Vista. Turn right on Monte Vista Drive and follow it to El Camino Grande. A right turn here brings you once more to Highway 9. Cross it again, and proceed straight on Austin Way, which swings around to the left and comes out again on the highway at La Hacienda Inn.

Journey's End

The Inn

La Hacienda Inn, 18840 Saratoga – Los Gatos Road, (Highway 9) Los Gatos 95030; (408) 354-9230. A motel, with continental breakfast included and a restaurant on the premises; moderately expensive.

Surrounding a large, inviting pool and patio in a garden setting, 20 comfortable ranch-style guest rooms in the foothills of the Santa Cruz Mountains.

The Way Back

By Public Transportation: Take Santa Clara County Transit bus 27 along the Saratoga — Los Gatos Road (Highway 9).

By Foot: The shortest return route is along busy Highway 9; unfortunately, there are no back roads that go all the way through to Saratoga.

Chapter 34
Saratoga to Los Gatos

A 10½-mile hike through El Sereno Open
Space Preserve from a rustic motel to
a garden motel or traditional inn.

The Night Before

Getting There

See chapter 32.

Saratoga and the Inn

See chapter 32 for description of the town and the Saratoga
Motel.

A Look at the Day's Walk

A five-mile demanding climb from the historic town of Saratoga
brings the intrepid hiker to 1,036-acre undeveloped El Sereno
Open Space Preserve. The chaparral-covered hills here once served
as a breeding farm for race horses, before being purchased from
the Charles E. Moore estate for public use. A 3½-mile trail along
the ridge top, with spectacular vistas of the Santa Clara Valley and
the Santa Cruz Mountains, leads to a gradual descent into the
village of Los Gatos.

The Route

Distance: 10½ miles.

Walking Time: 6 hours.

Grade: 5 miles, a moderate-to-steep uphill climb; 3½ miles, mostly level; 2 miles, a moderate-to-steep descent.

Upon leaving the Saratoga Motel, turn left on Big Basin Way, left again on Sixth Street, then right on Oak Street toward Bohlmann Road. The route continues uphill on Bohlmann for the next nearly five miles as it climbs the wooded ridge above Saratoga. About halfway up, be sure to bear right at the junction with Orbit Drive and continue on Bohlmann past the Camp Stuart Boy Scout area, where the road levels off a bit. A little way past the junction with McGill Road, Bohlmann Road ends at a cul-de-sac.

The first dirt road to your right (circled number 1 on the map), just past the 19090 Bohlmann mailbox, is your pathway to the El Sereno Open Space Preserve. A few minutes down this road climb through or over the boundary gate; after a half mile, bear left at the fork (2). As you continue south along the ridge, you glimpse beautiful Lexington Reservoir below to your right, with the Santa Cruz Mountains beyond. The route extends downhill through open chaparral and aromatic groves of bay laurel, oak and madrone.

About 2½ to 3 miles from the point where you entered the preserve, take the grassy, level path that forks off to the left (3) at a right bend in the road. (If you arrive at a hilltop utility tower, turn back — you've missed the left fork.) Follow this trail around the wooded hillside, veering right (4) at its junction with two others at a clearing. Soon you arrive at the first of two meadows from which you can enjoy glorious aerial views of the entire Santa Clara Valley. Continue to follow the trail through the brush, emerging in the second meadow and proceeding straight down the narrow path that bisects it. Take the hairpin turn left at the bottom (5), following this new trail through densely wooded glades. You may have to ford a stream or two, depending on the season. Pass through or over the preserve gate to the top of Sheldon Road in Los Gatos.

Take Sheldon as it winds its way downhill. Turn right on Overlook Road, right on Wissahickon Avenue, right on

Pennsylvania Avenue and right again on Bayview Avenue to its junction with West Main Street. Here, a left turn and a short stroll down Main bring you to your choice of Los Gatos inns.

Journey's End

Los Gatos

The picturesque town of Los Gatos, named in 1840 for two wildcats seen battling in the vicinity, was slow to develop from its rural beginnings. Since World War II, however, and especially in recent years with the growth of the electronics industry, the town has boomed. Nevertheless, Los Gatos manages to maintain a small-town atmosphere in keeping with its Spanish heritage and incredibly beautiful setting in the foothills of the Santa Cruz Mountains.

The Inns

Los Gatos Hotel, 31 East Main Street, Los Gatos 95030; (408) 354-4440. An inn, with continental breakfast included; moderately expensive.

A winsomely renovated, century-old European-style establishment with 22 rooms.

Los Gatos Garden Inn, 46 East Main Street, Los Gatos 95030; (408) 354-6446. A motel, with continental breakfast included; moderately expensive.

In a garden setting around a heated pool, 28 Spanish-style bungalows.

Village Inn, 235 West Main Street, Los Gatos 95030; (408) 354-8120. A motel; moderately expensive.

A pool and 23 comfortable units.

The Way Back

By Public Transportation: Take Santa Clara County Transit bus 27 along Saratoga — Los Gatos Road (Highway 9). (Call (408) 287-4210 for schedule.)

By Foot: An alternate route back, which would allow you to sample another hike from this book, is a reverse of the Saratoga-to-La Hacienda hike described in chapter 33. To start this reverse trip, take the bus or walk to La Hacienda Inn, located about two miles west of Los Gatos along Saratoga - Los Gatos Road (Highway 9).

Chapter 35
Saratoga Gap to Sanborn-Skyline County Park

An 11¼-mile hike through Castle Rock
State Park from a rustic motor lodge
to a forest hostel.

The Night Before

Getting There

See chapter 32.

Saratoga and the Inn

See chapter 32 for description of the town and the Saratoga Motel.

A Look at the Day's Walk

This hike's format is atypical in that to begin the hike it is necessary to drive about 6½ miles from the Saratoga Motel to Saratoga Gap. From the 2,634-foot elevation of Vista Point at Saratoga Gap, you hike seven miles of rugged trails through the spectacularly beautiful Castle Rock State Park, culminating at Castle Rock, where mountain climbers practice their skills on the 80-foot sandstone monolith.

The route then continues another 4½ miles into contiguous Sanborn-Skyline County Park, through fir and bay laurel forests and a second-growth redwood grove and to historic Sanborn Park Hostel for a well-earned night's rest before the hike back to Saratoga Gap.

The Route

Distance: 11¼ miles.
Walking Time: 6 hours.
Grade: Mostly gradual descents and level terrain.

From the motel, drive west on Big Basin Way (Highway 9) about 6½ miles to the Vista Point parking lot at Saratoga Gap, which is the intersection of Highway 35 (Skyline Boulevard) and Highway 9. After parking your car, walk west along Highway 9 a few yards to the Skyline-to-the-Sea Trail — Castle Rock Trail sign (circled number 1 on the map.)

The Skyline-to-the-Sea Trail is a 37-mile network of trails from the Castle Rock State Park entrance (on Highway 35) to the Pacific. For our route, the portion through Castle Rock Park utilizes a combination of the Castle Rock Trail and Indian Rock Road to arrive at Park Headquarters and the campgrounds. However, you may use a combination of the Skyline and Loghry Woods trails. Choose either route; both arrive at the same point. If you use the latter combination, continue with the route described here from the campgrounds.

To use the Castle Rock Trail, take it toward Castle Rock campground. This trail goes steeply downhill, then uphill, and finally it reaches a paved road. At this junction, ignore Indian Rock Way and continue straight ahead on Indian Rock Road. Remain on the main road, ignoring the side roads leading to private residences.

At a junction with many roads, ignore the first turn to the right and the second and third turns (to the left); veering right onto Castle Rock and Indian Trail Road, which eventually becomes a tree-bordered dirt path. Passing through the gate 1½ miles from Saratoga Gap, enter Castle Rock State Park.

Along the way, stop to enjoy the remarkable views of the Santa Cruz Mountains to the west; if the day is clear, you may even catch a glimpse of the Pacific in the distance. This mountain range has three state parks: Portola at the northern end, Butano directly west and Big Basin to the southwest.

At a trail marker, make a hairpin turn to the right, following the signs to the campground (2). The narrow trail continues uphill and finally into the camp. You might stop for lunch at one of the picnic tables here before turning right at the Park Headquarters and continuing on the Skyline-to-the-Sea Trail. The trail sign indicates this leg's eventual destination, which is the main parking lot at the entrance to Castle Rock State Park.

Ignoring the turnoff to Oak Meadow Camp, continue on the Skyline-to-the-Sea Trail through a madrone forest. At a junction, proceed straight ahead on this trail toward the parking lot.

Now, as the route leads along the sheer rock face of the ridge, the beauty of Castle Rock State Park begins to reveal itself. But despite the spectacular views of Butano Forest below, be very attentive to your footing here.

Ignore the turnoff to Ridge Trail, continuing on the Skyline-to-the-Sea Trail toward Castle Rock Falls. Soon you arrive at the large, oak-shaded platform overlooking the falls, where you may wish to rest after your dramatic journey along the mountain ledge.

Proceed along Kings Creek, ignoring the junction with the Ridge Trail to Goat Rock. Cross the creek and, at a junction marked Castle Rock, take the right turn for a quarter-mile detour to see the mammoth rock for which the park is named.

As you proceed uphill toward the rock at the top, notice the marker indicating the continuation of the trail on the left side of the rock. When you're ready to continue, return to that point and turn left, following the signs to the parking lot.

Walk through the parking lot, cross Highway 35 (Skyline Boulevard), and turn right. Just a few steps down the shoulder of the road to your left, note the posts and fence opening that mark the entrance to Sanborn-Skyline Park. Enter the park, and, almost immediately, turn right onto the Skyline Trail (3). For the next 1½ miles it parallels Skyline Boulevard, leading you through lovely groves of fir, oak and madrone and affording occasional glimpses of the Santa Clara Valley and Bay below.

At the junction, proceed straight ahead, following the Sanborn Trail (4) as it wends its way through the spectacular Todd Creek Redwoods groves. After a mile or so, take the left-fork San Andreas Trail (5), which descends steadily down the slope in switchbacks. At the intersection with the service road, continue straight ahead downhill on the San Andreas (6). Soon a sign directs you left (7) toward Welch Lodge; this is the Sanborn Park Hostel of your journey's end.

Journey's End

The Inn

See chapter 32 for description of Sanborn Park Hostel.

The Way Back

By Public Transportation: None available.

By Foot: Except hitchhiking, the only way back to Saratoga Gap is by foot. Since retracing the route from the gap involves considerable climbing, you may wish to consider a shorter alternative — seven miles in all.

Start by following the original route back through Sanborn Park. However, instead of crossing over to Castle Rock, stay on the Skyline Trail, which parallels Highway 35 all the way back to Saratoga Gap.

The Santa Cruz Mountains

Some of the most beautiful virgin redwood forests in existence are located in the rugged Santa Cruz mountain range bordering the Pacific, and hiking here offers an opportunity to explore them. Trekkers enjoy a variety of lodgings, including rustic forest cabins, luxury resorts and ocean-front hostelries. Cool shaded rivers, deep forests and wind-swept beaches make this area an ideal choice for summer months.

Chapter 36
Felton to Davenport

A 13½-mile trek over country roads
from a rustic motel to a seaside inn.

The Night Before

Getting There

By Public Transportation: Take Santa Cruz Metropolitan Transit
District bus 33, 34 or 35 to the Felton Transit Center. (Call (408)
425-8600 for schedule.) Then walk a half mile south on Highway 9
to Griffin's.

By Car: From Highway 17, take the Mount Hermon Road exit.
Follow Mount Hermon Road five miles to Felton; Griffin's is a half
mile south on Highway 9.

Felton

In this hamlet set high in the Santa Cruz Mountains, some
residents live interspersed among great redwoods. In Felton,
history buffs might wish to visit the 1892 covered bridge — the
tallest in the nation — that spans the San Lorenzo River just off
Graham Hill Road. Narrow-gauge-railroad enthusiasts will certainly enjoy riding the fully operational 1880 steam train that makes a
six-mile round trip from the Roarding Camp Station, half a mile
south of Graham Hill Road.

The Inn

Griffin's Resort Motel, 5250 Highway 9, Felton 95018; (408) 335-4412. Inexpensive to moderately expensive.

Thirteen rustic units on a redwood-shaded bank of the San Lorenzo River. Most have kitchens; some, fireplaces.

A Look at the Day's Walk

This ambitious trek along the back roads crossing the Santa Cruz Mountains to the sea is recommended only for the intrepid hiker who is prepared for a full day on the road. From the forested town of Felton on the San Lorenzo River, you climb to the top of the ridge and over, walk through isolated Bonny Doon and, finally, arrive at Davenport in time to see the sun setting over the Pacific.

The Route

Distance: 13½ miles.
Walking Time: 8 hours.
Grade: 4½ miles, a gentle-to-moderate uphill climb; 9 miles, a gentle descent.

From your motel, walk north one mile along Highway 9 to Bennett Street which becomes Felton Empire Road (circled number 1 on the map). Take this road heading west on its 4½-mile climb through the dappled sunlight of redwood forests.

At the top of the ridge, cross Empire Grade Road (2) and continue straight ahead on a gentle descent toward Bonnie Doon.

Turn left at Marin Road (3), heading into the open meadows of Bonnie Doon's rural outskirts.

At the intersection with Pine Flat Road (4), take Bonny Doon Road toward Davenport in the west. Soon the ocean becomes visible ahead; when you reach Highway 1 (5), you can cross it and climb the bluff overlooking the Pacific. Davenport is one mile to the north, where the sign "Cafe Home Cooking" welcomes you to your inn.

Journey's End

Davenport

Named for a whaler, Capt. John Davenport, the seaside town of Davenport is an ideal place for January-to-May whale watching.

Some of the original buildings from its thriving seaport days remain to delight the eye, but it is the superb beach here that convinces the traveler to linger a while.

The Inn

New Davenport Bed and Breakfast Inn, 32 Davenport Avenue, Davenport 95018; (408) 425-1818 or 426-4122. With continental breakfast included and a restaurant on the premises; moderately expensive.

The oldest original building in Davenport; six guest bedrooms furnished with antiques and brightly colored rugs. Upstairs units have ocean views.

The Way Back

By Public Transportation: Take Santa Cruz Metropolitan Transit bus 40 to the Santa Cruz Transit Center. Transfer to bus 35 and take it to Felton. (Call (408) 425-8600 for schedule.)

By Foot: Take the bus to Santa Cruz, then reverse the Felton-to-Santa Cruz walk described in chapter 39.

Chapter 37
Brookdale to the
Boulder Creek Country Club

A 5½-mile walk by the San Lorenzo River
and through the redwoods from a picturesque lodge
to a country resort.

The Night Before

Getting There

By Public Transportation: Take Santa Cruz Metropolitan Transit District bus 35 to Brookdale; the bus stop is adjacent to Brookdale Lodge. (Call (408) 425-8600 for schedule.)

By Car: From Highway 17, take the Mount Hermon Road exit and drive north on Mount Hermon Road five miles to Highway 9. Take Highway 9 north four miles to Brookdale Lodge.

The Inn

Brookdale Lodge, P. O. Box 176, 11570 Highway 9, Brookdale 95007; (408) 338-6443. A motel with a restaurant on the premises; inexpensive.

Set among giant redwoods on the site of a turn-of-the-century logging camp, the lodge first opened its doors in 1924. Spacious, simply furnished motel units.

A Look at the Day's Walk

Hiking the back roads of the Santa Cruz Mountains is a perfect activity for a warm summer day. Your walk begins alongside the sun-dappled San Lorenzo river from Brookdale to Boulder Creek. From here, the route takes you on a gentle climb through giant redwoods that shade the quiet road to the Boulder Creek Country Club (and, just a few miles beyond your lodge, Big Basin State Park).

The Route

Distance: 5½ miles.
Walking Time: 3½ hours.
Grade: 2 miles, level terrain; 3½ miles, a gentle uphill climb.

Leaving the lodge, walk north on Highway 9 for about a half mile. (Alternately, you may take the road behind the lodge — Alta Via — north a half mile to its intersection with Highway 9. From here you must walk south a short distance to find Irwin Way, across the road.

Irwin Way leads off Highway 9 on the right a short way past the large Rivercroft sign (circled number 1 on the map). Take Irwin as it winds across a bridge and alongside the San Lorenzo River for about 2½ miles.

At Junction Avenue (2), turn right and pause for a rest at the picnic spot beside the cool river. Afterward, stay on the paved road and turn left on Middleton Avenue (3) to Highway 9, where you enter the town of Boulder Creek.

Cross Highway 9 at Middleton and walk north to West Park Avenue (4). This road, which parallels Big Basin Way, begins a gentle climb alongside Boulder Creek; take it to its end at Oak Avenue (5). Here, cross to Big Basin Way and continue right, uphill, through forests of giant redwoods that continue to the Big Basin State Park preserve. At the crest of the hill, the green meadows of the Boulder Creek Country Club welcome you to your lodging for the night.

Journey's End

The Inn

Boulder Creek Country Club, 16901 Big Basin Way, Boulder Creek 95006; (408) 338-2111. A hotel-resort, with a restaurant on the premises; moderately expensive.

A luxury condominium resort with 18-hole golf course and six tennis courts, full kitchens, fireplaces, decks, TV, swimming. (On holiday weekends, a two-night stay may be required.)

The Way Back

By Public Transportation: Santa Cruz Metopolitan Transit District bus 35 runs every half hour. (Call (408) 425-8600 for schedule.)

By Foot: The only alternative to retracing your steps is to take Big Basin Way to Highway 9 (Central Avenue), then walk back, right, on Highway 9 to Brookdale. This route allows you to see the small mountain town of Boulder Creek.

Chapter 38
Boulder Creek Country Club to Santa Cruz

A 10½-mile hike through Big Basin State Park
from a country resort to a garden inn.

The Night Before

Getting There

By Public Transportation: The spectacular setting of Big Basin State Park makes this hike well worth including here, though with a shuttle at both the beginning and the end its requirements are unusual. The wide-ranging routes maintained by the Santa Cruz Metropolitan Transit District (SCMTD) make possible the arrangements suggested (as well as a number of variations).

To get to Boulder Creek Country Club from Santa Cruz take SCMTD bus 35. After a night there, catch the 8:52 a.m. SCMTD bus — number 37 — for the 25-minute ride to Big Basin State Park, where the day's hike begins.

The Big-Basin-to-the-Sea Trail takes you to Waddell Beach on Highway 1, from which a 4:45 p.m. (or 5:45 p.m.) bus, SCMTD 40, will transport you in 40 minutes to the Babbling Brook Inn in Santa Cruz. The next day, you can take the one-hour return trip to your car in Boulder Creek via SCMTD bus 35, which runs regularly all day.

The many variations on this theme include starting and ending your trip in either Santa Cruz or Boulder Creek. For help in planning, request a copy of the bus schedule from the Santa Cruz Metropolitan Transit District, 230 Walnut Avenue, Santa Cruz 95060; (408) 425-8600.

By Car: Take Highway 9 to Boulder Creek; then take Highway 236 (Big Basin Way) west to the Boulder Creek Country Club.

The Inn

See the preceding chapter for description of the Boulder Creek Country Club.

A Look at the Day's Walk

As one walks these trails, gazing in awe at virgin redwoods as tall as 300 feet and more than 2,000 years old, one can imagine why the Indians appear to have avoided these lands. Perhaps they, like us, could feel the presence of the gods walking here.

It was not until the middle of the nineteenth century that this area was invaded by lumbermen who cut down these coast redwoods, yet by 1900 the future of *Sequoia sempervirens* already looked bleak. Fortunately for us, a San Jose artist named Andrew Hill formed a group of conservationists calling themselves the Sempervirens Club, and in 1902 they succeeded in convincing the legislature to create California's first state park, Big Basin.

The Route

Distance: 10½ miles.

Walking Time: 5 – 5½ hours.

Grade: 1 mile, a moderate uphill climb; 9½ miles, a gentle descent.

Entering Big Basin Park, you are immersed all at once in the astounding landscape that characterizes today's walk. Here, at the Headquarters Lodge, where 1,500-year-old redwoods tower 200 feet or more above you, the last leg of the 28-mile-long Skyline-to-the-Sea Trail begins. Follow the Redwood Trail sign opposite the Headquarters Lodge to the trailhead, taking care to stay on the Skyline-to-the-Sea toward Berry Creek Falls for the next nearly four miles. The first mile of the trail climbs steadily uphill through giant redwoods, oaks and ferns to the junction with the old Big

Basin Trail. From here on in, it's almost all downhill. The path now follows Kelly Creek Canyon to the first glimpse of Berry Creek Falls, which is easily viewed from the relaxing vantage point of the Leask Grove Bench.

At the falls, cross the bridge and follow Skyline-to-the-Sea signs toward Waddell Beach. A short climb to the intersection with Howard King Trail leads you to the old logging road that runs the next 5½ miles along Waddell Creek, past Camps Herbert, Twin Redwoods and Alder, and through Rancho Del Oso to trail's end. Soon the canyon widens and groves of alder rim the stream. Woods begin to yield to meadow as you see the first blue of the Pacific before you. Continue out through the park gate; cross Highway 1 to Waddell Beach, and take SCMTD bus 40 to Santa Cruz and your inn.

Journey's End

Santa Cruz

Franciscan padres founded Mission Santa Cruz in 1791, and the town, populated first by vagabond colonists and later by whalers and loggers, grew up around the Mission plaza. By the late 1800s Santa Cruz's sunny, protected beaches and mild temperatures had already begun to attract throngs of vacationers. The mile-long beach and boardwalk, the fishing pier and the carnival attractions provide ample explanation for its continuing popularity as a coastal resort.

The Inn

Babbling Brook Inn, 1025 Laurel Street, Santa Cruz 95060; (408) 427-2437. Continental breakfast included; expensive.

Beside Laurel Creek, surrounded by gardens, gazebo and covered foot bridges. Most of the 12 guest bedrooms have garden views; all are individually decorated in Country French style.

A great many attractive motels, too numerous to be listed here, are located in the East Cliff and West Cliff Drive waterfront area. Any motel guide can help you make a suitable choice.

The Way Back

By Public Transportation: See under Getting There at the beginning of this chapter.

By Foot: Retrace the described route.

Chapter 39
Felton to Santa Cruz

A 9½-mile hike through Henry Cowell State Park
from a riverside motel to a resort hotel.

The Night Before

Getting There

See chapter 36.

Felton and the Inn

See chapter 36 for a description of the town and Griffin's Resort
Motel.

A Look at the Day's Walk

This hike through Henry Cowell State Park begins with a pleasant stroll along the San Lorenzo River or through the magnificent
Redwood Grove. The "Big Trees" grove, as it was originally called,
is primeval redwood forest boasting such giants as a 285-foot tree
dedicated to Theodore Roosevelt. It was for the protection of
these coast redwoods that Joseph Welsh and Henry Cowell purchased this part of the Mexican land grant Rancho del Rincon in
the 1860s.

The route continues to the top of a forested ridge, where a large
observation platform has been built that's perfect for picnicking
and sunbathing. Here you can enjoy views across the mountains to

Monterey Bay. The stands of ponderosa pine that are found at this site are rare in the Santa Cruz area.

The gradual descent leads you into the lush Pasatiempo Golf Course area of Santa Cruz for the evening.

The Route

Distance: 9½ miles.

Walking Time: 5 hours.

Grade: 1 mile, gentle climb; 1 mile, gradual descent; 7½ miles, mostly level terrain.

You can flip a stone across the San Lorenzo River from Griffin's to the River Trail in Henry Cowell Park, so you have a choice of starts, depending on the seasonal flow of the river. If the stream looks invitingly fordable, simply wade across and turn right on the first dirt path you come to on the other side. Otherwise, walk north on Highway 9 to the park entrance and turn right, into Henry Cowell. In a short while, pick up the dirt path — a sign identifies it as the River Trail (circled number 1 on the map) — and follow it through the posts and alongside the river (passing the motel on the opposite bank).

You may wish to detour shortly to explore the magnificent Redwood Grove at your left. When you're finished, come back to the River Trail, which continues to parallel the river through groves of oak, bay laurel and redwood, touching the paved Pipeline Trail from time to time.

In 1½ miles or so, continue under the railroad overpass, and, a quarter mile farther on, follow the uphill trail marked "River Trail to Pipeline" (2). Cross the Pipeline Trail, and turn left on the Eagle Creek Trail (3), following it through the redwoods to its junction with the Pine Trail (4). A gentle climb through stands of ponderosa pine leads, in a little over a mile, to the Observation Deck. Here, you may wish to stop for a picnic lunch, with grand views of Santa Cruz and the blue Pacific.

When you are ready to leave your lofty perch, walk directly downhill, following the Pine Trail until it intersects the Powder Mill Trail a half mile or so down the road. Turn right on Powder

Mill (6), then left toward the Graham Hill Trail (7). Cross Powder Mill Creek, then climb uphill on the opposite bank, arriving at the park exit on Graham Hill Road.

Turn right on Graham Hill Road, left on Sims Road, then right on Pasatiempo Drive. Follow Pasatiempo Drive as it curves through and around the golf course for 1¾ miles, then through the club entrance, where a left turn brings you to the front door of the Pasatiempo Inn.

Journey's End

Santa Cruz

See chapter 38.

The Inn

Pasatiempo Inn, 555 Highway 17, Santa Cruz 95060; (408) 423-5000. A hotel-resort, with a restaurant on the premises; moderately expensive.

Adjacent to the MacKenzie-designed 18-hole Pasatiempo Golf Course are 57 modern, spacious units, a large pool and outdoor patio dining.

The Way Back

By Public Transportation: Take Santa Cruz Metropolitan Transit bus 35, which leaves regularly for Felton. Inquire at the inn for the schedule and the location of the bus stop. (Or call (408) 425-8600 for information.)

By Foot: As an alternate hike back, you can retrace your steps through the Pasatiempo area. At Henry Cowell Park take the Graham Hill Trail to the Powder Mill Trail. At the Observation Deck, however, take the Ridge Trail west and north to its junction with the River and Pipeline trails. From this junction, if you chose the river route yesterday, take the Pipeline Trail through the Redwood Grove on the way back to the motel.

Chapter 40
Pescadero to Pigeon Point

A 12¾-mile hike through Butano State Park
from a forest guest house to a lighthouse hostel.

The Night Before

Getting There

By Public Transportation: Take SamTrans bus 90H to Half Moon
Bay, then 90C to Pescadero. (Call (415) 761-7000 for schedule.) From
Highway 1, walk east on Pescadero Road, south on Cloverdale
Road to Canyon Road, then east to Redwood Avenue and east to
Madrone Avenue.

By Car: From Highway 1, turn east on Pescadero Road, south on
Cloverdale Road to Canyon Road, then east to Redwood Avenue
and east to Madrone Avenue.

Pescadero

The grounds occupied by tiny Pescadero are within the bounds
of the original 1833 Rancho El Pescadero land grant to Juan Jose
Gonzales. Sitting on Pescadero Creek in a peaceful valley three
miles from the ocean, it ironically resembles a typical New
England village. Perhaps that is due to the fact that a number of its
residents hail from that part of the country.

The Inn

Rynders, P. O. Box 478, Pescadero 94060: (415) 879-0319. A guest house,
with continental breakfast included: moderately inexpensive.

This hideaway deep in a redwood forest along a shady creek offers a separate cottage guest room for the ultimate in vacation privacy.

A Look at the Day's Walk

Butano State Park, nestled in a deep ravine of the Santa Cruz Mountains, is redwood country. Its secluded, ferny trails, beautiful at any time of year, seem particularly well suited to a summer ramble, when the cool shade of the giant trees offers welcome respite from the sun. A mile southwest of your guesthouse hideaway, you pick up the fire trail that enters the park and gently climbs the wooded slope overlooking the ravine. Your descent through the redwoods is a return to the forest primeval — a trail sensitively designed for those who treasure wilderness. Leaving the park, you follow a winding country lane, then Highway 1 along the beach to the Pigeon Point Lighthouse.

The Route

Distance: 12¾ miles.
Walking Time: 6 hours.
Grade: 3½ miles, gentle uphill climb; 2½ miles, gentle-to-moderate descent; the remainder, mostly level.

From your Butano Creek guest house, follow Canyon Road southwest alongside the creek to Cloverdale Road. Turn left at Cloverdale and, just a few steps along, take the left turnoff leading to the trailhead (circled number 1 on the map). Climb over the gate and begin the 3½-mile ascent on Butano Trail. This fire road rises very gently, first through pasture land and then, as you near the top of the ridge, through fir forests.

About a mile up the trail, the Mill Ox Trail branches off to the right. If you wish to shorten your walk by a few miles, turn off to the right here, then turn downhill on the Jackson Flat Trail when it intersects. This alternative, which limits the transit of park considerably, nevertheless, gives some sense of its magnificent redwood groves.

Continuing to the top of the ridge on Butano Trail yields some fine panoramic views of the park. Along the way, notice a fire road branching off to the left, then another beside an abandoned hut. About a quarter mile further, you'll see the Jackson Flats Trail.

Turn right onto the Jackson Flats Trail at the signpost (2), and proceed downhill. Shortly, the trail swings right, becoming a narrow, sylvan path through giant redwoods and spreading ferns. Depending on the season, your way may seem overgrown from time to time, but close scrutiny will discern the trail from casual diversions away from it.

At the bottom, turn right on the park road (3), left on Cloverdale Road, and left again on lovely Gazos Creek Road, which winds 3½ miles through country pasture before intersecting with Highway 1, the Cabrillo Highway. Turn right on the highway, and follow it the remaining two miles to the Pigeon Point Lighthouse.

Journey's End

Pigeon Point

This promontory is named for the clipper ship *Carrier Pigeon*, which was wrecked here in 1853. The lighthouse, 148 feet above the sea, was built in 1872 and brings comfort to sailors for 18 miles around.

The Inn

Pigeon Point Lighthouse Hostel, Pescadero 94060; (415) 879-0633. A hostel; inexpensive.

An incomparable setting at the foot of the lighthouse on cliffs overlooking the waves. Cooking facilities are provided; because this hostel is situated far from towns and restaurants, be sure to carry your own food.

The Way Back

By Public Transportation: SamTrans bus 90C runs along Highway 1. (Call (415) 761-7000 for schedule.)

By Foot: The quickest route back is to retrace your steps but to remain on Cloverdale Road to Canyon Road rather than taking the loop into Butano State Park.

The Wine Country

The singular qualities of air, light and landscape that favor grape growing tend to prove equally salutary for wine-country visitors. Add to these the charm of historic towns and picturesque inns and you have all the ingredients for an ideal weekend in the country. Indeed, the growing popularity of just such weekending mandates that you book your lodging quite far in advance, especially during the spring and summer months.

Because the Napa and Sonoma County countryside is essentially rural, many of the treks in this section follow quiet back roads. Two of the area's parks that are accessible to inns also are included, and we urge you, given a layover of an extra day or two, to explore the day-hiking possibilities of the others.

Chapter 41
Sonoma to Boyes Hot Springs

A 4⅓-mile walk between
historic Sonoma inns and a luxury resort.

The Night Before

Getting There

By Public Transportation: Greyhound buses depart for Sonoma
from San Francisco at 5 p.m., Monday through Friday. (In San Francisco, call (415) 433-1500 for schedule, or call the toll-free number
for your area.) From the Sonoma Plaza, the Sonoma Hotel is visible; for the Thistle Dew Inn, walk a halfblock west on Spain
Street.

By Car: From Highway 101, take the Napa-Vallejo turnoff and proceed east on Highway 37. At Sears Point take Highway 121 North,
then follow Highway 12 to Sonoma. The inns are both in the
vicinity of the plaza.

Sonoma

A stroll around Sonoma Plaza is a stroll around some of the cor-
nerstones of California history. It was here in 1823 that the Franciscan fathers established their northernmost mission. The plaza
itself was laid out by the charismatic Gen. Mariano Vallejo, who in
1835 founded the Pueblo de Sonoma as a northern outpost of the
Mexican empire. A monument in the northeast corner of the
square marks the spot where, 11 years later, the California Bear
Flag flew bravely and briefly. The plaza green today, ringed by

historical buildings, restaurants and specialty shops, is as much the center of Sonoma as it was when Vallejo drilled his cavalry here almost 150 years ago.

The Inns

Sonoma Hotel, 110 West Spain Street, Sonoma 95476; (707) 996-2996. An inn, with continental breakfast included and a restaurant on the premises; moderately expensive.

Just off the Sonoma Plaza, restored in careful detail to its nineteenth-century appearance. Seventeen rooms individually decorated with period antiques.

Thistle Dew Inn, 171 West Spain Street, P. O. Box 1376, Sonoma 95476; (707) 938-2909. Continental breakfast included; moderately expensive to expensive.

Two restored Victorian homes surrounded by gardens and lawns on a quiet street just off the Sonoma Plaza. Six rooms, decorated in 1910 California Mission style.

A Look at the Day's Walk

This is a stroll for sybarites — those who prefer their country pleasures well laced with luxury. It starts simply enough at the Sonoma Plaza, proceeding eastward for a half mile. History buffs have the opportunity to explore a number of sites along the way; you may want to stop at the Mission for a detailed route map. At the Sebastiani Vineyards, wine enthusiasts may wish to spend some time in the tasting room. When you leave these attractions, you join the bike path that turns west toward Boyes Hot Springs. From the end of this path, you follow a quiet small-town road the remaining 1½ miles to Sonoma Mission Inn — the grand old pleasure palace of the Sonoma Wine Country.

The Route

Distance: 4⅓ miles.
Walking Time: 2 hours to all day (depending on your detours).
Grade: Level.

Walk east from your inn on West Spain Street, stopping according to your pleasure at the historical attractions along the way.

Turn left on Fourth Street to enter the Sebastiani Winery, which is open from 10 a.m.-5 p.m. daily for guided tours and tasting. Continue north on Fourth Street; pause to notice the site of the first California vineyard before turning left onto the bike path just ahead. After proceeding westward half a mile or so through a pleasant meadow, consider detouring once again at the Depot Hotel, circa 1870. This establishment was formerly a saloon and then a hotel for railroad travelers. Now, housing a fine restaurant, it's an ideal lunch spot. Less than a quarter mile beyond the hotel, turn right on the broad paved road for a tour of Lachryma Montis, General Vallejo's fine old Gothic Revival family home.

Return to the bike path, following it through the wide meadows and past modest neighborhoods to its end opposite the Casa Del Sol Apartments on Robinson Road. Turn right on Robinson, which is unmarked here, then left onto Verano Avenue. Follow Verano westward across Highway 12 and past Verano Park, and turn right on Riverside Drive just across the bridge. Stay on Riverside for the next mile or so, taking care to swing right at the junction with Craig, halfway along. Where you meet Boyes Boulevard, turn right on to it; then, just before Highway 12, enter the grand circular drive of the Sonoma Mission Inn.

Journey's End

The Inn

Sonoma Mission Inn, P. O. Box 1, Boyes Hot Springs 95416; (800) 862-4945 or (707) 996-1041. A hotel-resort, with continental breakfast included and a restaurant on the premises; very expensive.

The three-story, 97-room Spanish Revival-style hotel has been fully restored to its original 1926 elegance. Complete spa, Olympic-size pool, and tennis courts.

The Way Back

By Public Transportation: Sonoma County Transit bus 30 runs several times daily except Sundays. (Call (707) 576-7433 for schedule.)

By Foot: Especially since there is no Sunday bus service, you may be walking back to Sonoma; just reverse the route taken to Boyes Hot Springs. If you prefer town streets to the bike path, take Riverside Drive south all the way to West Napa Street. Then turn left on West Napa, following it back to Sonoma Plaza.

Chapter 42
Valley of the Moon to Santa Rosa

A 12-mile hike through Annadel State Park
from a country guest house
to a hotel-resort or a motel.

The Night Before

Getting There

By Public Transportation: Take the Greyhound bus for Santa Rosa
departing several times daily from San Francisco. (In San Francisco,
call (415) 433-1500 for complete schedule, or call the toll-free
number for your area.) Ask the bus driver to let you off at the Los
Guilicos School stop, about two miles past Kenwood. Walk back ¾
mile east on Highway 12 to Gee-Gee's on the right.

By Car: From Highway 101, take the Napa-Vallejo turnoff and proceed east on Highway 37. At Sears Point take Highway 121 north.
Then follow Highway 12 through Sonoma. Continue north; two
miles past Kenwood, just after Frey Road, Gee-Gee's is just off the
highway on your left.

Valley of the Moon

Favored by a mild climate and rich soil, this lush valley extending some 17 miles northwestward from Sonoma is a much
celebrated grape-growing center. Here, in 1824, the Franciscan
fathers planted the vineyards that established the Sonoma Valley
as the birthplace of California viticulture.

The Inn

Gee-Gee's, 7810 Sonoma Highway (Highway 12), Santa Rosa 95405; (707) 833-6667. A guest house, with continental breakfast included; moderately expensive.

A country house with four guest rooms on a landscaped acre surrounded by orchards and mountains. Swimming pool lawn games.

A Look at the Day's Walk

For Santa Rosans, Eden lies just east of Newanga Avenue in the guise of Annadel State Park. It is an unspoiled 5,000 acres of quiet lakes, woods and meadows, jeweled with wildflowers in springtime. You approach it from its back gate on Lawndale Road, just over a mile up the hill from Gee-Gee's. The wooded trail takes you up to Ledson Marsh; here you might enjoy having lunch while watching the ducks paddle by. Or perhaps you'd prefer to save your picnic for the banks of Lake Ilsanjo, a few miles down the road. From the lake, you follow Spring Creek all the way out to the streets of Santa Rosa, then stroll about three miles to the inns.

The Route

Distance: 12 miles.
Walking Time: 6½ hours.
Grade: 1½ miles, gradual uphill climb; 10½ miles, level terrain and gradual descent.

Leaving the guest house, turn right on Highway 12 and right again on Lawndale Road for the 1½-mile walk to the trailhead and Annadel Park. Just past 1160 Lawndale Road, turn right through the green gate onto Lawndale Trail (circled number 1 on the map).

You now begin a 1½-mile moderately steep climb through eucalyptus and oaks to the top of the ridge. At the top, pass the overhead power lines, ignoring a crossroads marked by numbered arrows pointing in all directions. Continue straight ahead, also passing the junction with Rhyolite Trail (2).

Remain on Lawndale Trail to its end ⅓ mile farther, ignoring an unmarked wide road going off to the left. At the junction with the

Marsh Trail (3), take the right fork, which leads around the upper end of Ledson Marsh.

Remain on the Marsh Trail, past the turnoff to the Rhyolite Trail (4) — this is the other end of the trail you met earlier. Just past this intersection is a long view of the marsh. The meadow to the left of the trail is a pleasant place to rest and contemplate the serene marsh, surrounded by redwood and eucalyptus. However, a bit farther on at Buick Meadow you arrive at a conveniently located picnic table, so if the hour is right you might save your picnic lunch for that spot.

Pass the junction with Two Quarry Trail (5), continuing on the fir- and oak-lined Marsh Trail, to the left. Do not take the turnoff to Ridge Trail (6), but proceed on the Marsh Trail past the enormous expanse of Buick Meadow and the turnoff to South Burma Trail (7).

When you reach the next junction, take the right fork onto Steve's S Trail (8), which heads downhill through a forest of oak, bay laurel and fir, with glimpses of Lake Ilsanjo in the distance.

At the bottom of the path, take the trail to the left (9), keeping the lake on your right. Continue past the turnoff to Canyon Trail on the left (10) and the unmarked road immediately afterward. Proceeding straight ahead, cross the spillway, where you have a vast vista of 26-acre Lake Ilsanjo (named for the property's former owners, Ilsa and Joe).

At the far end of the spillway, turn left on Spring Creek Trail (11), crossing the creek on some convenient rocks. Continue on Spring Creek Trail past the turnoff to Canyon Trail, following the stream.

At the second bridge crossing, ignoring the Rough Go Trail to the right (12), cross Spring Creek; then turn right and continue alongside the creek and through the parking lot to the exit at Newanga Avenue.

This has been a long hike, and you may wish to rest before walking the final three miles to the end of Newanga Avenue, right on Summerfield Road and left on Sonoma Avenue to Farmers Lane (Highway 12). From Farmers Lane turn right onto Fourth Street (the continuation of Highway 12) and cross the street to the motels.

Journey's End

Santa Rosa

"I firmly believe from all that I have seen that this is the chosen spot of all the earth as far as nature is concerned," wrote botanist Luther Burbank about Santa Rosa in 1875 (Matson, *North of San Francisco*). After establishing his experimental gardens in this attractive county seat 52 miles north of San Francisco, he continued to work here for 50 years. His Greek Revival home and the gardens where he worked are now open to the public. On view along with rare specimens of climbing plum, lily of the Nile and spineless cactus are beds of the Shasta daisy, which Burbank bred here.

The same favorable features of climate and geography that so enthralled Burbank accounted for Santa Rosa's phenomenal postwar growth and contribute to its thriving electronics industry. With a population of more than a million, the city has managed to retain an early small-town flavor while, for example, supporting the new Burbank Center for the Arts.

The Inns

Flamingo Resort Hotel, Fourth Street and Farmers Lane, Santa Rosa 95405; (707) 545-8530. A resort-hotel, with a restaurant on the premises; moderately expensive.

Beautifully landscaped grounds with Olympic-size pool and tennis courts; 140 attractively furnished guest rooms and suites.

Hillside Inn, 2901 Fourth Street, Santa Rosa 95405; (707) 546-9353. A motel; inexpensive to moderately expensive.

Thirty-four quiet, comfortable rooms. Swimming pool.

The Way Back

By Public Transportation: Available Monday through Saturday only. Sonoma County Transit: Take bus 30 from the corner of Farmers Lane and Montgomery Drive to Oakmont or Kenwood. On weekdays, the bus runs in the morning; on Saturday, in the afternoon. (Call (707) 576-7433 for schedule.) To reach Gee-Gee's, from the Oakmont stop walk east on Highway 12 approximately two miles; from Kenwood, walk the same distance west on Highway 12.

By Foot: Especially on Sundays, when there is no way of getting back to Gee-Gee's except by foot, you might choose the return route that allows further exploration of Annadel State Park. Retracing your route through the parking lot at the end of Newanga Avenue, pick up the Rough Go Trail instead of the Spring Creek Trail. Follow the Rough Go to the South Burma Trail, which joins the Marsh Trail just before Buick Meadow. From here, simply reverse the original route out to Lawndale Road and Highway 12.

Chapter 43
Valley of the Moon to Glen Ellen

A 3-mile stroll (and optional 4-mile loop)
through the vineyards from a ranch guest house
to a village motel.

The Night Before

Getting There

By Public Transportation: None available.

By Car: From Highway 101, take the Napa-Vallejo exit and proceed
east on Highway 37. At Sears Point take Highway 121 north; then
follow Highway 12 north to the ranch.

Valley of the Moon.

See the preceding chapter.

The Inn

Beltane Ranch, 11775 Sonoma Highway (Highway 12), P. O. Box
395, Glen Ellen 95442; (707) 996-6501. A guest house, with continental breakfast included; moderately expensive.

This nineteenth-century Southern-style ranch house is surrounded by extensive acreage on the slope of the Mayacamas Range. It
offers three comfortable, airy guest rooms with private balconies
overlooking the Sonoma Valley vineyards.

A Look at the Day's Walk

This Valley of the Moon ramble along level, shaded country roads to Glen Ellen is the perfect choice for the novice hiker and can easily be completed by lunchtime. However, Glen Ellen is the gateway to Jack London State Historic Park, and we highly recommend hiking an additional afternoon four-mile loop through the park.

Jack London State Park is the 800-acre former Beauty Ranch owned by the author of *The Call of the Wild* and *The Sea Wolf*. The House of Happy Walls, built by his wife after his death, is now a museum of London memorabilia. His grave and the remains of Wolf House, the 23-room stone mansion London built that was gutted by fire, are a short walk away.

The Route

Distance: 3 miles (extra 4 miles optional).
Walking Time: 1½ hours (optional loop, 3 hours).
Grade: Level (optional loop, steep 1½-mile ascent and descent).

Leaving Beltane Ranch, walk left a short distance along the highway to where Nuns Canyon Road comes from the left. Take the right dirt road across from it, through a cow pasture, to Dunbar Road. Turn right and walk along Dunbar to its junction with Henno Road. Here, turn left and follow Henno as it winds through the vineyards between the Mayacamas Range on your left and the Sonoma Mountains to the right. Along the way, you may wish to pay a visit to the Grand Cru Vineyards at 1 Vintage Lane. (The tasting room is open daily from 10 a.m. – 5 p.m.) At Warm Springs Road, turn left into the town of Glen Ellen and right on Arnold Drive. Walk along Arnold across the bridge to the London Lodge motel, not far from London Ranch Road.

After a stop for lunch, if you wish to take the four-mile loop into Jack London Park, follow London Ranch Road about 1½ miles on a steep uphill climb to the park entrance and museum. A one-mile loop from the entrance area circles the areas of historical interest within the park and returns to the parking lot. To leave, retrace your steps down London Ranch Road to Glen Ellen.

Journey's End

Glen Ellen

Before the turn of the century, the Glen Ellen region boasted eight hotels for vacationing San Franciscans. However, with the advent of the automobile other resort areas gained favor, and, by 1941, when the last railroad train had completed its run, the village had returned to its peaceful agricultural origins. Now it is known primarily as the former home of Jack London, as well as for its wines.

The Inn

London Lodge, P. O. Box 595, 13740 Arnold Drive, Glen Ellen 95442; (707) 938-8510. A motel, with a restaurant on the premises; moderately expensive.

In a quiet setting bordering two creeks, 22 large modern units. Pool.

The Way Back

By Public Transportation: None available.

By Foot: You may alter the return walk by taking Arnold Drive north to the junction with Dunbar Road; then turn left and remain on Dunbar to the dirt road that leads to Sonoma Highway (Highway 12).

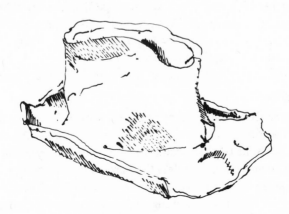

Chapter 44
Yountville: Yount Mill Road to Vintage 1870

A 3½-mile historic stroll between country inns.

The Night Before

Getting There

By Public Transportation: Greyhound runs three buses daily from San Francisco. (In San Francisco, call (415) 433-1500 for schedule, or call the toll-free number for your area.) Ask the bus driver to let you off at the Oakville stop and walk back, south 1½ miles, on Highway 29; just past Yount Mill Road, Sybron House sits above the road to your left.

By Car: From Highway 101, take the Napa-Vallejo turnoff, and proceed east on Highway 37. At Sears Point take Highway 121 north and continue on it east toward Napa. Then take Highway 29 north. About two miles north of the Yountville exit, watch for the tennis courts and the Sybron House sign at number 7400 on the right.

Yountville

Traveling through the vineyards on Highway 29, it wouldn't be difficult to drive by Yountville and miss it entirely. And what a loss that would be. This cameo town, founded by Napa Valley pioneer George Yount, proffers the particular kinds of enticements that make a visit to the wine country so satisfying. There are local wineries for tasting and touring, fine restaurants and quaint cafes for gourmet dining, and several historic country inns for stopping over. The former Groezinger Winery, now named Vintage 1870, houses a potpourri of specialty shops and boutiques for hours of browsing. Local citizens have fought to preserve the rural character of the community, and, indeed, within a block or two from the center of town, the beauty of open farmland and vineyard prevails.

The Inn

Sybron House, 7400 Saint Helena Highway (Highway 29), Napa 94558; (707) 944-2785. A guest house, with continental breakfast included; moderately expensive to expensive.

Four comfortable rooms in a new Victorian-style home on a hill overlooking the Napa Valley. Tennis court.

A Look at the Day's Walk

If some soft summer day finds you less up for a hike than for an amble, a back-roads stroll through historic Yountville might be ideal. Leaving your Sybron House eyrie, you follow shady Yount Mill Road through meadow and vineyard to the village center. Along the way are reminders of the nineteenth-century Yountville; at the end is an unusually wide selection of twentieth-century comforts. Explore the village before or after checking into your inn.

The Route

Distance: 3½ miles.
Walking Time: 1½ hours to half a day.
Grade: Level.

Descend the steep drive from Sybron House; turn right on Highway 29 and then, almost immediately, right again on Yount Mill Road. This pleasant country lane bisects vineyards, then winds alongside the narrow Napa River to its junction with Cook Road — the site of Yount's Kentucky Blockhouse (A), the first wooden building in the county. Here, in 1836, the gracious and resourceful George C. Yount built his two-story home on the 11,800-acre Mexican land grant awarded him by Gen. Mariano Vallejo. With the help of local Indians, he proceeded to plant the valley with vineyards and orchards, raise large herds of livestock, and erect mills. Later, he directed a surveyor to lay out the town, which then became known as Sebastopol.

Turn right, and continue on Yount Mill Road through the vineyards to Monroe Street. A right on Monroe, right on Jefferson Street and left on Jackson Street brings you to Pioneer Cemetery (B), where Yount is buried. Upon his death, in 1865, the name of the town was changed from Sebastopol to Yountville to honor his achievements here.

Leaving the cemetery, return to Yount Street and proceed south. Cross the bridge over Hopper Creek, and, on the right, just a few steps farther, pause to admire the graceful Yountville Community Church (C), built in 1876. A block south on the left is Yountville School (D), built in the 1920s but sporting the old Yount School bell, circa 1866.

Continue south past the Magnolia Hotel (E), which has charmed guests since 1873. At the foot of Yount Street, one block south, cross Washington Street to explore two late-nineteenth-century railroad depots (F): the Southern Pacific "Whistle Stop" and the older Napa Valley Railroad depot beside it.

You are now directly opposite the Vintage 1870 complex of shops (G), still in the guise of its earlier service as winery, distillery and stable. You may wish to browse or lunch here before retiring to your inn.

For the Webber Place and Bordeaux House Inn, walk north two blocks along Washington Street to Webber; turn left for Bordeaux House or right for the Webber Place. For Burgundy House Country Inn, continue three blocks north along Washington Street.

Journey's End

The Inns

Bordeaux House, P. O. Box 2766, 6600 Washington Street, Yountville 94599; (707) 944-2855. An inn, with continental breakfast included; inexpensive to very expensive (prices seasonal).

A sophisticated contemporary, styled after a French country inn. Six attractively decorated rooms with fireplaces and patios.

Burgundy House, P. O. Box 2766, 6711 Washington Street, Yountville 94599; (707) 944-2855. An inn, with continental breakfast included; inexpensive to very expensive (prices seasonal).

An 1870 stone-construction wine-country classic; six rooms individually decorated with French country antiques.

Magnolia Hotel, P. O. Drawer M, 6529 Yount Street, Yountville 94599; (707) 944-2056. An inn, with full breakfast included and a restaurant on the premises; expensive to very expensive.

An historic inn close by Vintage 1870; 11 rooms elegantly decorated with antiques. Swimming pool, jacuzzi spa.

The Webber Place, 6610 Webber Street, Yountville 94599; (707) 944-8384. An inn, with continental breakfast included; moderately expensive to expensive.

A family-style inn more than 100 years old, surrounded by shady lawn on a quiet street; four attractive, comfortably furnished rooms.

The Way Back

By Public Transportation: Greyhound runs three buses daily along Highway 29 with stops at Yountville and four miles north at Oakville. (Call (707) 944-8377 for schedule.) Ask the driver to drop you (please) at Yount Mill Road.

By Foot: Walk north on Washington Street, which parallels Highway 29 for most of the easy 2 — 2½-mile walk back to Sybron House.

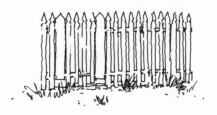

Chapter 45
Yountville to Napa

A 13-mile back-roads walk from a
hilltop guest house to a country inn.

The Night Before

Getting There

See the preceding chapter.

Yountville

See the preceding chapter for description of the town and Sybron
House.

A Look at the Day's Walk

If you are one for whom the lure of what's beyond the curve in
the road is irresistible, this trek in the Napa Valley is for you. After
a vigorous climb to the ridge top overlooking the vineyards, your
reward is a long, level stroll along a quiet, winding country road
guaranteed to satisfy the most insatiable wanderlust.

The Route

Distance: 13 miles.
Walking Time: 6½ hours.

Grade: 1 mile, moderate uphill climb; 12 miles, gradual descent and level terrain.

Walk down the driveway of Sybron House and turn right on Highway 29 for about one mile to Oakville Grade; here, cross the highway and turn left. Take this level road past the Stelling Vineyards, toward the mountain ridge ahead. You can see the peaceful Carmelite retreat above on the hillside.

Soon you begin the one-mile climb that is the most strenuous part of the day's walk. Before reaching the top, you will probably wish to rest a bit; be sure to take in the views of the Napa Valley behind you. As long as you're taking a break, you might like to stop in at the Vichon Winery, which offers tours and tasting.

At the top of the ridge, the road levels off, and then it begins winding downhill. At a junction after about one mile, make a hairpin turn to the left to follow Dry Creek Road on its southerly journey downhill.

This evergreen-lined seven-mile stretch of back road alongside the meandering Dry Creek is the epitome of country road trekking and rivals walking tours anywhere in the world. A picnic lunch could be spread at a number of points along the way, perhaps on a grassy knoll at one of the many bends in the road.

At the first intersection after the road levels out again, take the left turn onto Orchard Avenue. Walk about one mile past small houses and vineyards to Solano Avenue, where you turn right, taking this frontage road along Highway 29 to the stoplight (at Salvador Avenue).

Cross Highway 29 and turn left on the frontage road going north. Pass the inn, which unfortunately has no access at this point; turn right at the first available street. Take this street, which is the entrance to La Residence, to the right.

Journey's End

Napa

This spot was originally called Nappo by the Indians. The first white settlers here arrived in the 1830s, and by the midnineteenth-century Napa was a fairly good-sized town.

Napa's location at the head of the Napa River made it a natural trade center for products from the fertile valley. The Gold Rush added to its growth; as a winter home for miners, the town flourished. Today it is the county seat of the Napa Valley, known worldwide for its production of superb wines.

The Inn

La Residence, 4066 Saint Helena Highway North (Highway 29), Napa 94558; (707) 253-0337. An inn with continental breakfast included; moderately expensive to expensive.

In an 1870 Gothic Revival house built with a Southern flair by a New Orleans river pilot, seven large, comfortable guest rooms. Antique furnishings, air conditioning, spa.

The Way Back

By Public Transportation: Greyhound buses run from Napa to Yountville. (Call (707) 226-1856 for schedule).

By Foot: The shortest return is along Highway 29. Stay on the frontage roads wherever they are available.

Chapter 46
Angwin to Meadowood

A 7-mile downhill walk from a
country guest house to a secluded resort.

The Night Before

Getting There

By Public Transportation: None available.

By Car: From Highway 101, take the Napa-Vallejo turnoff and proceed on Highway 37 east. At Sears Point take Highway 121 north, and continue on it east toward Napa. Then take Highway 29 to Saint Helena. Just north of the city limits, pass the Krug Winery and turn right on Deer Park Road. Follow Deer Park 3½ miles uphill to its junction with Howell Mountain Road and White Cottage Road.

Guests of Forest Manor proceed from Deer Park Road straight ahead on Howell Mountain Road to its junction with Cold Spring Road. Turn right on Cold Spring and follow it to its end, where you'll see the number 415 mailbox on the left. Turn left up the private road for the inn.

Angwin

Situated 1,800 feet above sea level overlooking Napa Valley, this hilltop retreat was the Angwin Health Resort until the turn of the century. In 1909 the Seventh Day Adventist Church moved its liberal arts Pacific Union College here, and a new village grew around it. Angwin, with two-thirds of its tiny population composed of students and faculty, offers many cultural and educational activities as well as a market featuring the largest assortment of natural foods in Northern California. The vegetarian restaurant in town is open until 7 p.m. If you wish a wider choice of food, stop for dinner in Saint Helena.

The Inn

Forest Manor, 415 Cold Spring Road, Angwin 94508; (707) 965-3538. A guest house, with continental breakfast included; moderately expensive to expensive.

A gracious Tudor-style contemporary, surrounded by 20 acres of pines, with five comfortable guest rooms, including a suite with parlor and fireplace.

A Look at the Day's Walk

From your hilltop inn in Angwin, you descend all the way to the valley floor via wooded, little-trafficked Howell Mountain Road. Forestland, neighboring vineyards and fine vistas of the Napa Valley enhance this gentle downhill walk.

The Route

Distance: 7 miles.
Walking Time: 3½ hours.
Grade: Gradual descent and level terrain.

From Forest Manor, take Cold Spring Road, about half a mile to its beginning at Howell Mountain Road. Turn left on Howell Mountain Road and take it two miles to the junction with Deer Park Road. (A bicycle path going off to the left offers an alternate place to walk along part of the main road.)

Having reached the intersection by either route, take Howell Mountain Road as it winds four miles downhill. Broad views of the Napa Valley showcase terraced vineyards and Lake Hennessey in the foreground.

At the bottom of the ridge, turn right at Meadowood Lane and walk a half mile past vineyards to the inn.

Journey's End

Saint Helena

From the beginning, Saint Helena's identity has been intertwined so intimately with the grape vine as to render the two figuratively inseparable. When in 1853 Charles Krug, California's first wine commissioner, gave away parcels of his tract here to all interested homesteaders, the town was underway, and it has continued to flourish at the center of the Napa Valley wine industry ever since. Guests will enjoy visiting some of the handsome old wineries that ring the town, as well as strolling the picturesque main street.

The Inn

Meadowood, 900 Meadowood Lane, Saint Helena 94574; (707) 963-3646. A hotel-resort, with continental breakfast included and a restaurant on the premises; expensive to very expensive.

A lush 256 acres, with tennis courts, nine-hole golf course, and swimming pool. Sixty-eight tastefully appointed guest rooms and cottages, some with fireplaces, set amidst oak and madrone.

The Way Back

By Public Transportation: The Tri-City Bus Company provides door-to-door service for a nominal fee but asks that you call for your ride two to three days in advance. (Call (707) 963-4222, from 9 a.m. — 5 p.m. on weekdays and 8:30 a.m. — 4:30 p.m. on weekends.)

By Foot: Retrace the described route.

Chapter 47
Saint Helena: South to North
Along the Wine Way

A 2½- to 5-mile winery walk
between comfortable country inns.

The Night Before

Getting There

By Public Transportation: Greyhound runs three buses daily from San Francisco. (In San Francisco, call (415) 433-1500 for schedule, or call the toll-free number for your area.) From the Saint Helena stop at Pope and Main streets, for the Hotel Saint Helena, walk two blocks north on Main Street; for the Harvest Inn and Chalet Bernensis, walk one mile south on Main Street.

By Car: From Highway 101, take the Napa-Vallejo turnoff and proceed on Highway 37 east. At Sears Point, take Highway 121 north and continue on it east toward Napa. Then take Highway 29 north to Saint Helena. Chalet Bernensis and the Harvest Inn are at the left side of the highway at the south end of the city limits; Hotel Saint Helena is a mile north at the town center.

Saint Helena

See the preceding chapter.

The Inns

Chalet Bernensis, 225 Saint Helena Highway (Highway 29), Saint Helena 94574; (707) 963-4423. An inn, with continental breakfast included; moderately expensive.

A graceful 1884 Victorian next door to the Sutter Home Winery. Nine rooms, decorated with Early American and Victorian furnishings.

Harvest Inn, 1 Main Street, Saint Helena 94574; (707) 963-WINE. Continental breakfast included; expensive to very expensive.

An English Tudor-style contemporary inn, in a 21-acre working vineyard; 25 spacious rooms decorated with antiques. Fireplaces, swimming pool, spa.

Hotel Saint Helena, 1309 Main Street, Saint Helena 94574; (707) 963-4388. An inn, with continental breakfast included; moderately expensive to expensive.

A genteel two-story hotel, circa 1881, in the heart of Saint Helena's Main Street district. Eighteen rooms, richly furnished with antiques.

A Look at the Day's Walk

If your version of a Wine Country weekend builds on sophisticated pleasures, consider a stay in Saint Helena. Here inns cater to the comfort-loving and wineries to the educated palate. For gourmet dining, try La Belle Helene and the Miramonte Restaurant, renowned for the excellence of their tables.

The Wine Way walk starts just south of the city limits and heads north past the vineyards that rim Main Street. En route, you stop to explore the Silverado Museum and three vineyards. The inn that is your destination north of town is some 4½ – 5 miles from where you began. Or, if you start from the town center at the Hotel Saint Helena, the distance is shorter by half.

The Route

Distance: 2½ to 5 miles, depending on your inn.
Walking Time: 2 hours to all day.
Grade: Level.

In order to bypass some of the hubbub of Highway 29, begin the route by meandering down neighborhood lanes of Saint Helena. Turn down Lewelling Lane (right, from Harvest Inn; left, from Chalet Bernensis) and walk through the vineyards. The first right turn brings you to Sulphur Springs Avenue. Turn left on Sulphur Springs and right on South Crane Avenue; pass Crane Park, and turn right on Birch Avenue, left on North Crane, and right on Spring Street, until you arrive finally at the Main Street town center.

Turn left, walking north on Main, pausing to admire some of the wonderful old stone buildings that lend the town its gracious turn-of-the-century air. Here, guests of the Hotel Saint Helena pick up the route. Proceed north to Adams Street. Turn right onto Adams, cross Railroad Avenue, and follow the signs directing you left down Library Lane to the Silverado Museum. Here, an extensive Robert Louis Stevenson collection is on display.

When you leave the museum, return to Railroad Avenue and walk north again; little Lyman Park, with shade trees and gazebo, appears at your left. Walk through the park to Main Street, turn right, and proceed north once more.

At the northern end of town, three historic wineries offer daily guided tours and tasting. The first to appear, at the left after you cross Pratt Avenue, is on the imposing Beringer estate. The 1883 Rhine House, once the Beringer family home, now serves as a visitor center and tasting room. The stone winery and network of underground caves were built in 1877 and are set back into the hillside just behind the Rhine mansion.

Christian Brothers, just north, presents as grand a stone facade as any in the valley. Built in 1889 by a mining magnate, the winery was purchased by the Brothers, a teaching order, in 1950 and has been producing fine wine under their tutelage ever since.

Upon leaving Christian Brothers, continue north beside the splendid stone wall, then cross the highway and enter the vineyards of Charles Krug (which has been owned and managed by the Mondavi family since 1943). It was Krug who, in 1858, was the first to bring European wine-making techniques to the Napa Valley, thus pioneering the industry that now thrives. Here, peruse the 1874 stone winery and carriage house from Krug's time.

When you've walked back to the highway through the vineyards, turn right and continue north. The just-short-of-a-mile walk to Lodi Lane passes two more fine wineries: Markham, just past the Deer Park intersection, and Freemark Abbey, on the corner of Lodi Lane. Turn right on Lodi Lane, and follow the signs just up the road to the Wine Country Inn.

Journey's End

The Inn

The Wine Country Inn, 1152 Lodi Lane, Saint Helena 94571; (707) 963-7077. Continental breakfast included; expensive.

Contemporary comfort in old New England style; 25 rooms furnished with country antiques. Glorious valley views. Balconies, fireplaces, patios.

The Way Back

By Public Transportation: The Tri-City Bus Company provides door-to-door service for a nominal fee but asks that you call for your ride two to three days in advance. (Call (707) 963-4222 from 9 a.m. – 5 p.m. on weekdays and 8:30 a.m. – 4:30 p.m. on weekends.)

By Foot: Retrace yesterday's route, exploring some side lanes that look intriguing or wineries that you missed. The fastest route is straight down Highway 29.

Chapter 48
Saint Helena to Deer Run

*A 5-mile back-roads walk from a village
guest house to a mountain retreat.*

The Night Before

Getting There

See the preceding chapter for directions by public transportation
and by car to Saint Helena. Once there:

By Public Transportation: From the Saint Helena stop at Pope and
Main streets, walk three blocks north to Adams and turn left. For
both inns, walk two blocks on Adams, then turn right on Kearney.

By Car: For both inns, turn left off Highway 29 onto Adams Street
and right on Kearney Street.

Saint Helena

See chapter 46.

The Inns

Chestleson House, 1417 Kearney Street, Saint Helena 94574; (707)
963-3328. A guest house, with continental breakfast included;
moderately expensive to expensive.

From the big front porch of this Victorian house, guests enjoy a
view of the Atlas Mountains. Three rooms, furnished with
antiques.

Cinnamon Bear Bed and Breakfast, 1407 Kearney Street, Saint Helena 94574; (707) 963-4633. A guest house, with continental breakfast included; moderately expensive.

A brown-shingled Victorian house with broad porches and stuffed bears everywhere. Four comfortable guest rooms.

A Look at the Day's Walk

Visitors to the Wine Country often limit their exploration of the area to those magnificent stone structures in which the grapes are fermented and bottled. This hike takes you primarily to the source — the vineyards themselves. Spring Mountain Road passes a number of vine-planted hillsides. (Among the structures passed are those of Spring Mountain Winery, the setting for the "Falcon Crest" TV series.)

Since the route ends in a hilltop hideaway far from restaurants and stores, it will be necessary for you to carry your dinner with you. The friendly folk at Deer Run will allow you the use of a barbecue and outdoor picnic table. Mention it (as well as the possibility of arranging wine tastings; see The Route) to them when you make your reservations.

The Route

Distance: 5 miles
Walking Time: 3½ hours.
Grade: A moderate uphill climb.

From both inns, turn left and walk to Madrona. Turn left again to Spring Mountain Road.

Arriving from either direction, follow Spring Mountain Road as it leaves the town behind and climbs gradually up the tree-shaded hillside. Small houses give way to rural countryside and finally, to large terraced vineyards.

Spring Mountain Winery, the setting for the TV series "Falcon Crest," is on the left, unmarked but recognizable by the wide stone entranceway. You pass many other fine vineyards as well; none is open on a drop-in basis, but your hosts at Deer Run can arrange visits for you upon request.

At the top of the ridge, you will see the large sign to Deer Run on your left.

Journey's End

The Inn

Deer Run, 3995 Spring Mountain Road, Saint Helena 94574; (707) 963-3794. A guest house, with continental breakfast included; moderately expensive.

A secluded mountain retreat in the forest above the vineyards. Two large, modern guest rooms, one with a fireplace. Pool.

The Way Back

By Public Transportation: The Tri-City Bus Company provides door-to-door service for a nominal fee but asks that you call for your ride two to three days in advance. (Call (707) 963-4222 from 9 a.m. — 5 p.m. on weekdays and 8:30 a.m. — 4:30 p.m. on weekends.)

By Foot: Retrace the described route.

Chapter 49
Napa Valley: Larkmead to Old Bale Mill

A 5¾-mile hike through Bothe — Napa Valley
State Park between country inns.

The Night Before

Getting There

By Car: From Highway 101, take the Napa-Vallejo turnoff and proceed east on Highway 37. At Sears Point take Highway 121 north
and continue on it east toward Napa. Then take Highway 29 north.
About four miles past Saint Helena, turn right on Larkmead Lane,
just opposite the Bothe — Napa Valley Park entrance. Larkmead
Inn is a quarter mile down the lane on the right, just before the
Kornell Winery.

The Inn

Larkmead Country Inn, 1103 Larkmead Lane, Calistoga 94515;
(707) 942-5360. Continental breakfast included; inexpensive.

An early-twentieth-century Victorian surrounded by vineyards
on a quiet country lane. Four comfortably elegant rooms,
decorated with antiques.

A Look at the Day's Walk

It would be difficult to imagine any more pleasant beginning
than the fragrant vineyard stroll down Larkmead Lane to the front
door of Bothe — Napa Valley State Park. Once arrived at this

lovely preserve of redwood canyon, rugged brushy slope and rushing stream, you may wish to stop for a morning plunge in the park swimming pool (which opens mid-June to Labor Day at 10:30 a.m.) before continuing. Then you follow the wooded canyon alongside Ritchey Creek, and perhaps climb Coyote Peak for choice glimpses of the Napa Valley below. Returning to the canyon floor, you walk along the History Trail past the 100-year-old cemetery, leading to Bale Grist Mill State Historic Park. Here you may explore the Old Bale Mill, built in 1846 by Edward Bale, then landlord of the entire northern half of the Napa Valley. A half-mile walk on Saint Helena Highway delivers you to the front door of the Bale Mill Inn.

The Route

Distance: 5¾ miles.
Walking Time: 3 hours.
Grade: Mostly level terrain; gentle hills.

Leaving the inn, turn left and walk to Highway 29. Cross the road and enter Bothe — Napa Valley State Park (circled number 1 on the map), following the paved road that crosses a stream and continues into the park. Turn right on a paved road opposite the pool (2) and proceed to the trail that heads uphill and winds to the right. This trail takes you through a maple grove in the ranger-residence area.

At a junction (not shown on the map) veer left and continue on the trail to another junction (3). Here, take the Redwood Trail to the left as it heads uphill along Ritchey Creek.

When you arrive at the next intersection, take Coyote Peak Trail (4) to the left as it proceeds rather steeply uphill and away from the creek. Eventually you arrive at a junction where the Coyote Peak Trail splits in two (5). The left fork heads steeply uphill to 1,100-feet high Coyote Peak; if you are feeling ambitious, take this quarter-mile strenuous climb to the top. The point about halfway up with a beautiful view of the Napa Valley would make a great spot for a picnic lunch. At the top, however, is a lovely grove of trees rather than the open viewpoint you might prefer as a reward for such an arduous climb. Return to the junction (5) to continue the hike.

After your foray to the peak, continue on the trail as it leads by switchbacks all the way down again to Ritchey Creek. You may want to stop on the shady shores of the creek before beginning the last half of the hike. If you wish to extend the walk a bit, turn left and take Canyon and Spring trails farther into the park.

From the base of the Coyote Peak Trail at creekside, cross the stream and walk a few paces to the turnoff on the right to Redwood Trail (6). Shortly, make another, more difficult crossing of the creek, and then continue along the Redwood Trail all the way back to your original entry point to the trail opposite the pool, near the park entrance.

Here, turn right, along a paved road leading through the picnic area to the Pioneer Cemetery. Proceed straight on the path through the cemetery and take the History Trail (7) through the Bale Grist Mill State Historic Park.

This pleasant trail through groves of manzanita and madrone passes the Mill Pond and eventually leads to a marker pointing to the Bale Grist Mill. Detour off the trail to explore this rustic nineteenth-century site, returning to the marker to proceed.

Continue out of the park, walking through the parking lot and down the paved road to Highway 29. Turn right and walk a half mile to the inn on the right.

Journey's End

The Inn

Bale Mill Inn, 3431 Saint Helena Highway (Highway 29), Saint Helena 94574; (707) 963-4545. Continental breakfast included; moderately expensive.

A rustic country inn exuding Napa Valley charm. The decor of each of the five rooms recreates the ambiance of a legendary historical figure.

The Way Back

By Public Transportation: The Tri-City Bus Company provides door-to-door service for a nominal fee but asks that you call for your ride two to three days in advance. (Call (704) 963-4222 from 9 a.m. - 5 p.m. weekdays and 8:30 a.m. - 4:30 p.m. on weekends.)

By Foot: An easy mile walk north on Highway 29 will return you to Larkmead Lane.

Chapter 50
Calistoga to Mountain Home Ranch

A 5- to 6½-mile back-roads hike
from a Calistoga inn to a mountain resort.

The Night Before

Getting There

By Public Transportation: Greyhound runs three buses daily from
San Francisco. (In San Francisco, call (415) 433-1500 for complete
schedule, or call the toll-free number for your area.) From the
Calistoga stop on Grant Avenue, walk the half block back to
Highway 29 (Lincoln Avenue) and turn right. The Mount View
Hotel is just ahead on your right; the Calistoga Inn, a few blocks
farther on your left; and the Wine Way Inn is a block or so farther
at the junction of Lincoln Avenue and Highway 28 (Foothill
Boulevard).

By Car: From Highway 101 take the Napa Valley turnoff and proceed east on Highway 37. At Sears Point take Highway 121 north,
and continue on it east toward Napa. Then take Highway 29 north
approximately 26 miles to Calistoga. At the junction of Highways
29 (Lincoln Avenue) and 128 (Foothill Boulevard) the Wine Way
Inn is at your left. For the Calistoga Inn, turn right on Lincoln
Avenue and find the inn on your right. The Mount View Hotel is a
few blocks farther on your left.

Calistoga

Tourism has always been Calistoga's number one business. In 1862 Sam Brannan, who had founded the town two years earlier, opened the elegant Springs Hotel, envisioning the spa as California's answer to Saratoga, the New York mineral-springs resort. Indeed, the charming hamlet at the foot of Mount Saint Helena has attracted visitors ever since, including Robert Louis Stevenson, who after his 1880 honeymoon stay immortalized the area in his story "The Silverado Squatters." Whether you come to partake of the curative waters and mudbaths, sample the nectar of the local vineyards, experience the thrills of gliding from the Calistoga Soaring Center or just relax in the splendor of the natural surroundings, you will certainly come away enriched.

The Inns

Calistoga Inn, 1250 Lincoln Avenue, Calistoga 94515; (707) 942-4101. Continental breakfast included, with a restaurant on the premises; inexpensive.

Since the early years of the century, the inn by the side of the Napa River on Calistoga's main street has welcomed travelers. Fifteen rooms, simple and tastefully decorated.

Mount View Hotel, 1457 Lincoln Avenue, Calistoga 94515; (707) 942-6877. An inn, with continental breakfast included Monday through Friday and a restaurant on the premises; moderately expensive to expensive.

Fully refurbished in Art Deco style on the site of the old European Hotel in central Calistoga. Thirty-four rooms and suites, individually decorated. Swimming pool, hot tub, live music nightly.

Wine Way Inn, 1019 Foothill Boulevard (Highway 29), Calistoga 94515; (707) 942-0680. Continental breakfast included; moderately expensive.

This 1915 family home with the Mayacamas Mountains as a backyard has been recently refurbished to function as a small inn. Guests are received with warm hospitality and accommodated in six rooms furnished with nineteenth-century antiques.

A Look at the Day's Walk

Walking the back roads of the Bay region's Wine Country is a bit like being magically transported to the chateau region of France.

The softly curving hills, the rows of terraced vineyards and the occasional stone winery in the distance are all here to be savored.

This route takes you from the town of Calistoga up the back roads and into the hills above to ranch lodgings.

The Route

Distance: 5 to 6½ miles (depending on your choice of inns).
Walking Time: 3 to 4 hours.
Grade: 2 miles, moderately steep uphill climb; the remainder, gently rolling hills.

From the Mount View Hotel and the Calistoga Inn, walk south to Foothill Boulevard (Highway 29). Cross to Kortum Canyon Road, directly opposite Lincoln Street.

From the Wine Way Inn, turn left to Kortum Canyon Road.

Proceed up Kortum Canyon Road as it climbs through tall stands of pines and redwoods to the top of the ridge. After a bit, the paved road ends; continue on the dirt road, ignoring the occasional private roads leading off to either side.

Take a rest at the top of the ridge, looking out over the peaceful hills and vineyards. A bit farther on, where the road becomes little more than a fire road, you may wish to stop for a picnic lunch on one of the level grassy areas.

At the junction with Sharpe Road, a pleasant, paved back road, 2½ miles from Calistoga, turn right. Proceed on Sharpe Road through open rolling meadows and oak-studded ranch land to Petrified Forest Road. At the stop sign, turn right and walk to the turnoff marked "Triple S Ranch."

Turn left on Mountain Home Ranch Road and proceed about one mile to Triple S Ranch Resort. Or, if you are staying instead at the Mountain Home Ranch, continue another 1½ miles past the Rainbow Ranch to your lodging.

Journey's End

The Inns

Triple S Ranch Resort, 4600 Mountain Home Ranch Road, Calistoga 94515; (707) 942-6730. A hotel-resort, with a restaurant on the premises; inexpensive. Open April 1 to December 31.

Very basic cabin accommodations on a large working ranch with walnut and apple orchards. Horses for hire, pool.

Mountain Home Ranch, 3400 Mountain Home Ranch Road, Calistoga 94515; (707) 942-6616. A hotel-resort, with a restaurant on the premises. In summer, all meals included; the rest of the year, continental breakfast only. Inexpensive to moderately expensive.

An expansive, woodsy resort; 24 units ranging from inexpensive rustic cabins to large modern cottages and lodge rooms. Two large pools, lake fishing, tennis.

The Way Back

By Public Transportation: The Tri-City Bus Company provides door-to-door service for a nominal fee but asks that you call for your ride two to three days in advance. (Call (707) 963-4222 from 9 a.m. — 5 p.m. on weekdays and 8:30 a.m. — 4:30 p.m. on weekends.)

By Foot: For the most direct route, take Petrified Forest Road east to Highway 128 and turn right to Calistoga.

Appendix A

Treks for Novices and Hardy Hikers

Area	Treks for Novices	Treks for Hardy Hikers
San Francisco	1, 2, 3, 4	
The North Bay	16	9, 10, 14
The East Bay	19 (the short way) and 24	20
The South Bay	31, 32, 33	29, 34, 35
The Santa Cruz Mountains	37	36, 38, 40
The Wine Country	41, 43, 44, 49	42, 45

Appendix B

Budget and Luxury Treks

Area	Budget	Luxury
San Francisco	3	
The North Bay	9, 14, 15	6, 7, 16
The East Bay	24, 24, 26	
The South Bay	27, 32, 35	
The Santa Cruz Mountains	40	
The Wine Country		41

Appendix C
Extended Walking Tours

Treks can be linked together in the order indicated to form walking tours of from two- to eight-days' duration. Give some thought to augmenting your provisions for the longer excursions.

Bay Area Regions	Treks	Route
San Francisco	1 and 2	Union Square to Pacific Heights
San Francisco	4 and 5	The Panhandle to Fisherman's Wharf
San Francisco	3, 6, 7, 8, 9, 10, 11, 12	San Francisco to the North Bay
The North Bay	13 and 17	Mill Valley to Tiburon
The North Bay	12, 11, 10, 9, 8, 7, 6, 3 (each reversed)	The North Bay to San Francisco
The North Bay	16, 8, 9, 10, 11, 12	Mount Tamalpais to Inverness
The East Bay	21 or 22 and 23	Berkeley to the Claremont
The East Bay	20 and 25	Kensington to Walnut Creek
The East Bay	20 and 26	Kensington to Martinez
The East Bay	26 (reversed) and 25	Martinez to Walnut Creek
The South Bay	29, 30, 31	Burlingame to Woodside, plus loops
The Santa Cruz Mountains	37 and 38	Brookdale to Santa Cruz
The Santa Cruz Mountains	39 (reversed) and 36	Santa Cruz to Davenport
The Wine Country	44 (reversed) and 45	Vintage 1870 to Napa
The Wine Country	47 and 48	Saint Helena; elements of the two walks can be combined

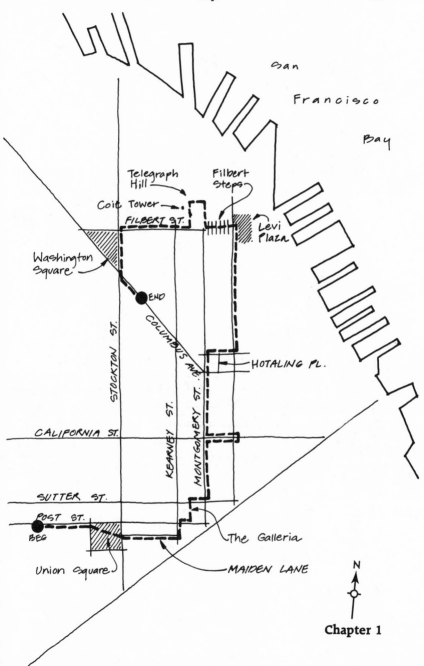

San

Francisco

Bay

Telegraph Hill

Filbert Steps

Coit Tower

FILBERT ST.

Levi Plaza

Washington Square

END

COLUMBUS AVE.

STOCKTON ST.

HOTALING PL.

KEARNEY ST.

MONTGOMERY ST.

CALIFORNIA ST.

SUTTER ST.

POST ST.

BEG

The Galleria

Union Square

MAIDEN LANE

N

Chapter 1

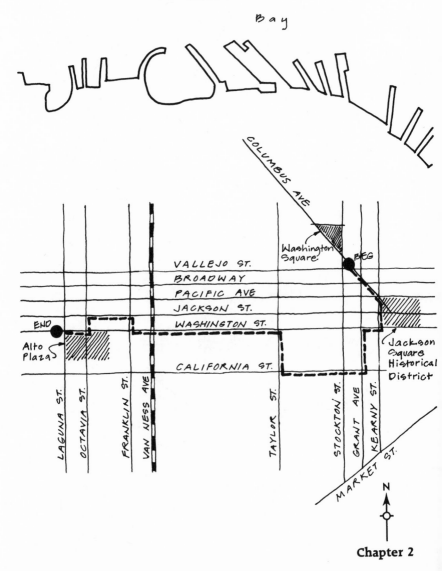

San Francisco Bay

COLUMBUS AVE

Washington Square

BEG

VALLEJO ST.
BROADWAY
PACIFIC AVE
JACKSON ST.
WASHINGTON ST.

END

Alto Plaza

Jackson Square Historical District

CALIFORNIA ST.

LAGUNA ST.
OCTAVIA ST.
FRANKLIN ST.
VAN NESS AVE
TAYLOR ST.
STOCKTON ST.
GRANT AVE
KEARNY ST.
MARKET ST.

N

Chapter 2

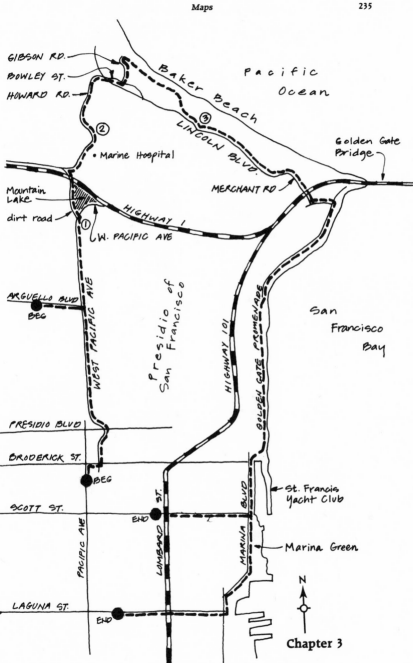

Chapter 3

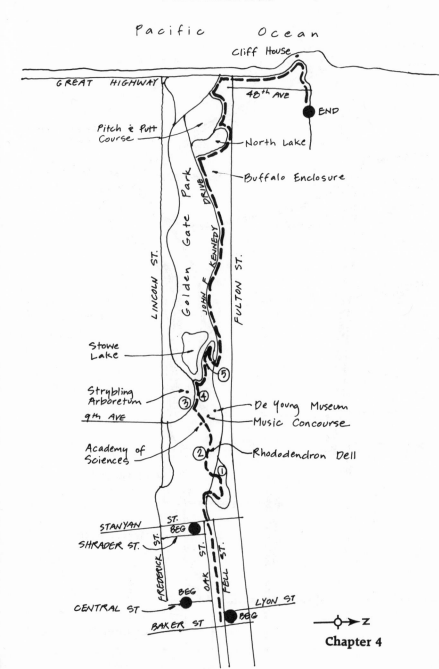

Chapter 4

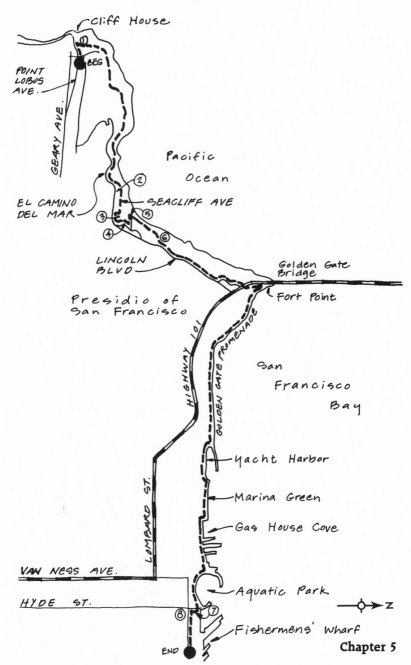

Chapter 5

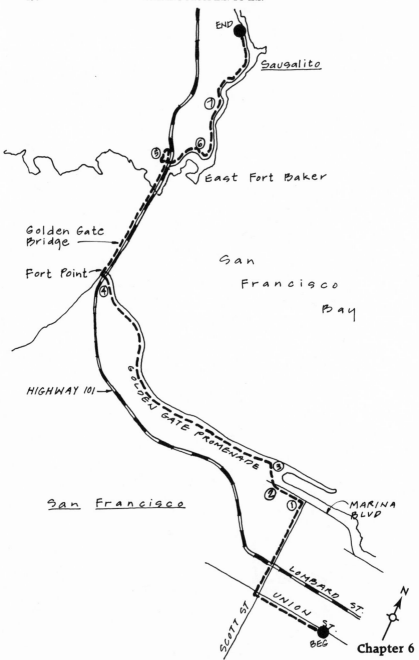

Sausalito

East Fort Baker

Golden Gate Bridge

Fort Point

San Francisco Bay

HIGHWAY 101

GOLDEN GATE PROMENADE

San Francisco

MARINA BLVD

LOMBARD ST.

UNION ST.

SCOTT ST.

BEG

END

N

Chapter 6

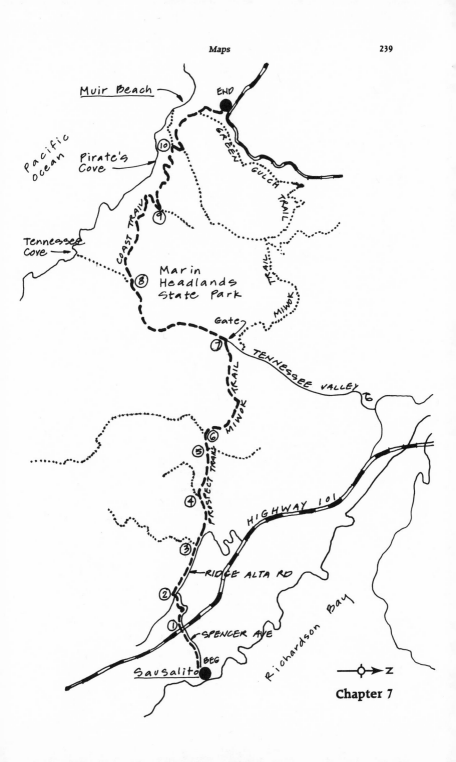

Chapter 7

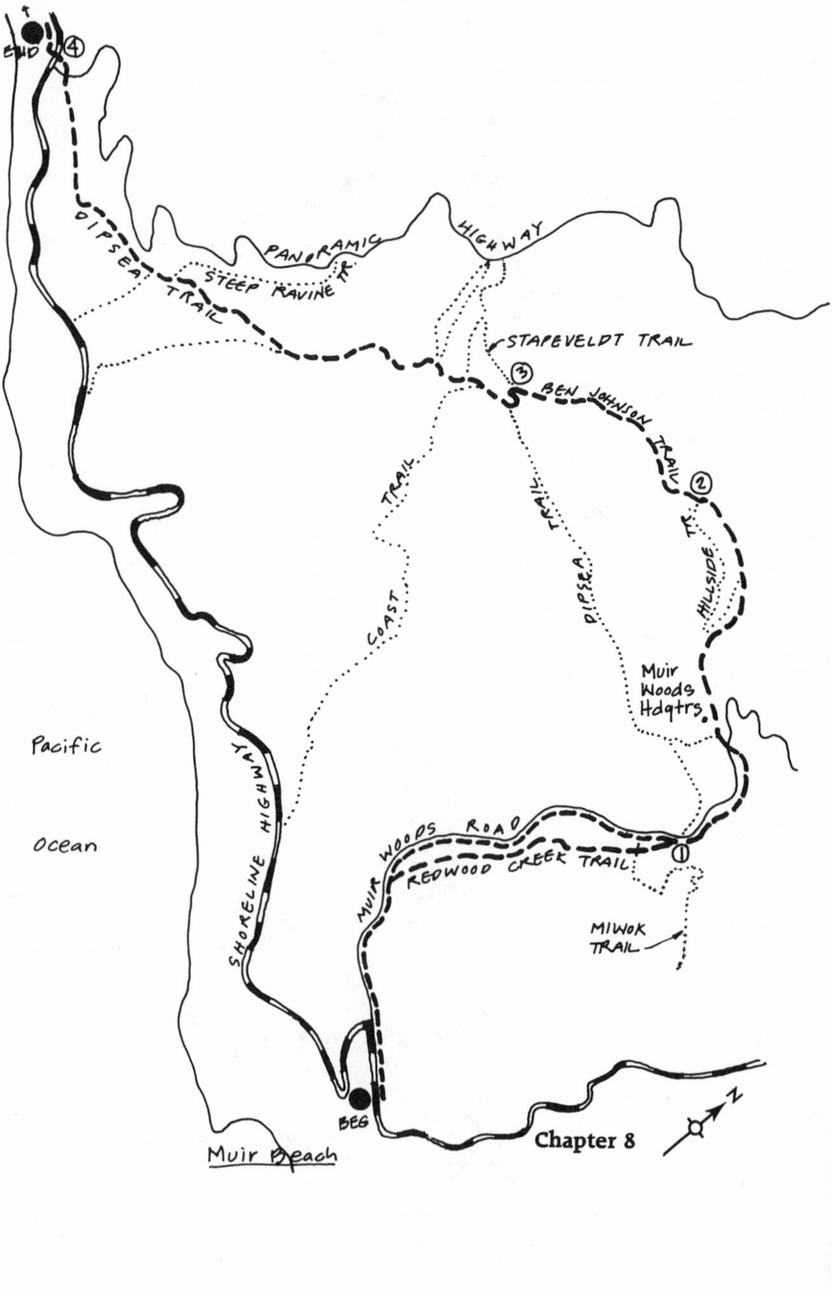

END ④

PANORAMIC HIGHWAY

DIPSEA TRAIL

STEEP RAVINE TR.

STAPEVELDT TRAIL

③ BEN JOHNSON TRAIL

②

HILLSIDE TR.

COAST TRAIL

DIPSEA TRAIL

Muir Woods Hdqtrs.

Pacific

Ocean

SHORELINE HIGHWAY

MUIR WOODS ROAD

REDWOOD CREEK TRAIL

①

MIWOK TRAIL

BEG

Muir Beach   Chapter 8   N

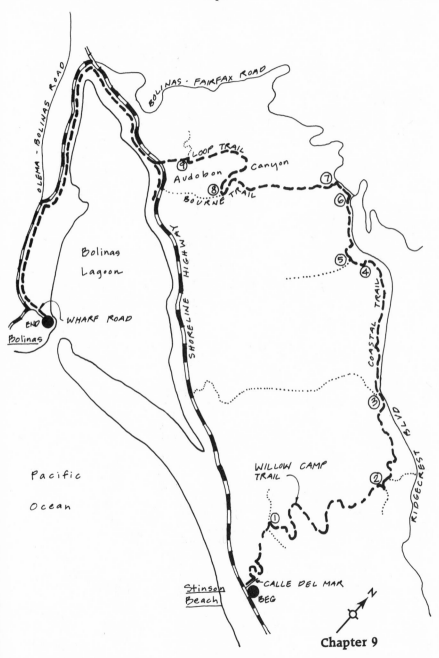

Chapter 9

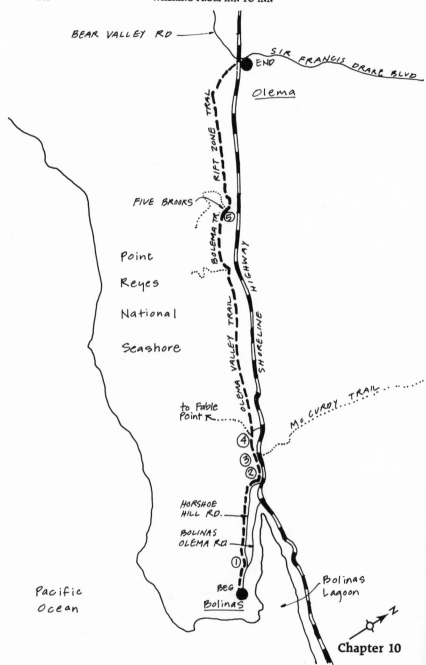

BEAR VALLEY RD

SIR FRANCIS DRAKE BLVD

END

Olema

RIFT ZONE TRAIL

FIVE BROOKS

⑤

BOLEMA TR.

SHORELINE HIGHWAY

Point

Reyes

National

Seashore

OLEMA VALLEY TRAIL

Mc CURDY TRAIL

to Fable
Point

④

③

②

HORSHOE
HILL RD.

BOLINAS
OLEMA RD

①

Pacific
Ocean

BEG
Bolinas

Bolinas
Lagoon

N

Chapter 10

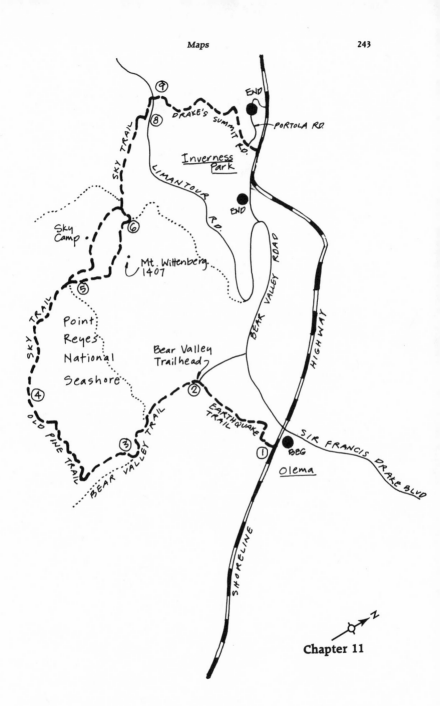

Chapter 11

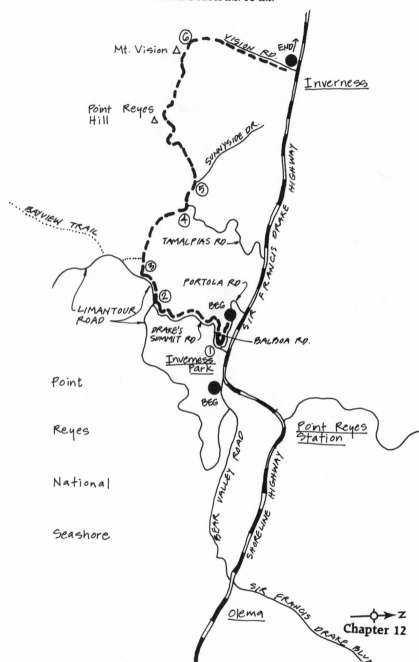

Chapter 12

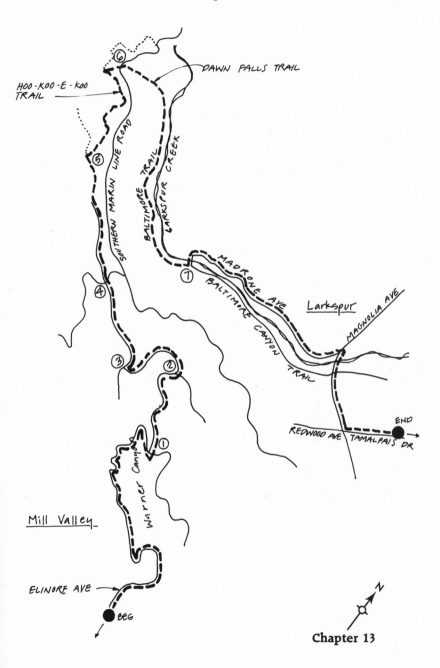

DAWN FALLS TRAIL

HOO·KOO·E·KOO
TRAIL

SOUTHERN MARIN LINE ROAD

BALTIMORE TRAIL

LARKSPUR CREEK

⑥

⑤

④

③ ②

①

MADRONE AVE

BALTIMORE CANYON

TRAIL

Larkspur

MAGNOLIA AVE

END

REDWOOD AVE   TAMALPAIS DR

Warner Canyon

Mill Valley

ELINORE AVE

BEG

N

Chapter 13

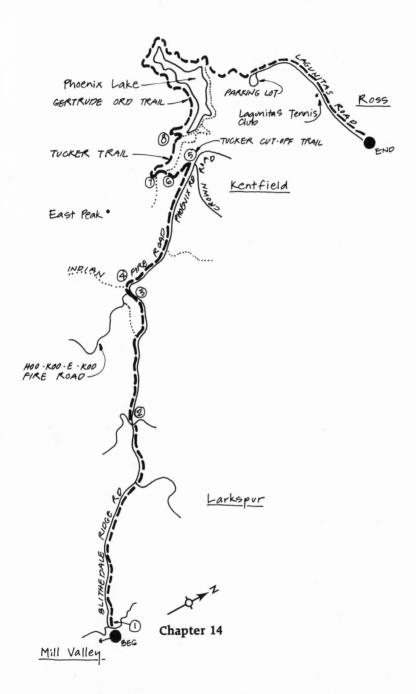

Phoenix Lake

GERTRUDE ORD TRAIL

PARKING LOT

Lagunitas Tennis Club

LAGUNITAS ROAD

Ross

END

⑧

TUCKER CUT-OFF TRAIL

TUCKER TRAIL

⑤

Kentfield

⑦ ⑥

CROWN ROAD

PHOENIX RD

East Peak •

FIRE ROAD

INDIAN ④

③

HOO·KOO·E·KOO
FIRE ROAD

②

Larkspur

BLITHEDALE RIDGE RD

N

①

Chapter 14

BEG

Mill Valley

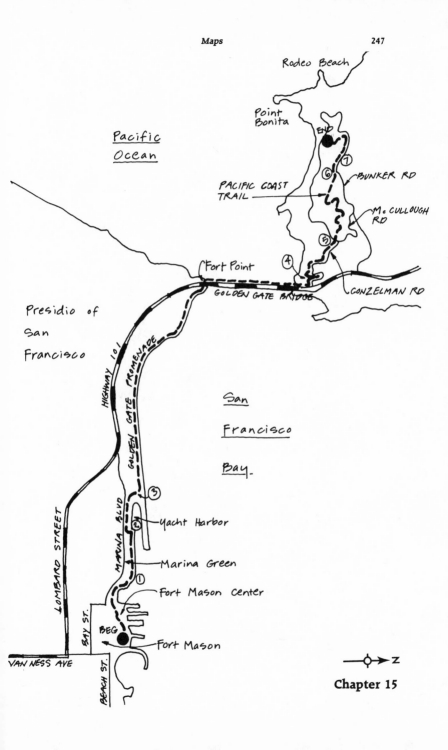

Chapter 15

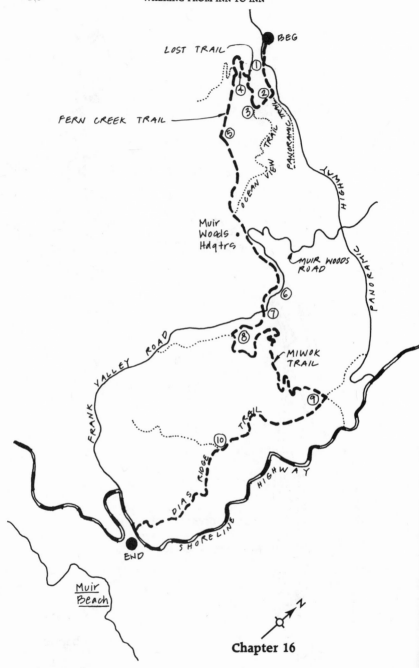

LOST TRAIL

BEG

①

④

②

③

⑤

FERN CREEK TRAIL

PANORAMIC TRAIL

OCEAN VIEW TRAIL

HIGHWAY

Muir
Woods
Hdqtrs

MUIR WOODS
ROAD

PANORAMIC

⑥

⑦

⑧

MIWOK
TRAIL

FRANK VALLEY ROAD

⑨

⑩

DIAS RIDGE TRAIL

SHORELINE HIGHWAY

END

Muir
Beach

N

Chapter 16

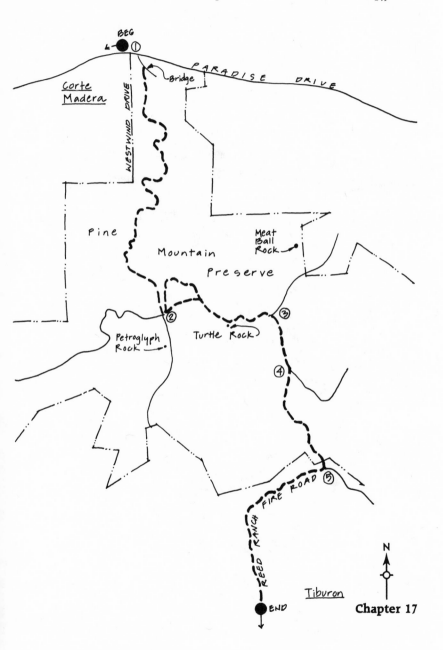

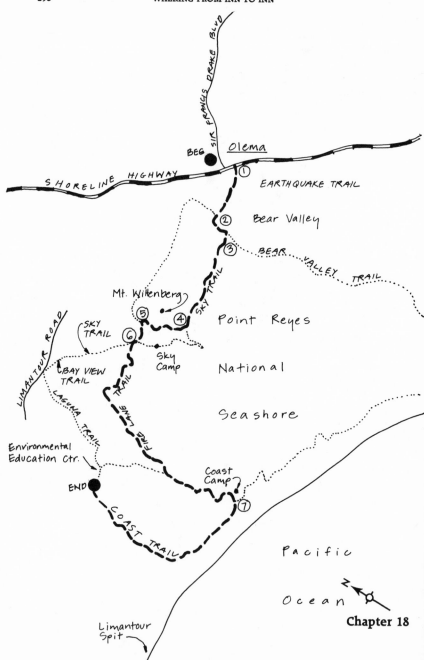

Chapter 18

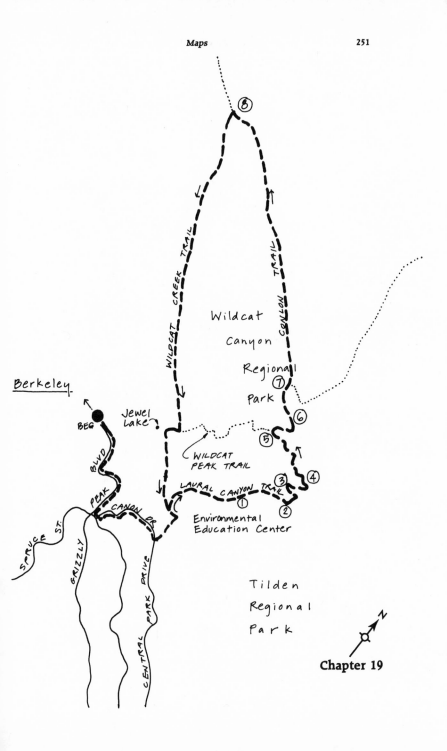

Berkeley

Wildcat
Canyon
Regional
Park

Jewel
Lake

BEG

WILDCAT CREEK TRAIL

CONLON TRAIL

⑧

⑦

⑥

⑤

④

③

②

①

WILDCAT
PEAK TRAIL

LAURAL CANYON TRAIL

Environmental
Education Center

PEAK BLVD

CANYON DR

SPRUCE ST.

GRIZZLY

CENTRAL PARK DRIVE

Tilden

Regional

Park

N

Chapter 19

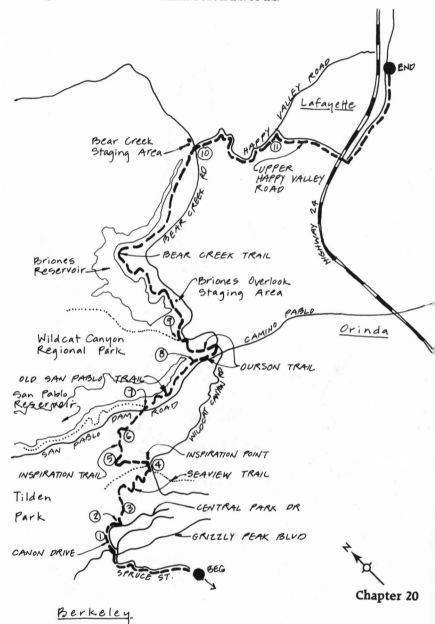

Chapter 20

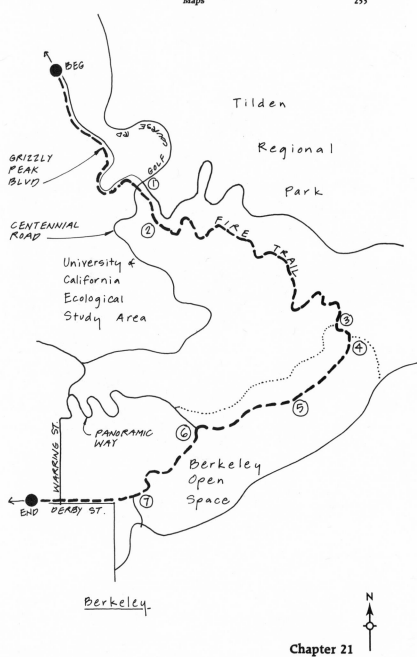

BEG

GRIZZLY
PEAK
BLVD

GOLF COURSE RD

CENTENNIAL
ROAD

①

②

Tilden

Regional

Park

FIRE TRAIL

③

④

University of
California
Ecological
Study Area

⑤

⑥

WARING ST.

PANORAMIC
WAY

Berkeley
Open
Space

END   DERBY ST.

⑦

Berkeley

N

Chapter 21

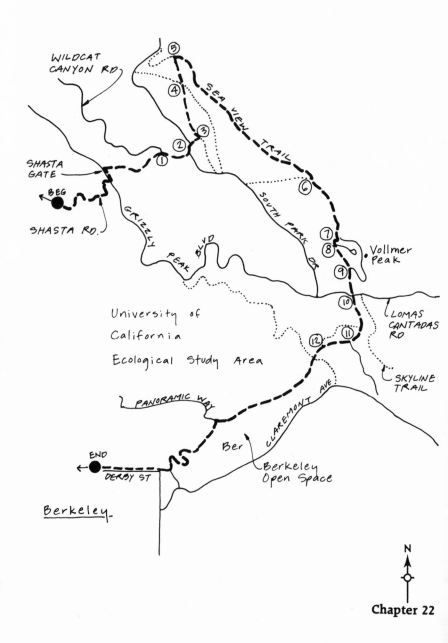

N

Chapter 22

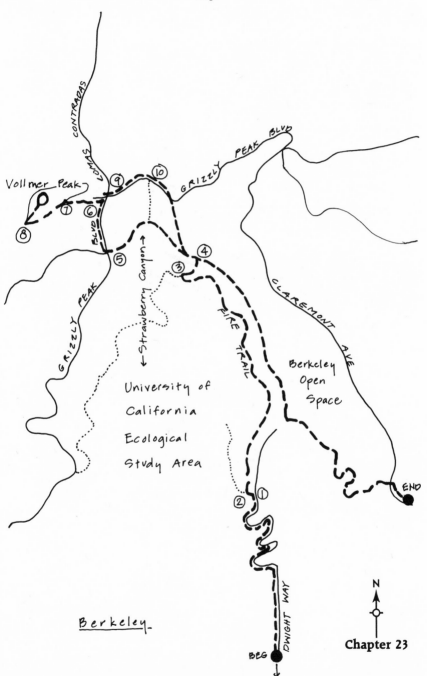

Berkeley

N
Chapter 23

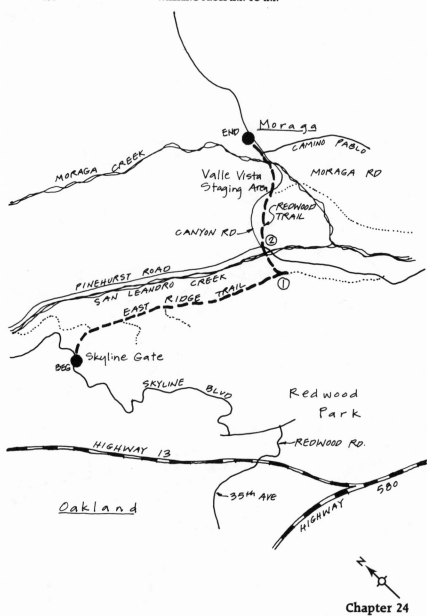

Chapter 24

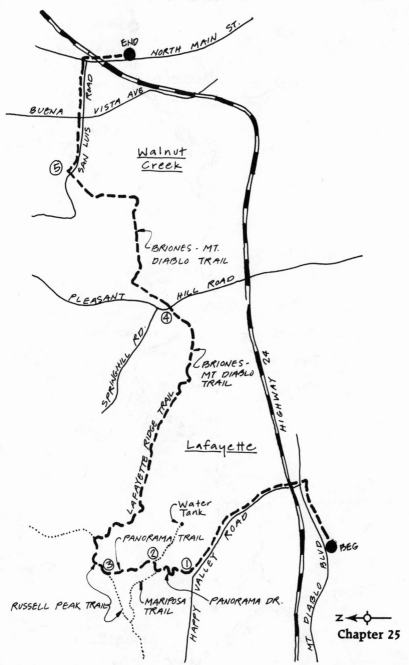

END NORTH MAIN ST.

BUENA VISTA AVE.

SAN LUIS ROAD

Walnut Creek

⑤

BRIONES · MT. DIABLO TRAIL

PLEASANT HILL ROAD

④

SPRINGHILL RD.

BRIONES - MT DIABLO TRAIL

LAFAYETTE RIDGE TRAIL

HIGHWAY 24

Lafayette

Water Tank

PANORAMA TRAIL

②

③

①

RUSSELL PEAK TRAIL

MARIPOSA TRAIL

PANORAMA DR.

HAPPY VALLEY ROAD

MT. DIABLO BLVD.

BEG

N

Chapter 25

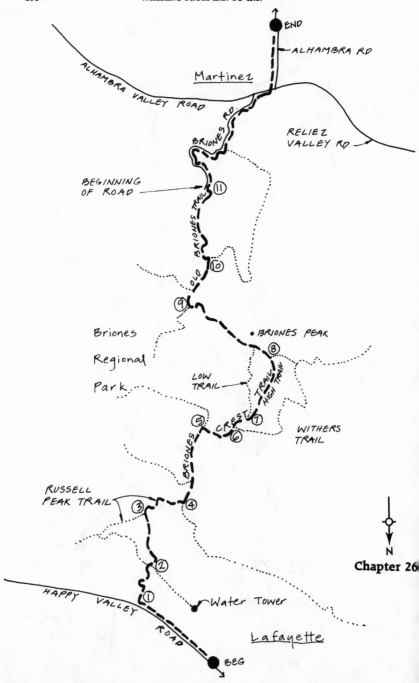

Chapter 26

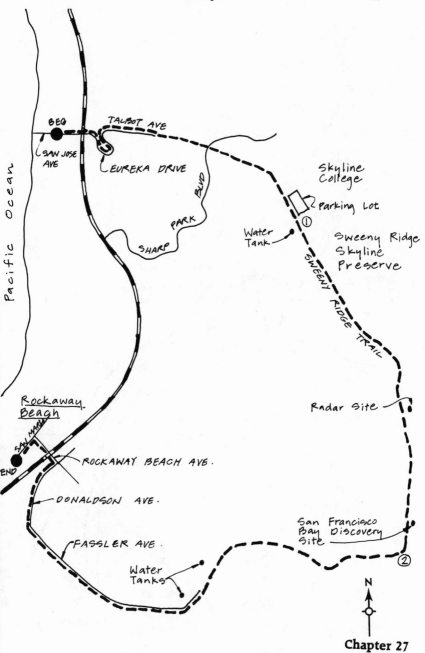

Chapter 27

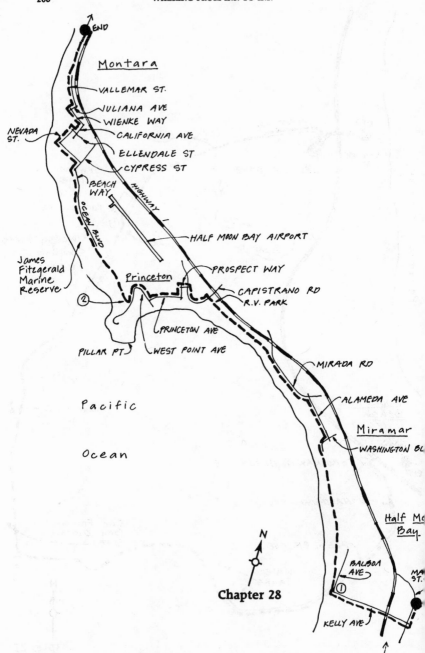

Chapter 28

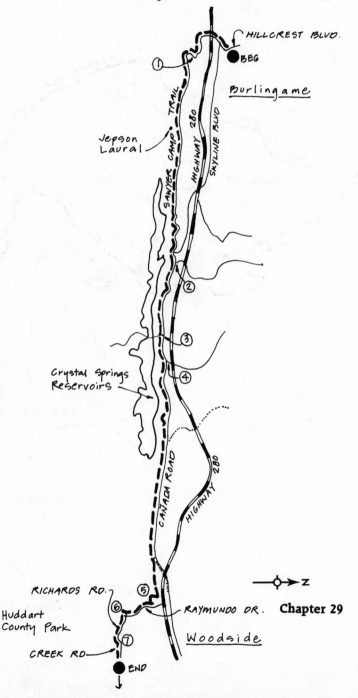

HILLCREST BLVD.

① BEG

Burlingame

Jepson Laural

SAWYER CAMP TRAIL

HIGHWAY 280

SKYLINE BLVD

②

③

④

Crystal Springs Reservoirs

CANADA ROAD

HIGHWAY 280

RICHARDS RD.

⑤

Huddart County Park

⑥

RAYMUNDO DR.

Chapter 29

Woodside

CREEK RD.

⑦

END

Z

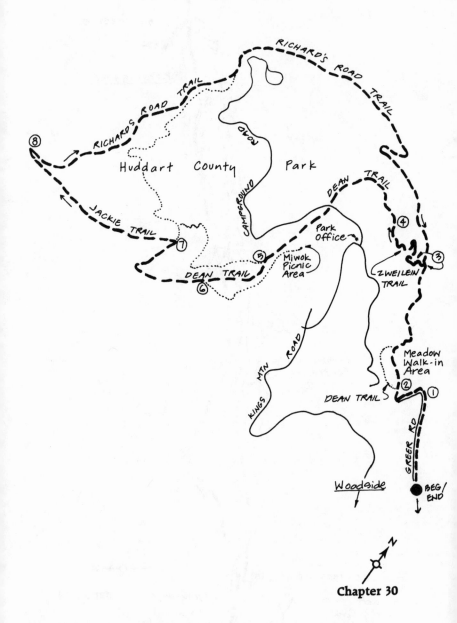

Chapter 30

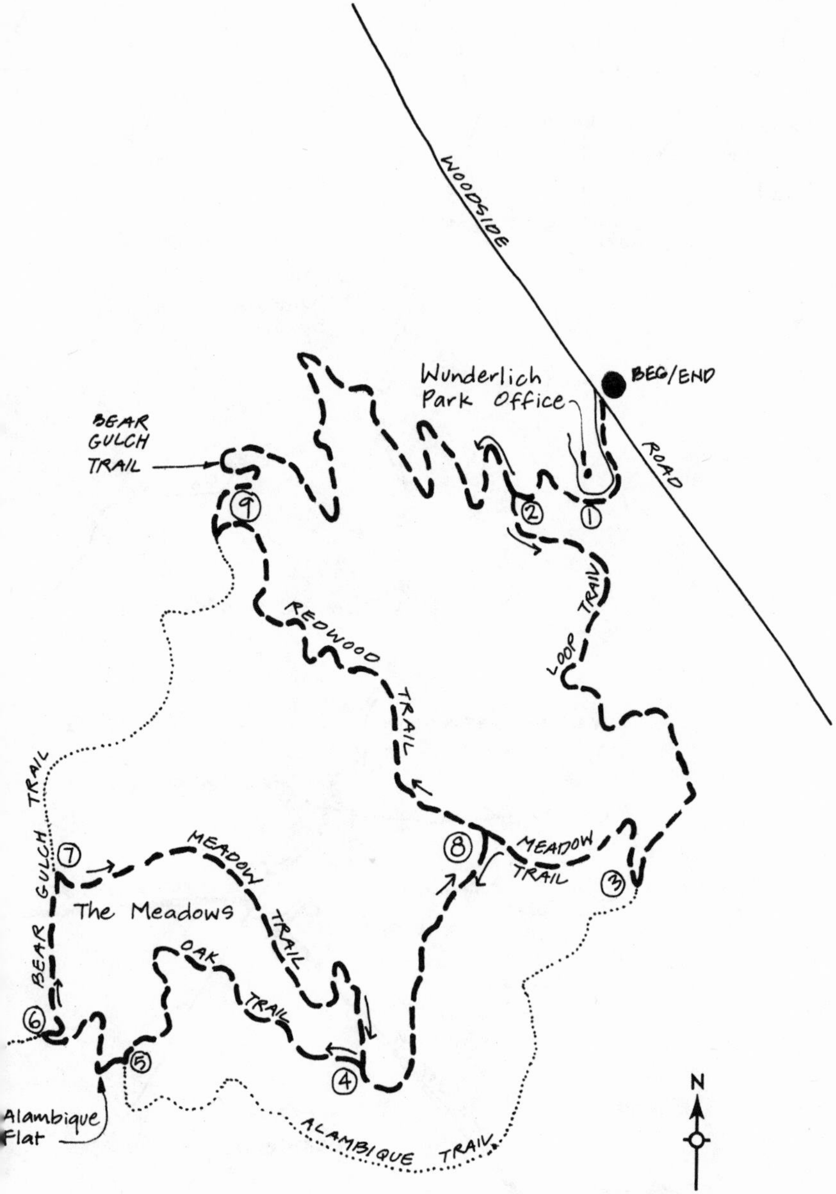

WOODSIDE

Wunderlich
Park Office

BEG/END

BEAR
GULCH
TRAIL

ROAD

②

①

LOOP TRAIL

⑨

REDWOOD TRAIL

BEAR GULCH TRAIL

MEADOW TRAIL

⑧

MEADOW TRAIL

③

⑦

The Meadows

OAK TRAIL

⑥

⑤

④

Alambique
Flat

ALAMBIQUE TRAIL

N

Chapter 31

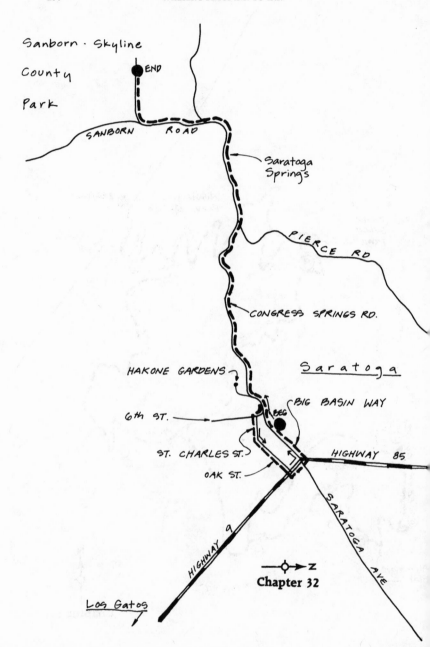

Sanborn · Skyline
County
Park

END

SANBORN   ROAD

Saratoga
Springs

PIERCE RD

CONGRESS SPRINGS RD.

<u>Saratoga</u>

HAKONE GARDENS

BIG BASIN WAY

6th ST.

BEG

ST. CHARLES ST.

HIGHWAY 85

OAK ST.

HIGHWAY 9

SARATOGA AVE

⟶◇➤ z
Chapter 32

<u>Los Gatos</u>

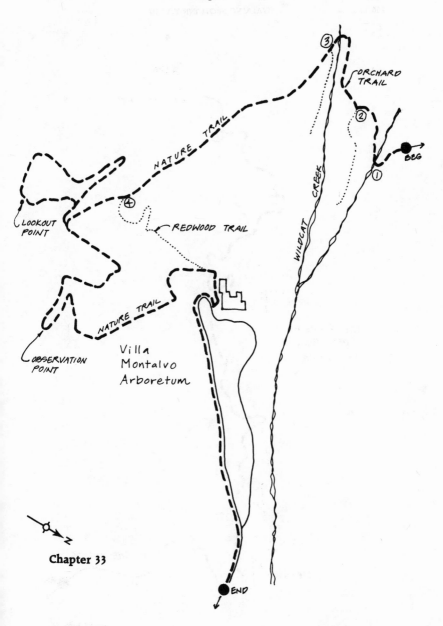

ORCHARD
TRAIL

NATURE TRAIL

③

②

①

BEG

WILDCAT CREEK

LOOKOUT
POINT

④

REDWOOD TRAIL

NATURE TRAIL

OBSERVATION
POINT

Villa
Montalvo
Arboretum

N

Chapter 33

END

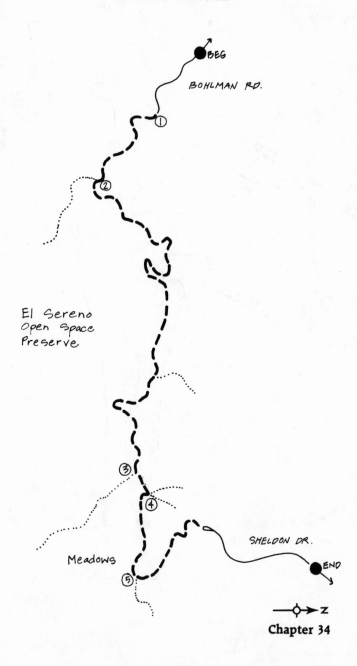

BEG

BOHLMAN RD.

El Sereno
Open Space
Preserve

SHELDON DR.

END

Meadows

Z

Chapter 34

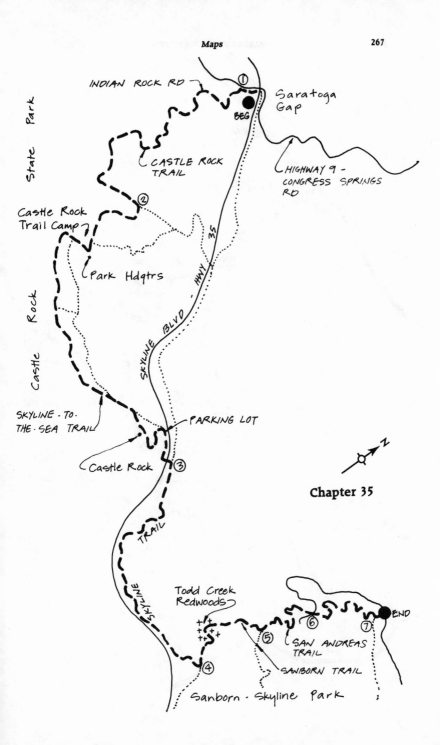

INDIAN ROCK RD

Saratoga Gap

① BEG

CASTLE ROCK TRAIL

HIGHWAY 9 - CONGRESS SPRINGS RD

State Park

②

Castle Rock Trail Camp

Park Hdqtrs

SKYLINE BLVD - HWY 35

Castle Rock

Castle Rock

SKYLINE - TO - THE · SEA TRAIL

PARKING LOT

Castle Rock

③

N

Chapter 35

SKYLINE TRAIL

Todd Creek Redwoods

④

⑤

⑥

⑦ END

SAN ANDREAS TRAIL

SANBORN TRAIL

Sanborn · Skyline Park

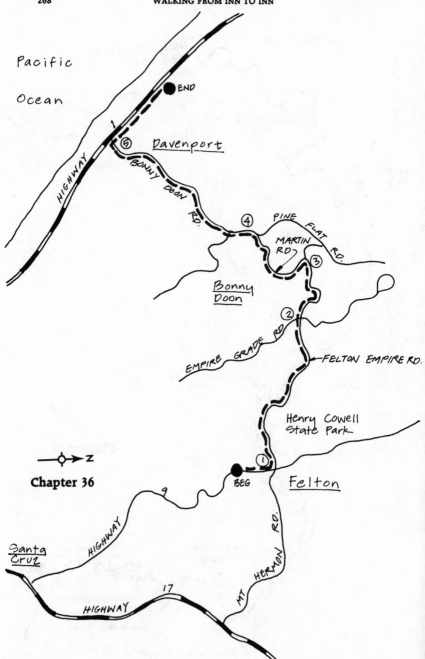

Pacific Ocean

END

Davenport

⑤

BONNY DOON RD.

④ PINE FLAT RD.

MARTIN RD.

③

Bonny Doon

②

EMPIRE GRADE RD.

FELTON EMPIRE RD.

Henry Cowell State Park

①

BEG   Felton

Chapter 36

Santa Cruz

HIGHWAY 9

HIGHWAY 1

HIGHWAY 17

MT HERMON RD.

N

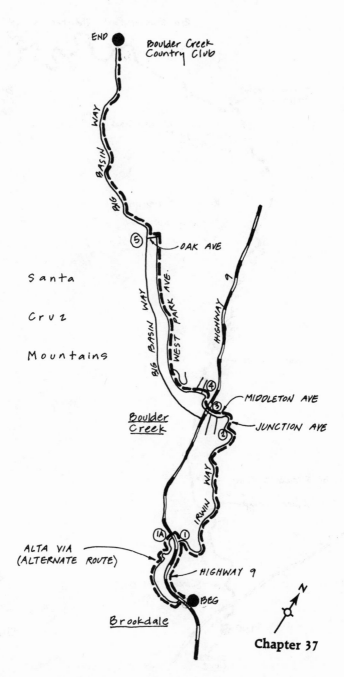

END ● Boulder Creek
Country Club

BIG BASIN WAY

Santa

Cruz

Mountains

⑤ OAK AVE

BIG BASIN WAY

WEST PARK AVE

HIGHWAY 9

④

MIDDLETON AVE

③

Boulder Creek

② JUNCTION AVE

IRWIN WAY

ⒶA ①

ALTA VIA
(ALTERNATE ROUTE)

HIGHWAY 9

● BEG

Brookdale

N

Chapter 37

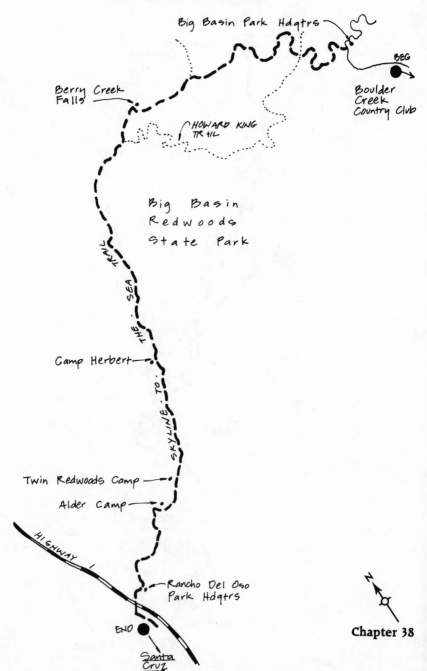

Big Basin Park Hdqtrs

BEG

Boulder
Creek
Country Club

Berry Creek
Falls

HOWARD KING
TRAIL

Big Basin
Redwoods
State Park

THE SEA TRAIL

Camp Herbert

SKYLINE TO

Twin Redwoods Camp

Alder Camp

HIGHWAY 1

Rancho Del Oso
Park Hdqtrs

END

Santa
Cruz

N

Chapter 38

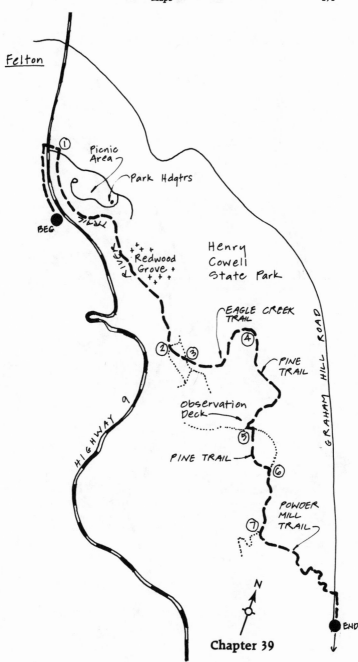

Felton

① Picnic Area

Park Hdqtrs

BEG

Trail

River

Redwood Grove

Henry Cowell State Park

EAGLE CREEK TRAIL

② ③ ④

PINE TRAIL

Observation Deck

⑤

PINE TRAIL

⑥

POWDER MILL TRAIL

⑦

HIGHWAY 9

GRAHAM HILL ROAD

N

END

Chapter 39

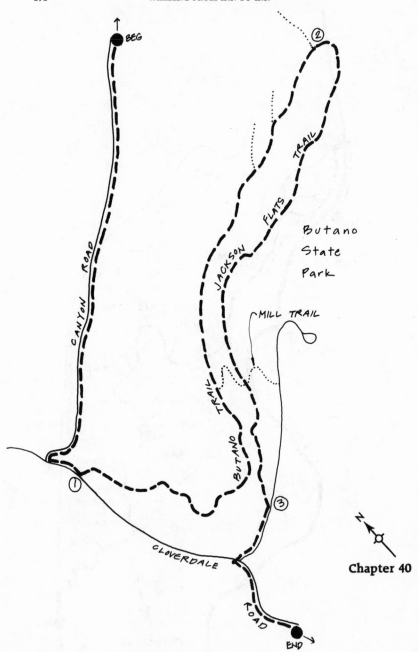

BEG

CANYON ROAD

②

Butano State Park

JACKSON FLATS TRAIL

MILL TRAIL

BUTANO TRAIL

①

③

CLOVERDALE

N

Chapter 40

ROAD

END

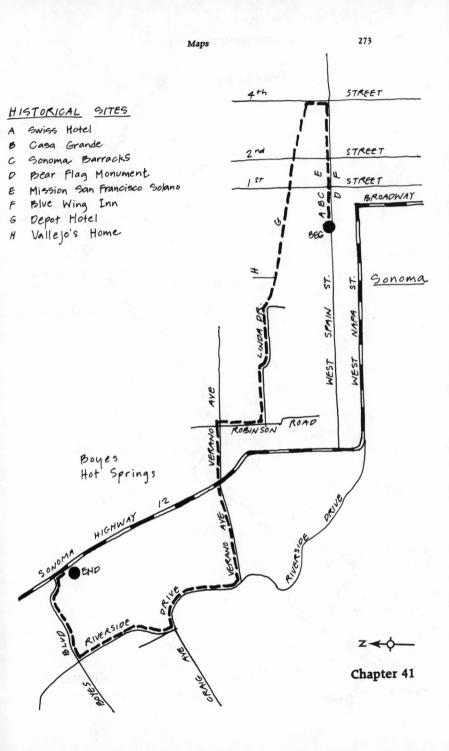

HISTORICAL SITES

A Swiss Hotel
B Casa Grande
C Sonoma Barracks
D Bear Flag Monument
E Mission San Francisco Solano
F Blue Wing Inn
G Depot Hotel
H Vallejo's Home

Chapter 41

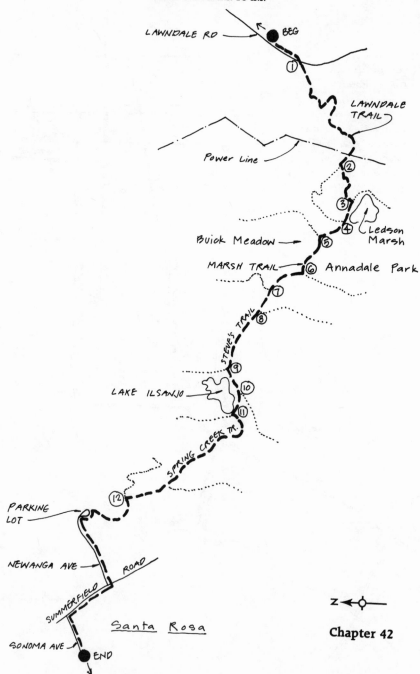

LAWNDALE RD

BEG

①

LAWNDALE TRAIL

Power Line

②

③

④ Ledson Marsh

Buick Meadow →

⑤

MARSH TRAIL ⑥ Annadale Park

⑦

⑧

STEVE'S TRAIL

⑨

⑩

LAKE ILSANJO

⑪

SPRING CREEK TR.

⑫

PARKING LOT

NEWANGA AVE

ROAD

SUMMERFIELD

Santa Rosa

SONOMA AVE

END

Z ←◇→

Chapter 42

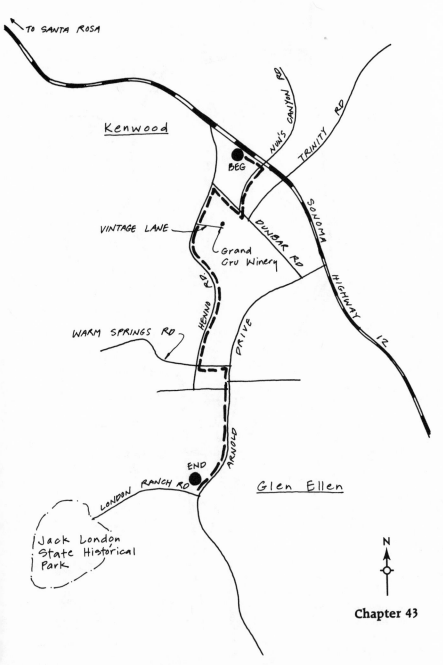

TO SANTA ROSA

Kenwood

NUN'S CANYON RD

TRINITY RD

BEG

SONOMA

VINTAGE LANE

DUNBAR RD

Grand Cru Winery

HIGHWAY 12

HENNO RD.

DRIVE

WARM SPRINGS RD

END

ARNOLD

LONDON RANCH RD

Glen Ellen

Jack London State Historical Park

N

Chapter 43

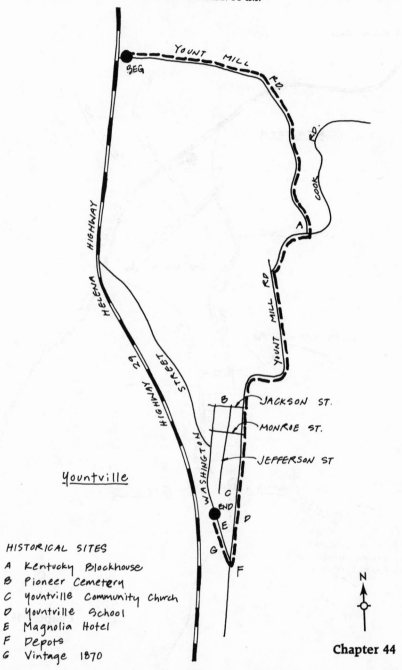

Yountville

HISTORICAL SITES

A   Kentucky Blockhouse
B   Pioneer Cemetery
C   Yountville Community Church
D   Yountville School
E   Magnolia Hotel
F   Depots
G   Vintage 1870

Chapter 44

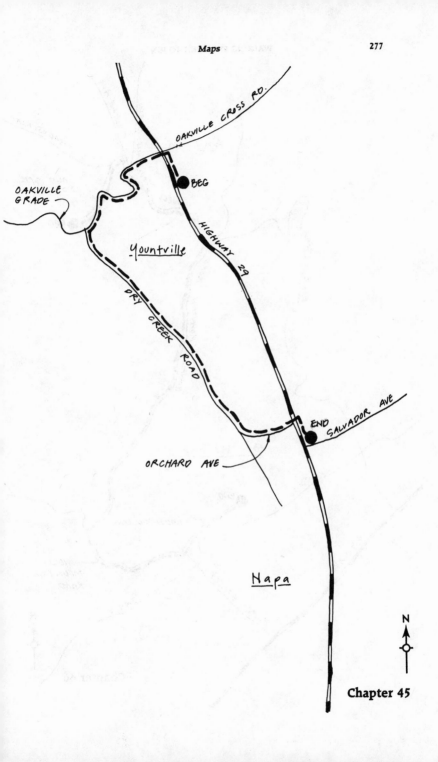

OAKVILLE CROSS RD.

OAKVILLE GRADE

BEG

HIGHWAY 29

Yountville

DRY CREEK ROAD

END   SALVADOR AVE

ORCHARD AVE

Napa

N

Chapter 45

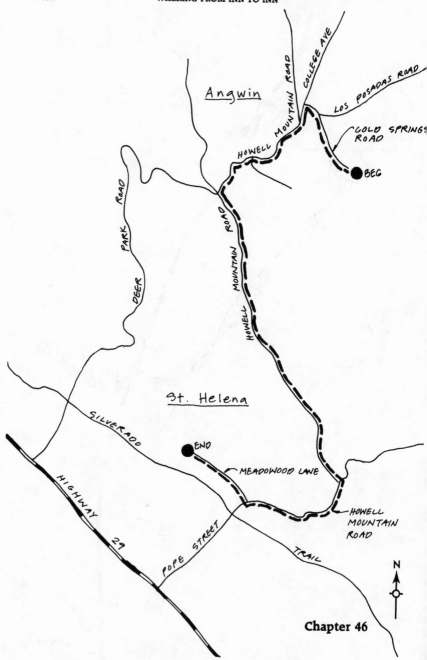

Chapter 46

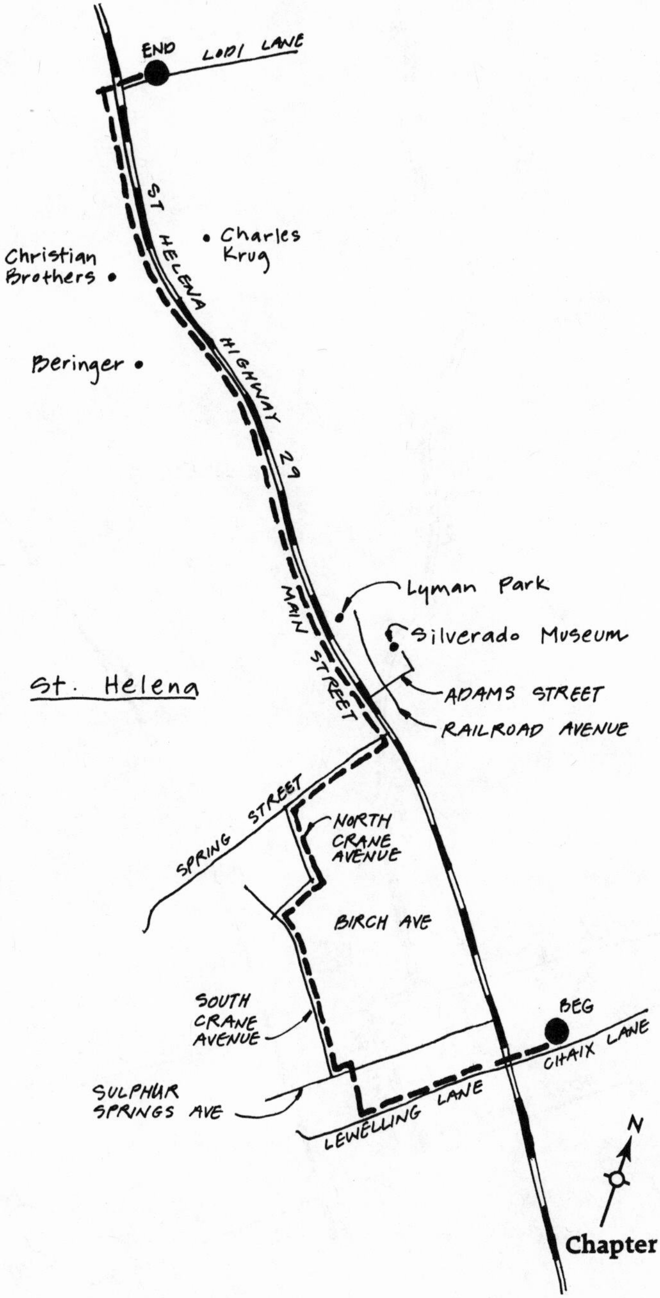

END LODI LANE

ST. HELENA HIGHWAY 29

• Charles Krug

Christian Brothers •

Beringer •

Lyman Park

Silverado Museum

ADAMS STREET

RAILROAD AVENUE

MAIN STREET

St. Helena

SPRING STREET

NORTH CRANE AVENUE

BIRCH AVE

SOUTH CRANE AVENUE

SULPHUR SPRINGS AVE

LEWELLING LANE

BEG

CHAIX LANE

N

Chapter 47

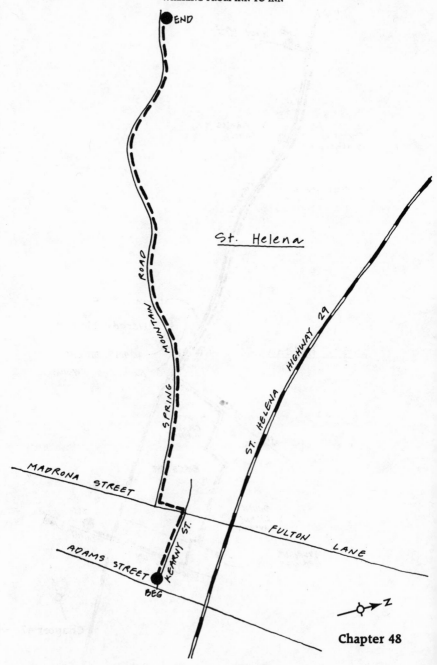

Chapter 48

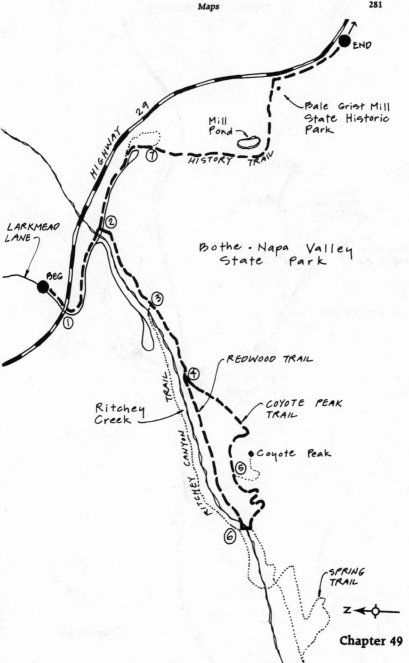

END

Bale Grist Mill State Historic Park

HIGHWAY 29

Mill Pond

⑦ HISTORY TRAIL

LARKMEAD LANE

②

BEG

①

③

Bothe · Napa Valley State Park

REDWOOD TRAIL

④

COYOTE PEAK TRAIL

Ritchey Creek

RITCHEY CANYON TRAIL

Coyote Peak

⑤

⑥

SPRING TRAIL

Z ←⊙→

Chapter 49

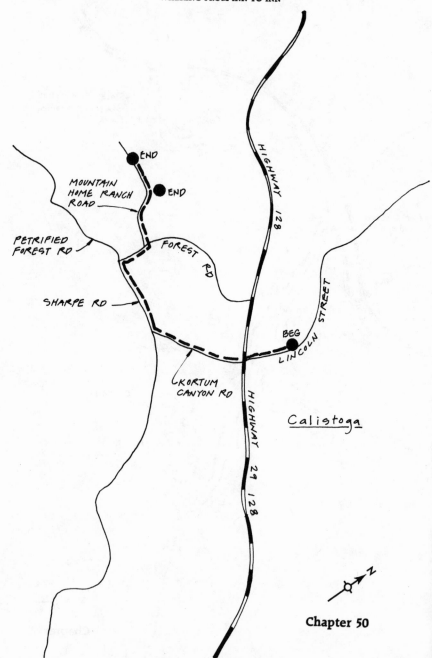

Chapter 50

Bibliography

Benet, James. *A Guide to San Francisco and the Bay Region.* New York: Random House, 1963.

Brant, Michelle. *Timeless Walks in San Francisco.* Richmond: Lompa Press, 1975.

Brown, Vinson, and George Lawrence. *The California Wildlife Region.* Healdsburg: Naturegraph, 1965.

Coplin, Maxine. *A National Guide to Guest Homes.* Mill Valley: Home on a Range, 1981.

Dalbey, Alice. *The Visitors Guide to Point Reyes National Seashore.* Riverside: The Chatham Press, 1974.

Delehanty, Randolph. *San Francisco: Walks and Tours in the Golden Gate City.* New York: Dial Press, 1980.

Doss, Margot Patterson. *Golden Gate Park at Your Feet.* San Rafael: Presidio Press, 1978.

———— *Paths of Gold.* San Francisco: Chronical Books, 1974.

———— *San Francisco at Your Feet.* New York: Grove Press, 1964.

Futcher, Jane. *Marin: The Place, the People.* New York: Holt, Rinehart & Winston, 1981.

Geary, Ida. *Marin Trails.* Fairfax: Tamal Land Press, 1969.

Hansen, Gladys, ed. *San Francisco: A Guide to the Bay and Its Cities.* American Guide Series. New York: Hastings House, 1947.

Hart, John. "A Park for All Reasons." San Francisco Examiner: *California Living.* Oct. 17, 1982.

Kensington Improvement Club. *A Survey of Kensington.* Berkeley: Kensington Improvement Club, 1978.

Knight, Diane. *Bed and Breakfast Homes Directory for California.* Cupertino: Knightime Publications, 1982.

Los Gatos-Saratoga Branch, American Association of University Women, in cooperation with The Saratoga Historical Foundation. *Saratoga Historical Walking Tour.* Saratoga.

Mason, Jack. *Olema, Dear Valley.* Inverness: Northshore Press, 1976.

———— Summer Town: *The History of Inverness, California*. Inverness: Northshore Books, 1974.

Matson, Robert. *North of San Francisco*. Santa Rosa: North of San Francisco Publications, 1975.

Moffitt, Mary R. *Old Yountville Walking Guide.* Napa: Napa Landmarks, Inc., 1979.

Mullen, Barbara Durr. *Sonoma County Crossroads*. San Rafael: CM Publications, 1974.

Myrick, David F. *San Francisco's Telegraph Hill.* Berkeley: Howell-North Books, 1972.

Newey, Bob. *East Bay Trails.* Hayward: Footloose Press, 1981.

Olmsted, Nancy. *To Walk With a Quiet Mind.* San Francisco: Sierra Club Books, 1975.

Omduff, Robert. *An Introduction to California Plant Life*. Berkeley: University of California Press, 1974.

Shepherd, Susan. *In the Neighborhoods*. San Francisco: Chronical Books, 1981.

Smith, Arthur C. *The Natural History of the San Francisco Bay Region*. Berkeley: University of California Press, 1968.

Sonoma League for Historic Preservation. *Sonoma Walking Tour*. Sonoma, 1980.

Taber, Tom. *Exploring California's Coast: From Bodega Bay to Monterey*. San Mateo: Oak Valley Press, 1977.

Thompson, Bob. *Sunset Guide to California Wine Country.* Menlo Park: Lane Publishing Co., 1979.

Whitnah, Dorothy L. *An Outdoor Guide to the San Francisco Bay Area*. Berkeley: Wilderness Press, 1976.

In addition to the material found in the above publications, a great deal of information has been culled from printed material provided by the chamber of commerce of each of the municipalities, and by the city, county, state and national park agencies that administer the hiking lands included in this book.